SWEDISH MILITARY INTELLIGENCE

SWEDISH MILITARY INTELLIGENCE
Producing Knowledge

Gunilla Eriksson

EDINBURGH
University Press

Edinburgh University Press is one of the leading university presses in the UK. We publish academic books and journals in our selected subject areas across the humanities and social sciences, combining cutting-edge scholarship with high editorial and production values to produce academic works of lasting importance. For more information visit our website: edinburghuniversitypress.com

© Gunilla Eriksson, 2016

Edinburgh University Press Ltd
The Tun – Holyrood Road
12(2f) Jackson's Entry
Edinburgh EH8 8PJ

Typeset in 11/13 Sabon by Servis Filmsetting Ltd, Stockport, Cheshire

A CIP record for this book is available from the British Library

ISBN 978 1 4744 1344 2 (hardback)
ISBN 978 1 4744 1345 9 (webready PDF)
ISBN 978 1 4744 1346 6 (epub)

The right Gunilla Eriksson to be identified as the author of this work has been asserted in accordance with the Copyright, Designs and Patents Act 1988, and the Copyright and Related Rights Regulations 2003 (SI No. 2498).

CONTENTS

List of figures vi
Acknowledgements vii

1 Introduction 1
2 Framework for Researching Intelligence Knowledge 20
3 Intelligence in Swedish Political Culture 41
4 The Institutional Setting 46
5 The Swedish Military Intelligence Directorate 55
6 Practice for Producing Knowledge 62
7 Practice for Creating Knowledge 94
8 The Intelligence Worldview 118
9 The Representation of NATO 140
10 The Representation of Russia 148
11 The Representation of Terrorism 157
12 The Intelligence Discourse 168
13 The Intelligence 'Style of Thought' and 'Collective of Thought' 190

Bibliography 213
Index 223

FIGURES

2.1	Fairclough's model for discourse applied in the context of intelligence	25
4.1	The institutional setting	49
4.2	The work process for the MUST	52
5.1	Overview of the MUST organisation	58
12.1	Language practice for the term terrorism	180

ACKNOWLEDGEMENTS

Conducting intelligence-related research is always a quest that is a little bit trickier than other social and political research, caused by an aura of secrecy and delicacy surrounding the issue. Coincidentally it is also one of the more exciting topics situated between high politics, institutional and organisational issues, and sociological and psychological aspects.

During my journey to research what characterises intelligence knowledge and how it is produced within the Swedish military intelligence, I have had the privilege of meeting extraordinary people. I have had the pleasure of discussing and working with Professor Jan Olsson and Professor Mats Lindberg at Örebro University, and Professor Jan Willem Honig, Kings College, London. To all three of you I say special thanks for both creative ideas and encouragement as well as for constructive critical comments. I also would like to thank Professor Jim Nyce, Ball State University, Professor Peter Jackson, University of Glasgow, and Professor Wilhelm Agrell, Lund University, for constructive and critical remarks on earlier drafts.

At the Armed Forces Headquarters and at the Swedish Military Intelligence and Security Service I would like to acknowledge support from General Stefan Kristiansson (retired), General Mats Engman and Colonel Pär Blid for sanctioning the very idea of a contemporary intelligence research project. Furthermore, I express my appreciation to General Gunnar Karlson for not only acknowledging my research findings, but for inviting me to take part in most constructive and engaged discussions on the current and future challenges of intelligence.

I also want to express gratitude to my respondents for taking time to answer my questions in interviews, in a most straightforward and cordial way. Further, I would like to thank the staff at the archives and the administrative staff for aiding me. I also have had the pleasure of enjoying the collegial support from fellow researchers at the Department of War Studies at the Swedish Defence University. I would also like to thank colleagues and friends who patiently and critically read and commented on earlier texts and drafts of this book.

For moral support and for hours of pondering life's and science's big questions I thank Ulrica Pettersson, PhD, at National Defence University and Lund University. Without you, I would have been lost. Very special thanks go to my family and friends, and my urban family Anna for always believing in me and encouraging me to find new ways. Last, to my darling daughter, Nike. You have brought such joy to my life. Always making sure to remind me of what is truly important – You.

Chapter 1

INTRODUCTION

INTELLIGENCE – A SPECIAL KIND OF KNOWLEDGE

During my six years as an intelligence professional in the Swedish Military and Security Directorate (Militära Underrättelse och Säkerhetstjänsten – the MUST) I produced and consumed intelligence assessments of different scope and focus. During this time my curiosity about the phenomenon of knowledge within intelligence analysis grew. I tried to make sense of and categorise what the contribution of the intelligence service really was to the political policymaking process. At the same time there was (and still is) a vibrant debate among scholars and practitioners over the problems of intelligence analysis.[1] The debate on intelligence analysis is primarily concerned with the issue of why it often comes to 'wrong conclusions'. Additionally, the debate is concerned with the question of why intelligence services seem ineffective in providing timely intelligence to policy decisions, and what could make the analysis and input to policy more efficient.

My initial curiosity later changed to a more critical reading of intelligence and its special kind of knowledge. The intelligence service – not only in Sweden but also all over the world – produces knowledge on security issues, conflicts, war and complex political processes. The knowledge is often produced within a tight time frame, with only some of the relevant information available, which makes the intelligence analysis task more challenging and difficult. In spite of these difficulties intelligence knowledge is used to contextualise, explain and predict events in the real world. Its fundamental aim is to underpin strategic action and help security policymakers to make informed decisions; consequently it has a great impact on how security issues are understood and how security and foreign policy is shaped. Yet history shows that on numerous occasions intelligence has affected policy outcome in the wrong direction and grave consequences have followed.[2]

In my critical reading of intelligence products, I noticed what seemed like peculiarities. For instance, the text of the assessments seemed to contain a high degree of repetitiveness in wording and substance. Furthermore, the conclusions seemed to be articulated as objective truths. They were formulated with objective truth claims and the arguments and evidence in support of the conclusions were mostly diffuse or hidden in the background of the text. Moreover, many of the assessments often came to wrong conclusions (history being the judge). These observations led me to suspect that there was more to the story of intelligence knowledge than careful data collection and objective truth, suggesting that there were hidden aspects of the intelligence analysis to be uncovered and critically examined. Among other things, several implicit assumptions seemed to be made, regarding the kind of empirical data considered relevant and sufficient, and the mode of interpretation and explanation. Furthermore, the knowledge production seemed to be surrounded with unarticulated norms and specific procedures, constituting a social context of a specific character, with a possible effect on the knowledge produced.

All these observations lead me to formulate critical questions in a more systematic way: What kind of knowledge does intelligence produce? Are there some inherent methodological and theoretical conventions (paradigms) that might obstruct or at least hamper the emergence of valid descriptions and explanations? In which social context does intelligence emerge? Are there some traits in the social context of knowledge production (inherent norms and values, routines or organisational patterns) that might constrain or hamper the emergence of valid knowledge?

This study adopts a perspective on intelligence as a knowledge producer, whose knowledge is vital for policy processes and policy outcomes. My understanding of knowledge, and with knowledge claims like intelligence analysis, is that knowledge never consists of empirical data alone. All knowledge includes implicit and explicit valuations concerning the scope and direction of knowledge, as well as implicit and explicit theoretical assumptions underpinning the attempts at explanation and understanding. This is the common view within the philosophy of science.[3]

Another common view in the philosophy and theory of science, held by sociologists and historians of different intellectual communities, is an emphasis on the social context of knowledge production. All knowledge, it is believed, is produced within a specific social and institutional setting that affects the individuals engaged in producing knowledge and the character of the knowledge itself. For example, a newspaper editorial office is different from a policy agency or a scientific academic institute; they constitute different social milieus with different aims, valuations, assumptions and norms – implicit and explicit – for what is considered a valid piece of knowledge, sufficient empirical underpinning or an interesting informative story. All knowledge is produced in social contexts, and all knowledge is produced within and affected by the prevailing linguistic discourse (terminological and conceptual) in the context at hand. This would also hold for the intelligence analysis, and in the case of my investigation, the MUST and its annual strategic estimates on the security situation of Sweden.

I assume, as a foundational starting point, that the knowledge production and knowledge products in the MUST, the annual strategic intelligence estimates (described below), are influenced by both explicit and implicit methodological and theoretical assumptions, constituting a kind of 'specific intelligence knowledge'. I also assume, as a second foundational starting point, that this paradigm is upheld and carried out in a social context that is equally important and fruitful to investigate. My immediate aim in this study was twofold: to investigate the character of intelligence knowledge and the social context in which it is produced.

Thus, the aim of the study is to investigate the intellectual and substantial content of the strategic intelligence estimates produced at the MUST, and to investigate the social milieu and the social context of the knowledge production. For this twofold investigation I used three kinds of source material. My first and most important source was the annual Swedish Armed Forces Strategic Intelligence Estimates (hereafter referred to as the 'estimates') through the years 1998 to 2010.[4] The second important source was several lengthy and highly valuable interviews with the analysts, including managers, working at the MUST. Without the interviews many of the insights and results in this study would not have occurred.[5] Finally, I had source material based on participant observation. I participated in and made observations at working meetings and seminars during the production process of the 2010 estimate. (I included my experiences from my years as an active analyst. Although these were not systematically recorded, they constitute valuable background knowledge and pre-understanding of the knowledge production at the MUST.)[6]

The use of *analysis of text* is inevitable because the purpose of the intelligence service is to produce assessments and analyses, which are done mainly in written assessments and briefs. *Interviews* were used to identify, understand and question the way issues were framed and understood and how this came about in everyday life in the institution of the intelligence service. *Observations* were used to investigate and study the everyday life of the intelligence analysts and to engage in the way they talk about and argue the issues and topics. Observation allowed access to the world of the analysts and to study the processes surrounding and, to some extent, shaping them.

INTELLIGENCE AND KNOWLEDGE

Intelligence research, which has grown in recent years, might be said to be a disparate field.[7] Intelligence research involves diverse issues such as giving accounts of the intelligence impact in historical events, describing covert action and explaining intelligence failures. The problems of the intelligence process in general,[8] and of intelligence analysis in particular, are usually framed using various kinds of diagnoses aimed at 'fixing intelligence'.[9] The literature on explaining and trying to 'fix' intelligence failures engages in discussing the analytical (and other) difficulties revealed through turbulent events such as Pearl Harbour,[10] the Cuban Missile Crisis, or the US and UK belief that weapons of mass destruction (WMD) existed in Iraq prior to the Second Gulf War.[11] In general, this kind of intelligence research shares an assumption that the unique character of intelligence calls for in-depth historical case studies. In addition the research area of intelligence failures tends to focus on the impact and constraining effects of failures on the organisational and structural issues within the services[12] and/or the limits of cognitive and psychological conditions for the intelligence analysis.[13]

The debate over the problems in intelligence analysis discusses the failure of intelligence to make accurate predictions and also problematises the relationship between intelligence and policy. Although a vast amount of intelligence research is devoted to try and 'fix' the intelligence malfunctions and prevent intelligence failures, there is little or no interest in trying to critically investigate the intelligence as a producer of knowledge. However, some approaches within intelligence research take into account the epistemic challenges inherent in intelligence analysis. Additionally, some research discusses the relationship of intelligence to policy. A brief overview of these perspectives will bring us closer to the focus of this book.

In intelligence research on the problems of intelligence analysis, some approaches examine the analysis through a discussion of the basis on which the analysis is made. This research brings focus to issues of the character of and the conditions for the production of knowledge. In his writings, Sherman Kent[14] brought focus to the issues of what kind of knowledge intelligence analysis should engage in and its relation to policy. In his discussion of what kind of issues intelligence analysis should focus on, Kent argues that there are three kinds of *'known'*: *'the knowable and known'* (facts), *'the knowable and unknown'* (secrets) and *'the unknowable'* (mysteries). The latter two are the focus of assessments and predictions, and should, according to Kent, be based on logic and objective reasoning.[15] Kent's reasoning takes a normative approach, arguing for the intelligence to speak truth to power and offer an objective and neutral assessment and estimations on issues relating to foreign and security policy. Kent further argues that the relationship between intelligence and policy is (and should be) separated, because the intelligence should not be affected by policy objectives.

Kent elaborates on what are and should be defining features of intelligence analysis, to enhance the chances of attaining objective analysis. Kent further argues that the intelligence analysis and policymaking are conducted with two widely separated goals: one with the aim of achieving objective knowledge (and accurate estimates), and one with the aim of achieving political objectives. Therefore, Kent argues, the two (equally important) state functions should be kept apart.[16] The aim of objectivity in intelligence analysis has come to imply being an advocate for specific political policy objectives. The aim of objectivity in intelligence has come to imply speaking *truth* to power, suggesting that the analyses presented are not laden with (theoretical) assumptions.

More recent research concerned with knowledge in intelligence analysis has engaged in a variety of epistemic issues. This is done, for instance, by identifying and discussing the epistemic character of the intelligence analysis. The researchers argue that intelligence has not engaged enough with epistemic issues to make the analysis as reliable as it could be. In general, this research argues for structural as well as methodological revisions to allow for a more reflexive and critical approach for the analysts in their analytical work.[17]

The aim of objectivity within intelligence is visible in research discussing the relationship between intelligence and policy. The focus on the intelligence–policy relationship leads to a tendency to cover how the boundaries between intelligence and policy should be defined, why the communication between intelligence and policymaking does not run as smoothly as desired[18] and the impact that intelligence has had on policy decisions.[19] Hence, a frequent assumption in the related research is that an intelligence service should be an independent provider of an analysis, untainted by policy objectives and political will. Johnson states: 'Perhaps the greatest paradox of intelligence is that so much effort and funding go into the gathering of information for policy makers, only to have them ignore it. . . . Speaking truth onto power is a notoriously difficult endeavour.'[20]

In the process of 'speaking truth to power', the knowledge of the truth plays different roles in policymaking. In his classic study *Strategic Intelligence and National Decision*, Roger Hilsman covers the impact of intelligence on policymaking and discusses the foundations of the intelligence analysis.[21]

Hilsman's primary focus is on how the intelligence might contribute to making decisions on policy issues. The study reveals a consensus among policymakers and intelligence personnel that intelligence has (and should have) made vital contributions in the policy process by providing descriptive background information and by making sure that the policymakers have all the relevant 'facts'. The study argues that a primary function of intelligence *'is backing the operator up with the facts, protecting him by supplying him with facts to defend his position'*.[22] Hence, Hilsman argues that the intelligence role of policymaking becomes a way of rationalising policies made or actions already taken.

Much like Kent, Hilsman argues that the intelligence function, analysis and personnel should not be involved with policy recommendations or policymaking. In his opinion, some distance should exist between the functions of policymaking and of intelligence analysis, otherwise intelligence officials would become tainted, and unable to maintain the objectivity and impartiality needed to present the correct and relevant facts.

Hilsman also points towards factors and attitudes that make it difficult to achieve objective and impartial knowledge. Hilsman's findings

Introduction

are relevant to this study. Although his primary purpose was not on discussing knowledge production, Hilsman expresses concern about how doctrines and attitudes within intelligence influence the environment for thinking.

> The opinions the operators offer on the proper role of intelligence and the reasoning they use to support those opinions seem to fall into a recognizable pattern, and both the nature of this pattern and the mere fact of its existence seem to suggest that these officials tend to share a set of attitudes and assumptions which shape their thinking on this problem of a role for intelligence.[23]

Hilsman argues that despite their intention to provide basic information (facts) to the political decision makers, intelligence analysts seem to be affected by other factors that influence the process, production and products of the intelligence service.[24] Though expressing it as an unproven hypothesis, he suggests intelligence professionals have 'shared assumptions and attitudes' that affect analytical products:

> a set of shared assumptions and attitudes – assumptions about the role of facts and of theory, attitudes toward experience, feelings and anti-intellectualism, inclinations toward activism and simplism – that have channelled the thinking of these officials and shaped the solution they advocate.[25]

Additionally, more recent research discusses the impact of the social context for intelligence production. The research identifies a number of problems within the intelligence social context, where socialisation and ethnocentrism are commonly identified features.[26] Further, the research also discusses the problems of socialisation and conducting analytical work in hierarchical organisations, with no institutionalised reflective process of the analytical preconditions.[27]

Kent and Hilsman[28] underline important issues for this study. Kent brings focus to the importance of the 'thinking part' of the intelligence production – in his words the importance of the analytical tradecraft. However, contrary to my understanding of the possibilities of intelligence production, Kent seems to consider the intelligence role of speaking an objective truth (relying just on the right facts) onto power as both desirable and achievable. Hilsman's study, on the other hand, suggests there is a shared set of assumptions and beliefs in the context of intelligence production, a suggestion that would support my initial observations of the structure and content in the MUST estimates.

Nonetheless, neither Kent's nor Hilsman's studies offer much support in approaching how to further inquire into the characteristics of intelligence knowledge, its underlying assumptions and possible worldview and the social context situating it. However, the research tradition of critical policy analysis does so, with emphasis on the importance of disclosing ideas, assumptions and possible valuations underlying knowledge produced within policy processes. Furthermore critical policy analysis offers a few initial pointers on how these factors might be uncovered.

POLICY AND KNOWLEDGE

Modern policy analytical research challenges the formerly prevailing idea of rationalism, objectivism and exogenous knowledge in policymaking. Instead, critical policy analysts like Frank Fischer have argued the importance of exploring and understanding the knowledge in the formative part of the policy process. Critical policy analysis emphasises the importance of exploring and understanding ideas, norms and assumptions of the knowledge underlying policymaking.

Critical policy analysis rejects the idea that facts speak for themselves and acknowledges that facts are theory-laden, implying that knowledge in the policy process cannot be rendered with objective claims of indisputable truths.[29] Sonia Mazey argues this essential idea within critical policy research: *'Such thinking has opened up the research agenda to systematic and critical consideration of the impact of ideas, norms, knowledge and beliefs upon politics and policymaking . . ..'*[30] Mazey argues that the ideas and norms of knowledge are influential in policymaking and policy processes. This is further underlined by, for instance, Bacchi who argues for social research to engage in the more formative aspects of policymaking through discussing and challenging the construction of problem representation.

> Put simply, it is essential to think deeply about the assumptions and presuppositions that lie behind and shape selected policies. It is also essential to consider the implications that flow from these presuppositions and how particular forms of rule have come to be.[31]

Introduction

The critical policy analysis acknowledges that the way in which knowledge is constructed within policy processes matters for how the policy areas are understood and, ultimately, influences policy decisions.

In a similar fashion, in discussing environmental regulation, Lidskog et al. discuss how knowledge and policy interact and what underlies the construction of environmental regulation. They argue that *'rules and knowledge are co-constructed in the very same process'*.[32] The argument put forward is that knowledge affecting policy and regulation is constructed and negotiated within and between various kinds of actors (not only within the scientific community and/or the state).[33] Their research focus encompasses understanding how knowledge is incorporated into policy; in other words, how actors establish epistemic authority to affect the regulatory policy on environmental issues.[34] However, this study has a different though related focus. Instead of examining the negotiation between policy actors, it focuses on the knowledge creation within one such actor – the intelligence service; thus, it does not encompass an ambition to discuss how the intelligence knowledge might affect or be incorporated in policy decisions. That is a research field of its own. Nevertheless, both studies acknowledge that knowledge relevant to policy is embedded in a social context and is affected by and produces discourses.

The critical policy analysis argues that studies should instead focus on understanding and exposing discourses through the articulatory possibilities within the policy process. Bacchi underlines the constitutive role of representation of what is perceived as problems within policy knowledge. She argues that the representation of the problem (that the policy decisions are set to answer) matters for how the policy is designed. Bacchi also argues that the way the knowledge producers articulate the problem and problem area is influenced by discourses and create discourses of their own through their articulatory role.[35]

Fischer emphasises that policy knowledge – used for making policy decisions – is affected by *'subjective presuppositions and assumptions that direct our perceptual processes in pre-shaping what are otherwise generally taken for empirical factors'*.[36] In line with this, Schön and Rein argue that the limits set on how to understand and cope with the complexities of different issues and societal problems are powerful stories and influence policy outcome: *'Each story constructs its view of social reality through a complementary process of naming and framing. Things are selected for attention and named in such a way as to fit the frame constructed for the situation.'*[37] Moreover, they argue that the underlying assumptions for policy knowledge are most often tacit, implying that the members of the policy process do not actively reflect on them or pay them conscious attention.[38]

Critical policy research involves asking questions concerning assumptions and articulation of knowledge. This position also suggests a change in the approaches and methodological choices for analysing policy. '*A discourse approach seeks to show that we need a much more refined understanding of the interactions that construct reality, in particular, the way the empirical is embedded in the normative.*'[39] Critical policy analysis underlines the need to embrace a more hermeneutic and interpretative approach when analysing knowledge within policy and the policy process by investigating discourses and discursive practices.

Hence, critical policy analysis directs attention to underlying and implicit ideas, assumptions and value judgements and seeks to make these factors visible. The ideas, assumptions, and valuations in policy knowledge are usually buried in the shape of facts and empirical arguments. Fischer argues that these ideas and assumptions are '*advanced through a dramaturgy of objective description, which masks the performative function of political language*'.[40] The critical approach to policy analysis suggests that using the ideas of discourse and discourse analysis will reveal the underlying assumptions and presuppositions within the knowledge produced.

The emphasis and ideas within critical policy analysis offer pointers on how an inquiry aimed at uncovering ideas, assumptions and possible valuations within knowledge production may be approached. The arguments underline the importance of critically examining intelligence knowledge. Further, they suggest the importance of studying the character of intelligence knowledge by infusing the ideas of discourse and discourse analysis into an institutional context. The focus of this study, of intelligence as a producer of knowledge for policy purposes, is motivated through the emphasis made by critical policy analysis.

INVESTIGATING INTELLIGENCE KNOWLEDGE PRODUCTION

In this study, I view the intelligence service as an institution that produces fundamental knowledge for policy formation and decision concerning national security and foreign policy. Critical policy analysis, being my overall theoretical perspective, suggests that knowledge in policy processes not only consists of empirical facts and alleged objective truth claims. In addition, it also contains theoretical and methodological assumptions together with values and valuations, not to mention various distortions caused by adherence to one or another established political stream of ideas.

Therefore, this study examines the character of knowledge within the intelligence service. The foremost aim is to investigate how intelligence analysis contains assumptions and valuations that eventually lead to an established knowledge-steering political worldview. This study also examines another aspect of intelligence analysis. Like all types of knowledge, intelligence knowledge is produced within a set of institutional and social conditions. Thus, the second aim is to investigate how these institutional and social conditions influence knowledge production as well the character of the knowledge, especially the issue how the eventual assumptions and valuations of intelligence analysis are upheld, changed or reaffirmed.

Hence, the overall purpose of this study is to examine the characteristics of knowledge in intelligence analysis and also to investigate how that knowledge is affected by the social context of its production, the military intelligence service.

To generate a theoretical foundation to support and structure this twofold purpose of research, an analytical framework as well as more elaborated research questions are constructed and argued for in Chapter 2.

OUTLINE OF THE BOOK

This chapter has underlined the importance of conducting research knowledge produced within intelligence analysis by using the arguments emphasised by critical policy analysis. In order to do so, Chapter 2 provides a theoretical framework (and some modest methodological considerations) for researching intelligence knowledge. To further develop the viewpoint on the foundations for knowledge underlined by critical policy analysis, the study is further situated through discussion of New Institutionalism in relation to the ideas of critical discourse analysis on how to approach knowledge production.

The next three chapters briefly describe the traits of the Swedish political, institutional and organisational context. It is within this context that the MUST is situated. Chapter 3 starts with a brief overview of the specifics of the political culture in the Swedish context of relevance to intelligence. Chapter 4 aims at furthering the understanding of the social practice of the MUST by describing and examining its formal institutional setting. The chapter reveals the founding ideas of the intelligence process, and the institutional structure in which the work process for the MUST is placed. Chapter 5 describes the research object – the organisational development and context of the MUST. This description outlines some of the conditions that affect the processes within which knowledge is produced as well as the formal organisation and aim and scope of the intelligence function.

To extend and deepen the inquiry into conditions under which intelligence knowledge is created, the next two chapters seek to uncover the informal social and textual discursive practices of the MUST. Chapter 6 examines the characteristics of the knowledge production process at the MUST. It seeks to identify and discuss the social discursive practice within the social context, by turning the focus to how the analysts carry out their analytical tasks and by questioning what structures their actions. Chapter 7 discloses what guides the analytical considerations and choices of the analysts by uncovering the textual discursive practice within the MUST. In addition, the chapter discusses how the analysts view distinctions between assumptions, facts and valuations.

A conceptual analysis of the central issues and concepts within the intelligence estimates, thus detecting whether a coherent worldview is evident in the estimates, is now presented. Chapter 8 argues that the worldview of intelligence analysis is founded within the assumptions of political realism. Thereafter the chapter elaborates on how this affects the intelligence analysis. Further, the representation of three issues (North Atlantic Treaty Organization (NATO), Russia and terrorism) are examined to identify how these issues are conceptualised and substantiated, and to detect possible valuations and implicit presuppositions. Chapters 9 and 10 discuss the construction and articulation of the concept of 'NATO' and 'Russia', respectively. The chapters also discuss how these assessments and conclusions are substantiated and it reveals possible valuations within this representation. Chapter 11 contains a conceptual analysis of and a discussion of how the concept of 'terrorism' is articulated, how it changes over time and whether it is used consistently throughout the estimates. Last, it seeks to uncover an identifiable intelligence knowledge discourse examining the language practice in the estimates. Chapter 12 discusses the language practice and the construction and use of qualifiers in the estimates. The goal is to uncover a possible intelligence knowledge discourse by disclosing how the discursive practices impact the knowledge produced.

The book concludes with a discussion of the social practice, discursive practices and the intelligence knowledge discourse, arguing that the social context of the MUST holds specific features for the social and textual discursive practices. Thereafter, it reflects and discusses how the empirical findings might contribute to the future policy and intelligence research agenda. This last chapter suggests a few modest changes on how intelligence knowledge production could be improved by reducing the constraining characteristic of the social and textual discursive practices in place.

Notes

1 This debate is most often situated with the US and the UK intelligence services as the frame of reference, although the problems of analysis are to various degrees valid for intelligence services worldwide. As for research into the nexus of intelligence and knowledge Persson et al. have made inquiries into Swedish intelligence. Although they pose the question of what kind of intelligence system or infrastructure Sweden should have (focusing on tactical and operational intelligence and the Intelligence, Surveillance, Target Acquisition, and Reconnaissance/Intelligence, Surveillance and Reconnaissance (ISTAR/ISR) capabilities), the research elaborates conditions and architecture for military intelligence analysis (Persson et al., *Från koncept till öppet system*). In addition, the MUST has also been the focus of research conducted at the Swedish National Defence University (NDU). Räsänen and Nyce investigate the approach to data in intelligence practice. They discuss the social construction of data within the MUST. Their research suggests that the intelligence practitioners use the concept of (raw) data being commonsensical, without acknowledging possible differences in the character of the facticities used as input in the intelligence analytical work (Räsänen and Nyce, 'The raw is cooked'). For further research on Swedish military intelligence see references in Chapter 4.
2 The Commission on the Intelligence Capabilities of the United States Regarding Weapons of Mass Destruction Report (2005) and Review of Intelligence on Weapons of Mass Destruction (2004).
3 See for instance Myrdal, *Objectivity in social research*; Kuhn, *The structure of scientific revolutions*; Popper, *Conjectures and refutations the growth of scientific knowledge*; and Törnebohm, *Studier av kunskapsutveckling*.

4 The estimates are produced by the MUST for the Armed Forces Headquarters, Department of Defence, Department of Foreign Affairs and the Swedish government. The estimates seek to explain world events and the MUST's strategic assessment contributes to the basis for making policy decisions over the next five to ten years in areas and issues of special interest to Swedish foreign and security policy and to the Swedish Defence Forces. The study included the text of estimates from 1998 (when it was first produced as a comprehensive intelligence estimate) to 2010 (when the structure of the estimate was changed substantially). The estimates make a contribution that may be described as an influential intelligence assessment. Thus, for a number of reasons, the estimates are of the utmost interest to the study of the knowledge produced within the intelligence service. First, the estimates are intelligence assessments that have been written annually for a long period of time, and, from an analytical perspective, this allows a researcher to grasp and illustrate changing discourses. Second, the estimates may be argued to be an important product for the intelligence service, given the amount of time and effort spent on producing them. This effort may be explained by the large number of intelligence consumers to whom they are disseminated. Third, the more holistic ambition of the estimates (in comparison to other intelligence assessments) suggests that this kind of text contains statements revealing a possible worldview and issues that signify and contain a possible 'style of thought'. This kind of estimate was established in 1998 as a result of requests for an overall and cohesive intelligence estimate from the Armed Forces and political policy-makers. The estimates used in this study are the entire report series, which contains annual estimates 1998–2001 (unclassified) and the estimates between 2002 and 2010 (classified). Quotations and references from the classified estimates have been approved by the MUST, following a process of declassification. The estimates produced in 1999–2002 are divided into one executive summary and two appendices, where the first appendix is the main assessment and the second contains more details. References here are made to all three documents and the numerical index identifies them.

5 The interviews are characterised as qualitative, in-depth, semi-structured expert interviews. A qualitative approach implies focusing on deep and nuanced understandings of specific aspects of the respondents' experience, situation and context. In this kind of interview, the respondents' experiences, perspectives and opinions about specific issues are sought. In this study the qualitative approach was realised through the focus of the interviews – characteristics of and conditions for intelligence knowledge production. The interviews were windows of opportunity to gain insight into the everyday world of the analysts. The in-depth interviews provided

Introduction   15

a way to understand how the analysts thought about their own knowledge process and the effect it might have on the knowledge produced. The interviews created a basis for uncovering conditions under which intelligence knowledge is produced – the social discursive practice. Kvale, *Doing interviews*, pp. 21–3; also Kvale, *InterViews*, p. 1.

6 Aronoff and Kubik argue that participant observation makes a vital contribution in understanding the interplay between social structure and context and the actions of individuals (emphasised as a vital problem within political science in relation to the study of power and within 'The New Institutionalism'). They further argue that participant observation allows the researcher to uncover the interplay of structure and individuals (agency) in the actions and processes of everyday life – stating that the aim is to focus on *'the fabric of meaning in terms of which human beings interpret their experience and guide their actions'* (Clifford Geertz quoted in Aronoff and Kubik, *Anthropology and political science a convergent approach*, p. 30). Observation is a research technique used for acquiring insights into contextual aspects of, for instance, processes that are institutionalised into a specific environment. It is productive in studies where the focus is on aspects that might be institutionalised in such a 'natural way' that the respondents would not even reflect on them when asked in an interview. An advantage in using observation is that it permits the researcher to capture aspects of social phenomena that could not be captured otherwise (for example, institutionalised behaviour or behaviour that groups are not able to describe). Observation is valuable if the research is primarily concerned with issues people might describe in a way that is inconsistent with their actions in their everyday life (Jorgensen, *Participant observation a methodology for human studies*, pp. 15–16; and Patel and Tebelius, *Grundbok i forskningsmetodik*, p. 94). Observation is especially held as a productive methodological technique where the context is of importance to the research focus and where process and practice is a part of the research focus, since they allow the researcher to observe 'events as they happen' and to collect material 'from the context in which they occur' (Dargie, 'Observation in political research', p. 66). In this study, the observations were used to uncover and grasp the discursive practice and the social context – the everyday (professional) life of the analyst. Observations made a valuable contribution to identifying and understanding the conditions for the intelligence knowledge production. Conditions that are a part of the social context of the intelligence service were not necessarily recognised by the analysts and therefore were not possible to access through interviews. Observation provided me with a technique for collecting materials that could capture these aspects of the analytical environment.

7 Scott and Jackson argue that scholars tend to approach intelligence research in three broad themes; international historians that seem to approach intelligence *'to seek to explain the relationship between organisational structure and policymaking. . . . focus on particular cases of espionage and individual biographies . . .'*. A second approach focuses on intelligence failures and successes, primarily concerned with structural and cognitive difficulties. A third approach focuses on *'the political function of intelligence means of state control'* (Scott and Jackson, *Understanding intelligence in the twenty-first century*, pp. 4–5).
8 For example, in the aftermath of the 9/11 event there has been an extensive debate over the structure and responsibilities of the organisations in the intelligence community in the US – arguing that the organisations need to be better coordinated and more cooperative to get better intelligence. See, for example, Betts, 'Two faces of intelligence failure'; and Armed Forces Communications and Electronics Association (AFCEA) Intelligence Committee, 'Making analysis relevant: More than connecting the dots'.
9 See, for example, Hatlebrekke and Smith, 'Towards a new theory of intelligence failure?; or Kuhns, 'Intelligence failures'.
10 See, for example, Wohlstetter, *Pearl Harbor warning and decision*.
11 See, for example, Betts, 'Two faces of intelligence failure'.
12 This is discussed in evaluative reports and public inquiries concerning the problems of performance of intelligence services. For example, the WMD Commission Report elaborates on the poor performance of the US intelligence services in assessing and predicting the status of WMD in Iraq prior to the Second Gulf War. The report acknowledges problems within intelligence analysis tradecraft and the organisation and structure. Although the WMD Commission Report indicated that of a lack of transparency existed between what were hypotheses and assumptions and what were confirmed conclusions, it paid little attention to these issues in the recommendations. Instead the vast majority of recommendations to fix the intelligence problems were dedicated to organisational and coordination issues, and managing reforms (The Commission on the Intelligence Capabilities of the United States Regarding Weapons of Mass Destruction Report, Chapter 8). The focus of organisational and structural issues as means to fix intelligence may also be found in intelligence research literature. Also see Nyce, 'Hindsights bias, scientism and certitude'.
13 The problems of intelligence analysis that result from cognitive and psychological issues are also discussed through use of expressions such as 'group think' and 'mirror imaging'. These concepts are found in evaluative reports such as the WMD Commission Report and the Butler Review (Butler, *Review of intelligence on weapons of mass destruction*). The cognitive and psychological approach of explaining intelligence problems and fail-

Introduction 17

ures may also be found in intelligence research such as Heuer, *Psychology of intelligence analysis*; and Bar-Joseph, 'The professional ethics of intelligence analysis'. References are often made to Janis, *Groupthink*. Janis argues for the influence of cognitive biases on collective decision making. The cognitive problems of intelligence analysts are also underlined, for instance, by Christina Shelton. Shelton lists (among other things) personal biases, politicised views and cultural unawareness as factors contributing to poor intelligence analysis (Shelton, 'The roots of analytical failure in the U.S. intelligence community').

14 Sherman Kent's thinking about intelligence has had significant impact on the ideas concerning intelligence in research and the practice of intelligence (for example, in terms of processes, organisations and structures). He is commonly referred to as 'the father of intelligence analysis' in an American context (although his ideas have spread well outside the US). As both a scholar and an intelligence professional, he has argued for further intelligence studies and a reflective approach within the intelligence services and the analytical tradecraft.

15 Kent, 'A crucial estimate relived'.

16 Kent, *Strategic intelligence for American world policy*.

17 See, for instance, Bruce, 'Making analysis more reliable', p. 186. Another example of epistemic conditions affecting the results of intelligence analysis is discussed by Christopher Mole. Mole argues that there is a tangible epistemological effect of the reluctance to share information (often present in intelligence analysis) on the analytical result (Mole, 'Three philosophical lessons for the analysis of criminal and military intelligence'). Epistemic problems of intelligence analysis is also discussed by Ben-Israel, 'Philosophy and methodology of intelligence'.

18 As Gregory Treverton puts it '*The output of intelligence is better understandings in the heads of people who must act or decide. Building these understandings is a continuous process . . .*'. The reason for intelligence services is to aid decision makers to be better informed, and thus better prepared, when making decisions. Because of an intertwined relationship between intelligence and policy, one possible overall theoretical framework for studying intelligence in its role as knowledge producer would be that of policy analysis. However, the role of the intelligence services as a producer of knowledge within policy processes has not yet been thoroughly discussed within academia (Treverton, *Reshaping national intelligence for an age of information*, p. 107).

19 See, for example, Hulnick, 'The intelligence producer-policy consumer linkage'; Kahn, 'An historical theory of intelligence'; Wirtz, 'The intelligence-policy'; or Russel, 'The subjectivity of intelligence analysis and implications for the U.S. national security strategy'.

20 Johnson, 'Introduction to intelligence studies literature', pp. 6–7.
21 Hilsman focuses on the doctrines of the intelligence services during the institutionalisation of the intelligence services in post-Second World War America. His study comprises an evaluative approach and an intention to seek improvements of the performance of the intelligence analysis. Hilsman refers to doctrines as the *'body of rules and principles . . . [It] grows up to define the organization's role, it's functions and responsibilities . . .'* (Hilsman, *Strategic intelligence and national decisions*, p. 7).
22 Hilsman, *Strategic intelligence and national decisions*, p. 43. Operators are defined as '. . . *the men who make policy and conduct operations*', and in that respect are equivalent to what is commonly referred to as consumers of intelligence (Hilsman, *Strategic intelligence and national decisions*, p. 37).
23 Hilsman, *Strategic intelligence and national decisions*, p. 39.
24 Hilsman, *Strategic intelligence and national decisions*, p. 49.
25 Hilsman, *Strategic intelligence and national decisions*, p. 51. A similar conclusion is drawn by Thomas G. Hart in his study of belief systems in security elites in Sweden in the 1970s. Hart examines the conceptual constraints and openness to new ideas and concludes that: *'But another interpretation which is intuitively more satisfying is that the more constrained elites are trapped by their fixed conceptual apparatus into adhering to the established modes of analysis, thus finding themselves in possession of the middleground, both cognitively and normatively'* (Hart, 'The cognitive dynamics of Swedish security elites', p. 218).
26 The primary constraints identified by Johnston are, among other things, time and the focus of current intelligence (marginalisation of strategic analysis), rewards and incentives not supporting qualitative analysis, the idea of intelligence analysis being a 'tradecraft' allowing analysis to be an individual and tacit process, and the process of conducting intelligence analysis tending to imply searching for confirmation of the available information and current view (Johnston, *Analytical culture in the U.S. intelligence community*, Chapter 2). Wilhelm Agrell underlines a critical view on the intelligence knowledge stating that it could be understood as *'the production or creation of institutional and social ignorance'*. Agrell argues that the intelligence analysis has not been able to keep up the ideas of conditions for producing knowledge to the possibilities of mass information present in today's intelligence work (Agrell, 'The next 100 years? Reflections on the future of intelligence'.
27 Hansen, 'An argument for reflexivity in intelligence work'.
28 The approaches used by both Kent and Hilsman (and by Johnston) in their intelligence research reveal a viewpoint that the key to understanding and inquiry is to study the intelligence analysis over time and through the daily

Introduction

routines and approaches used by the intelligence professionals. This is an approach I find appealing.

29 Fischer, *Reframing public policy*, p. 13.
30 Mazey also refers to related research with the founding notion of the importance of norms, values, ideas and shared belief systems with quite recent concepts being developed such as 'policy paradigm' and 'policy frames'. Mazey, 'Introduction: Integrating gender – intellectual and 'real world' mainstreaming', p. 336.
31 Bacchi, *Analysing policy: What's the problem represented to be?*, p. xiv.
32 Lidskog et al., *Transboundary risk governance*, p. 15.
33 Lidskog et al., *Transboundary risk governance*, p. 22.
34 Lidskog et al., *Transboundary risk governance*, pp. 113–32.
35 Bacchi, *Analysing policy: What's the problem represented to be?*, pp. 30–5.
36 Fischer, *Reframing public policy*, p. 14.
37 Schön and Rein, *Frame reflection: Toward a resolution of intractable policy controversies*, p. 26. Schön and Rein argue that framing implies power via the interpretation of the problematic situations, the possibility of articulating problems, and the function of creating boundaries for interpretation of the social world. They also point to the distinction between the practitioners and the scholars of policy study, where the practitioners rarely have the interest and ambition, or the possibility to bring new perspectives as the frames have already been formulated (Schön and Rein, *Frame reflection: Toward a resolution of intractable policy controversies*, p. xvii).
38 Schön and Rein define frames as *'policy positions as resting on belief, perception and appreciation, which we call frames'* (Schön and Rein, *Frame reflection: Toward a resolution of intractable policy controversies*, pp. 23–6).
39 Fischer, *Reframing public policy*, p. viii.
40 Edelman cited in Fischer, *Reframing public policy*, p. 61.

Chapter 2

FRAMEWORK FOR RESEARCHING INTELLIGENCE KNOWLEDGE

IN SEARCH OF THEORY

At present intelligence-related research is an area in progress. James Der Derian argues that '*[Intelligence is the] least understood and "under-theorized" area of international relations.*'[1] I agree with Der Derian and suggest that the under-theorisation extends far beyond the intelligence role within international relations, and is valid in the social sciences for all research concerning intelligence. Although the research area is under-theorised, there are theories and theoretical concepts that may be productively used to better understand and bring new perspectives to intelligence in general and to intelligence analysis in particular.[2] It is argued in this book that intelligence should not be viewed as *sui generis*, as is often done within intelligence research. Instead, established social theoretical concepts will be used to bring new insights to and investigate intelligence knowledge.

As discussed, the perspective of critical policy analysis emphasises that the knowledge (produced by the actors) within the policy process is influenced by ideas and assumptions formed within a discourse or paradigm. This implies that although knowledge in the policy process may be argued through factual arguments, additional approaches are needed. Hence, the critical policy analysis position emphasises the need to pay attention to how policy knowledge is produced, the assumptions and presuppositions on which it is based and the social context within which it is constructed.

In this chapter, I propose a theoretical framework for investigating intelligence knowledge production and the social context within which it is produced. In addition to the critical policy analytical perspective drawn upon in the introductory chapter, the theoretical framework is founded on ideas from New Institutionalism, socialised knowledge and critical discourse analysis.

A VIEW ON INSTITUTIONALISM

Since all knowledge is produced by individuals within a social context, we need to (theoretically) understand this social context. In a sense, all collective action is structured and ordered according to a set of accepted rules and practices within a social context. (An example of this is individuals coming together within an organisation such as the MUST with the aim of producing intelligence.) This situating of action in a structured social context may be conceptualised as an *institution*. The concept of institution includes the idea of a structured and formal set of rules and practices (often thought of as a formal organisation). It also includes a set of informal set of practices that affect the actions of individuals. Further, an institution is a structure of practices that are in place over time; for the institution to function there needs to be a sense of a shared understanding of the constitutive idea of that institution.[3] In other words, institutions are *'collections of interrelated rules and routines that define appropriate actions in terms of relations between roles and situations'*.[4] For this study, the understanding of institutions implies that the actions of individuals are affected by a formal set of rules and routines and by the informal expectations and practices embedded in the social context. These formal and informal practices are further specified conceptually through the concept of *logic of appropriateness*. However, the overall idea is that the actions of the individual actors (the intelligence analysts) are affected by the character of the formal and informal practices constituting the institution (the MUST). The structuring effect of the institution should not be considered equivalent to a constraining effect and should also be thought of as an equally important enabler of the collective action undertaken by the individuals of the institution.[5]

In addition, the institution should not be thought of as a static structure. Rather, there is interplay between the individuals (agents) within the institution and the structure and character of the practices in place. The idea of interplay between agent and structure holds a dualistic character, which Giddens argues allows both for the constraining and the contingent character. This implies that the actions of a (knowledgeable) agent are affected and constrained by the structure, although the agent still has the ability change the structure. This discretion in the dualistic relation between agent and structure accounts for possible institutional change.[6] This change is possible because the individuals are not to be considered purely as victims of circumstance of the structuring effect that the institution enforces. Instead, the resources and the agents by their knowledgeable actions can promote change in the structure, over time. Nevertheless, the agents' actions are affected by the structure in which they are embedded.[7]

The formalised rules and structure of an organisation may be understood as the practical materialisation of the normative conviction within the institution of how work ought to be conducted.[8] At the same time, the informal rules, ideas and norms have just as important a structuring effect on the actions of agents. As the institution practices the intended activity, it brings together roles and identities. The institution should also hold the resources to make that activity feasible.[9] March and Olsen states that an institution is:

> a relatively stable collection of rules and practices, embedded in structures of resources that make actions possible – organizational, financial and staff capabilities, and structure of meaning that explain and justify behaviour – roles and identities and belongings, common purposes, and casual normative beliefs. Institutions are organizational arrangements that link roles/identities, accounts of situations resources and prescriptive rules and practices.[10]

In a similar way, Schmidt argues that the concept and ideas of discourse is vital in advancing understanding of the constitutive effect that norms and frames ideas and narratives of institutions and the practices, and the agents within them.[11] To further understand the underlying ideas and norms within institutions, Schmidt argues that it is necessary to take discourse seriously and pay attention to the practices within institutions.[12] In addition, Schmidt argues that the contingent character of the relation between agents and institutions makes institutional change possible:

> They are simultaneously constraining structures and enabling constructs of meaning, which are internal to 'sentient' (thinking and speaking) agents whose 'background ideational abilities' explain how they create and maintain institutions at the same time that their 'foreground discursive abilities' enable them to commu-

nicate critically about those institutions, to change (or maintain) them.[13]

Thus, the possibility of institutional change would depend on the possibility of critical communication occurring among the agents. Even though the agents possess discursive abilities, constraints may discourage them from formulating and communicating possible criticism of practices and the institution. In other words, the norms and practices may encourage continuity and discourage change, even though the agents are knowledgeable and have discursive abilities.

The intelligence service has rules, procedures and routines within which the intelligence analysts conduct their knowledge production. The actions of people in institutions are determined by a mix of the rules and informal practices. March and Olsen argue that the actions of people in the institutions may partly be explained by the idea of rational competition, but also by the informal code (ideas and norms) and actors endowed with different kinds of resources.[14] The character of these rules, routines and procedures creates a set of circumstances that influence how knowledge is produced. March and Olsen argue that expectations also affect how agents act: *'Much of the behaviour we observe in political institutions reflects the routine way in which people do what they are supposed to do.'*[15] That is, actions undertaken in political and policy processes are defined not only by the formal institutional structure and consequentialism, but also by an expectation among the agents of how they are supposed to act.

Routines may be formed by either (formal or informal) rules or a *'code of appropriate behaviour'*.[16] March and Olsen argue that the people within institutions base their actions primarily on *'identifying the normatively appropriate behaviour'*[17] rather than on rationally calculating the expected gains. The individuals learn appropriate behaviour through socialisation and absorb it through *'exploration of the nature of things, of self-conceptions, and of institutional and personal images'*.[18] Appropriate behaviours create stability and provide guidance for performing expected tasks. They also provide *'vocabularies that frame thought and understandings and define what are legitimate arguments and standards of justification and criticism in different situations'*.[19] The rules and codes of appropriate behaviour also encompass worldview and values, thus constraining the recognition of possible perceptions, priorities and the direction of attention within given situations.[20]

Although appropriate behaviour evolves, the rules of appropriateness tend to be slow in changing.[21] The logic of appropriateness also holds a certain set of traditions and beliefs that are taken for granted.[22] Because the experts involved in policy processes are subject to the logic of appropriateness, they are influenced by biases and: 'seem to find facts and theoretical implications consistent with their policy preferences and forget facts and theoretical implications inconvenient for their purposes. Expert judgements are not magically shielded from personal commitments and professional biases.'[23]

Studying the characteristics of the logic of appropriateness within an institution may aid in understanding why its members act and conduct their profession in specific ways. In a sense, the aim of this study may be conceived of as a quest to investigate the logic of appropriateness for producing knowledge of a specific institution – the intelligence service. The perspective underlined by critical policy analysts – that policy knowledge is affected and imbued with ideas, assumptions and presuppositions – is supplemented by the ideas of the logic of appropriateness. This perspective holds that the actions of agents (in this case the analysts producing knowledge) are affected and guided by rules, routines and norms in the social context of the institution. Both critical policy analysis and New Institutionalism holds that knowledge should be understood in a social context; to investigate the social act of producing knowledge, this study turns to the critical discourse analysis and the ideas of socialised knowledge.

A VIEW ON KNOWLEDGE

Critical Discourse Analysis

Within social science, one approach to investigate knowledge is through the ideas of *'discourse'*. The concepts of discourse, discursive practice and social practice are situated within an understanding that knowledge is produced within a social context. Further, Norman Fairclough argues, that within critical discourse analysis discourse *'contributes to the construction of systems of knowledge and beliefs'*.[24] Fairclough argues that the critical element in discourse analysis aims at *'showing connections and causes which are hidden'*.[25] Based on this, I argue that discourse and discursive practices can further our understanding of the intelligence knowledge by uncovering and conceptualising the manner in

Framework

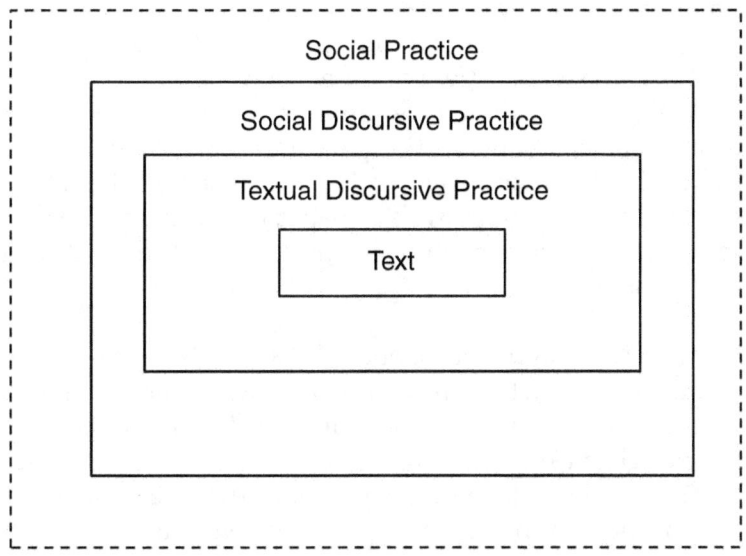

Figure 2.1 Fairclough's model for discourse applied in the context of intelligence

which meaning is assigned and interpreted in descriptions and explanations of the social world in intelligence knowledge.[26]

Discourse is a contested concept, although in this study it will be understood as constitutive of how the subject under investigation understands and brings meaning to social entities. Fairclough argues that within the framework of critical discourse analysis, discourses constitute the understanding of the social world (provides its meaning). Discourses, therefore, constitute and identify the key entities in the conception of a world and the formation of knowledge or, as Fairclough says, *'and it is these social effects of discourse that are the focused upon in discourse analysis'*.[27] Fairclough further underlines the constitutive role of discourse by arguing that *'language signifies reality in the sense of constructing meanings for it, rather than that discourse is in a passive relation to reality'*.[28] Theoretically, he situates his ideas in a model, with the three concepts of discourse, discursive practices and social practices (Figure 2.1).

Any discursive 'event' is seen as being simultaneously a piece of text, an instance of discursive practice, and an instance of social practice. The 'text' dimension attends to language analysis of the text. The 'discursive practice' dimension like 'interaction' in the 'text-and-interaction' view of discourse, specifies the nature of the process of text production and interpretation, for example which types of discourse are drawn upon and how they are combined. The 'social practice' dimension attends to issues of concern in social analysis such as the institutional and organizational circumstances of the discursive event and how that shapes the nature of the discursive event and how that shapes the nature of the discursive practice, and the constitutive/constructive effects of discourse referred to above.[29]

According to Fairclough, the relation between discourses, discursive practice and social practice are highly intertwined and all three need to be considered for a full understanding of the discourse to be possible. Fairclough makes a strong argument, with which I concur, for the necessity of acknowledging the influence that the social practice of an institution has on individuals, the discursive practice and thereby the discourse, in terms of social positioning, structural conformation and struggles and power.[30] Fairclough's model illustrates the interconnectedness between the discourse (text),[31] the discursive practice (production, distribution and consumption of text) and the social practice. The text is considered as a discursive event when the *'texts are made up of forms which past discursive practices, condensed into conventions, has endowed with meaning potential'*.[32] This implies that it is possible to find and expose a discourse by analysing the text. Because discourses articulate and structure knowledge within texts, it is vital to investigate the articulatory aspect of the discursive practice. The knowledge production within the intelligence service may be approached by the concepts of discourse, discursive practice and social practice.

For this study a refined understanding of the concept of discursive practice in Fairclough's model is suggested. In this model there is a further division within the concept of discursive practice (which includes the production, distribution and consumption of texts),[33] which I refer to as a distinction between a 'social discursive practice' and a 'textual discursive practice'.[34] This distinction is not seen as finite and mutually exclusive; rather, it is made to emphasise practice and ideas in relation to the characteristics of the process (form) of producing knowledge – social discursive practice. Textual discursive practice seeks to underline the analytical aspects (substance) underlying the process of creating knowledge and text. Hence, even on a theoretical level, there is interplay between all these concepts (also stressed by Fairclough). The discursive practices are viewed as non-static (hence, to a degree contingent on the possibility of change in discourse and discursive practice).[35] They nevertheless impose a social constraint on the discourses produced. The constraint varies depending on the institutional setting. Fairclough argues that the social constraint within a discursive practice is internalised in the production process and the constraints are the most non-conscious part of the discursive practice.[36] He argues that an analysis of a discursive practice should be undertaken from both a micro and macro perspective. The former should focus on *'how participants produce and interpret texts on the basis of their members' resources'*.[37] The latter should be undertaken to focus on *'the nature of the members' resources that is being drawn upon in order to produce and interpret texts, and whether it is being drawn upon in normative or creative ways'*.[38] The line between the discursive and the social practice is not necessarily distinct. Rather, Fairclough argues that the discursive practice is a part of social practice.

Critical discourse analysis provides a framework for the relation between consuming and producing knowledge in a social context through the concepts *social practice, social* and *textual discursive practice* and *discourse*. However, this investigation of knowledge in the context of the intelligence service demands further elaboration before these concepts can be used for an empirical investigation. Therefore, the framework of critical discourse analysis is supplemented with the general ideas of socialised knowledge.

Social Knowledge

Because intelligence analysis produces knowledge within a social context, the social aspect of knowledge must be conceptualised and investigated. The implication of the social context and the attached ideas, norms and assumptions within the scientific community are discussed within what may be broadly defined as the sociology of socialised knowledge. Within this field, it is held that all knowledge is produced and affected by its social context. Its argument over the interplay between social context and knowledge production has been widely accepted within related research fields, primarily through Thomas Kuhn in his *The Structure of Scientific Revolutions*.[39] Through his research, which is based on the evolution of diverse discoveries within the scientific community, Kuhn convincingly argued the impact of conventions of ideas, norms and worldviews within the context of knowledge production. Following the ideas invoked by Kuhn's and his concept (paradigm), the research tradition of the Strong Programme has been engaged with the social (as well as the psychological and cultural) aspects of scientific knowledge production.[40]

Kuhn and his successors and the Strong Programme use the scientific community as their object of study.[41] However, there are differences between the community of science and the community of intelligence. The scientific community represents a social context with a far more sophisticated and in-depth conscious approach with ontological and epistemological considerations than does the intelligence community. While the science and the scientific process holds critical examination, open discussion and transparency as being fundamental, intelligence is, to a great extent, characterised by closedness and secrecy. Similarly, the scientific community has a long tradition of questioning and furthering the ideas and concepts of theory of science; the intelligence community lacks an equivalent.

At the same time, the knowledge produced within the intelligence community differs from the everyday knowledge produced by laypeople – an alternative research approach within 'The Strong Programme'.[42] However, the general purpose and assumed focal point of the sociology of knowledge – *'we can study belief and knowledge in relation to their social context'*[43] – is important for this study. To provide a theoretical middle ground between the scientific community and laypeople's knowledge context, the intended meaning of the concepts of social and textual discursive practices will be elaborated. The elaboration is to a large extent founded on the essential ideas of Fleck's ideas on 'style of thought' (*Denkstil*) and 'collective of thought' (*Denkkollektiv*).[44] Nevertheless, references will be made throughout the discussion to highlight the similarities and the discrepancies to later ideas on socialised knowledge.

SOCIAL AND TEXTUAL DISCURSIVE PRACTICE

Textual Discursive Practice

The concept of 'style of thought' as well as the concept of textual discursive practice implies that the knowledge created is permeated with a specific system of thought. The development of scientific research and understanding of facts within science are highly dependent on the culturally and socially accepted ideas about the phenomena. Before there is science, there are preconceived ideas that create a system of logic and reason and thus a system of thought. Throughout history what have been accepted as valid facts have been constituted by a socially constructed and accepted convention created to explain various phenomena to keep an existing 'style of thought' intact. 'Once a structurally complete and closed system of opinions consisting of many details and relations has been formed, it offers enduring resistance to anything that contradicts it.'[45]

The 'style of thought' within a textual discursive practice create a strong resistance to change and functions as a constraint, making it difficult to contradict the system of thought (or its conclusions).[46] The form of scientific theories and scientific discoveries are socially embedded and the closed structure and stylistic consonance with other accepted theories serves a formative function for further advancing knowledge. The meaning and truth value of theories are a function of the community. This does not imply that truth is relative or subjective in the popular sense of the word. Rather, the 'style of thought' constrains criticism of the accepted knowledge within the thought system and makes irregularities seem unthinkable. Observations and facts that do not fit into the system of thought remain unrecognised, and if they become known, they are suppressed.[47] It is characterised by a mutual understanding of which problems and other conditions are of interest to the 'collective of thought'. In a similar fashion, Kuhn acknowledges this constitutive role of the paradigm in the scientific community. Kuhn argues: 'A paradigm, can for that matter, even insulate the community form[s] those socially important problems that are not reducible to the puzzle form, because they cannot be stated in terms of the conceptual and instrumental tools the paradigm supplies.'[48] Kuhn thereby concedes to the formative role of the paradigm concerning what scientific endeavours researchers undertake.[49]

A 'style of thought' (or a paradigm) holds a predefined worldview that implies articulatory power. However, the 'style of thought' is broader than worldview. The 'style of thought' within the textual discursive practice implies a specific and accepted language, it has become institutionalised and *'every contradiction seem unthinkable and impossible'*.[50] Language, therefore, plays a vital role in exposing and constituting an established textual discursive practice. For example, lack of criticism or awareness of conceptualisations could indicate that basic assumptions and presuppositions have become truth claims.[51]

In general, only facts compatible with the 'style of thought' are considered as valid. This implies that contradictory facts are considered inadmissible and possible incommensurabilities are not recognised. However, as time passes conformity declines and eventually new discoveries are possible and knowledge further develops. In this sense, the 'style of thought' (and ultimately the textual discursive practice) is not static and it has a contingency that allows for new scientific discoveries.[52]

Further, the constraining nature of a 'style of thought' implies that logical consistency is the primary momentum for knowledge produced. Fleck argues:

> contradictions in a belief are 'explained' and smooth over, [this] is a very instructive episode. It shows how logical consistency at all costs is sought in the system and how the logic of practice can be used. Any teaching endeavours to be within a logical system, but how often that is at the price of a *petitio princpii* (circle proof)! (. . .) Such a stylistically, closed system is not immediately open to change: everything needs first to be reinterpreted in terms of style.[53]

Hence, Fleck argues the endeavour to keep the style of thought consistent prevails over the use of logical arguments or interpretations of facts and indices. Kuhn concedes and refers to this as a consequence of the directing power that paradigmatic assumption has for science undertaken within normal science.[54]

As a consequence, when a 'style of thought' has permeated the process of establishing knowledge, it becomes difficult to sort out what is assumption and presumption and what are facts and proof for the conclusions drawn. The difficulty of sorting out the difference also implies that the knowledge created is greatly influenced by the existing knowledge, and that breaking away from this requires *'breach[ing] the specific laws of the thought structure'*.[55] This argument is further highlighted through the role of the individual scientist (agent) as the interpretive link between what is stated and the means by which what is stated can be supported by facts, proof or evidence, that is, qualifiers.[56] Implicitly, the mind of the scientist is permeated by a 'style of thought';

the researcher will only search for what is considered as inference proof within the textual discursive practice.[57]

Social Discursive Practice

The position of social knowledge implies the importance of the social context in which the individual's thinking and thought is both enhanced and constrained. Hence, the inevitability (and advantages) of the knowledge being a social act and the constraints that a 'collective of thought' exercises on the individuals and consequently on the knowledge act itself – the social discursive practice.[58]

The social discursive practice defines what is accepted as proof in the knowledge act and what assumptions are accepted as a frame of interpretation. Further, Fleck argues that the thought collective has a constraining effect on the development and heterogeneity of thought, as stability and search for continuity are defining features.

> The origin of her thinking is not in her, but in the social environment in which she lives, in the social atmosphere she breathes. She cannot think otherwise than what is determined by the influence of her mind that the social environment is inevitably exercising.[59]

That is, the individuals in a 'collective of thought' are seldom aware of the influence affecting their assumptions and thoughts: 'when a conception permeates a thought collective strongly enough, so that it penetrates as far as everyday life and idiom and has become the viewpoint in the literal sense of the word, any contradiction appears unthinkable and unimaginable'.[60] The 'collective of thought' has an articulatory power on the knowledge act itself. It is only what is accepted within the social discursive practice for the knowledge act that will be pursued and investigated.[61] Hence, the chances of finding empirical facts that contradict the assumptions are therefore highly unlikely. As a consequence, critique and reflection are often considered unimportant and superfluous. Further, the closedness of the 'collective of thought' that underlines the creation of knowledge is highly dependent on previously established accepted knowledge. The facts put forward must be consistent with the 'intellectual interests', deemed valid and expressed in accordance with the literary style accepted by the 'collective of thought'.[62] 'The literary style – a specific use of language – evolves within the social discursive practice. The meaning and understanding of words and terms change and become impregnated with more than just the lexical logic of the word.'[63] 'The language and the literary style within the "collective of thought" holds a specific meaning and use of words is significant to identifying the assumptions and preconceived understanding within a "style of thought".'[64] Therefore the use of language is an intermediary for the changes made in ideas and assumptions within both the discursive practices. Hence textual and social discursive practices of the intelligence service may be studied through analysing whether and how the meaning of concepts are portrayed and argued in the intelligence analysis.

Also, the individuals (agents) do not exercise equal impact in the knowledge acts within the collective. The social collective may be said to consist of two sets of members: an *esoteric circle* of initiated members and an *exoteric circle* of more distanced members.[65] The esoteric circle is the core of the 'collective of thought' and communicates the essence of and preconditions for the 'style of thought' throughout the exoteric circles. At the same time, the structuring influence and the articulatory power make questioning and critiquing virtually impossible. The individuals (in this case the intelligence analysts) are a part of a social context that embodies ideas and norms affecting the knowledge produced and the individuals need to relate to the group of individuals operating within this social context.

THE FRAMEWORK APPLIED

Framework for Researching the MUST

The theoretical point of departure for framing and structuring this study of the intelligence service is that the MUST is a producer of knowledge within policy processes. Thus, drawing on emphasis made within the critical policy analysis, the knowledge produced within the MUST affects how specific issues are framed and understood (and ultimately affect the policy formed). Also, this perspective underlines that knowledge produced within and for policy is affected by worldviews, preconceived ideas and discourse and, further, the knowledge produces (or reproduces) discourses of its own. Therefore, it is important to understand and investigate what constitutes such discourse and how it is conceived.

The intelligence service as a social and political actor within which knowledge is produced may be further framed by ideas of New Institutionalism. This perspective underlines that the actions within the MUST are situated within an institutional and organisational context affecting both the MUST and the individuals (agents) within it. They are affected by formal rules and by informal practices, thus creating a logic of appropriateness for the institution, which affects both the agent's actions and the knowledge produced. The institutional structure is not to be considered static; rather, the structuration by rules and practices holds contingency and may be altered by the actions of the agents. To conceptualise the relation between routines, norms and procedures that affect the agents within the context of the institution and the knowledge produced before the empirical study, we turn to the ideas of critical discourse analysis. In this study, the social context and its constraints within the discursive practice are of interest because they influence the analysts' process and the act of producing knowledge.

Critical discourse analysis suggests that producing knowledge for the policy process may be conceptualised by the use of the concepts of *social practice, social* and *textual discursive practice* and *discourse*. The social practice is interpreted as the formal and external institutional setting that affects the processes of the MUST and the analysts (agents). Further, structuration of the internal social context of the MUST is theoretically conceptualised by social and textual discursive practices. That is, the actions of the analysts are affected by the practices in place within the MUST, although at the same time the analysts hold the possibility of affecting the same practices by their actions (producing new practices or reproducing them). The knowledge produced through these practices constitutes an intelligence discourse, which can be uncovered through predicate and conceptual analysis of the text of the estimates.[66]

In this study the relation between the concepts in the model of critical discourse analysis is interpreted as: the *discourse* (knowledge found in the text of the estimate) and the *discursive practices* (the social conditions for interpretation and production of knowledge within the MUST) situated within a specific *social practice* (the external and formal institutional setting) of the intelligence service. Therefore, the model outlined in Figure 2.1 shows the relation when applied to the empirical case of the MUST. As shown above, the overall perspective in this study is critical policy analysis. This theoretical perspective implies that the knowledge itself is imbued with assumptions and presuppositions, both explicit and implicit, which are greatly influential in regard to the knowledge produced. The theoretical perspective also contains an understanding that these assumptions and presuppositions are upheld, changed or reaffirmed within a certain set of social and institutional features in the military intelligence service itself. Thus, in the overall purpose of this study, to examine the characteristics of knowledge in intelligence analysis and also to investigate how that knowledge is affected by the social context of its production, the military intelligence service, two research areas are posed.

The first research area is: What characterises the institutional and social context within which the intelligence knowledge is produced? Does the institutional and social context for producing intelligence knowledge constitute a specific 'collective of thought' and, if so, how can it be characterised?

The second research area is: What are the characteristics of intelligence knowledge in terms of assumptions and presuppositions that constitute the view of the world, define the objects of knowledge, assert the methodological considerations and establish the view on facts and the aesthetic norm of how estimates ought to be conveyed? Does intelligence knowledge constitute a specific 'style of thought' and, if so, how can it be characterised?

By investigating these two questions this book seeks to bring a new and critical perspective to the study of intelligence. It uses established theoretical perspectives to understand and contextualise the intelligence service as a knowledge producer within the political policy process. To conduct a study for the purpose of uncovering the conditions for intelligence knowledge production, I set out to critically study the intelligence service to try to a bring perspective into an established way of thought within a field of research.

Notes

1 James Der Derian quoted in Scott and Jackson, *Understanding intelligence in the twenty-first century*, p. 2.
2 For similar arguments see, for example, Fry and Hochstein, 'Epistemic communities', pp. 14–28 or for another example of a theoretically funded intelligence research see Grey and Sturdy, 'Historicising knowledge-intensive organizations'.

3 Peters, *Institutional theory in political science the 'New Institutionalism'*, pp. 18–19, 29ff. See also March and Olsen, *Rediscovering institutions*, p. 20ff.
4 March and Olsen, *Rediscovering institutions*, p. 160.
5 Peters, *Institutional theory in political science the 'New Institutionalism'*, p. 30.
6 Giddens, *Central problems in social theory action structure and contradiction in social analysis*, pp. 5–7, 55–59. See also Whittington, 'Putting Giddens into action', pp. 696–7.
7 Giddens, *Central problems in social theory action structure and contradiction in social analysis*, pp. 5–7, 55–59.
8 Selznick, 'Institutionalism "old" and "new"'.
9 Schmidt, 'Taking ideas and discourse seriously', pp. 13–15.
10 March and Olsen, *The logic of appropriateness*, p. 5.
11 Schmidt, 'Discursive institutionalism'.
12 Schmidt, 'Taking ideas and discourse seriously'.
13 Schmidt, 'Taking ideas and discourse seriously', p. 4. In this context *'background ideational abilities'* encompass human capacities, dispositions and know-how about how the world works (following the institution's logic of practice. *'Foreground discursive abilities'* encompass the agents' ability to think outside the institution (in a critical way). Schmidt, 'Discursive institutionalism', pp. 14–16.
14 March and Olsen, *Rediscovering institutions*, pp. 16–17 and Selznick, 'Institutionalism "Old" and "New"', p. 274.
15 March and Olsen, *Rediscovering institutions*, p. 21.
16 March and Olsen refers to rules as *'routines, procedures, conventions, roles, strategies, organizational forms, and technologies ... We also need the beliefs, paradigms, codes, cultures, and knowledge that surround, support, elaborate, and contradict those roles and routines'* (March and Olsen, *Rediscovering institutions*, p. 22).
17 March and Olsen, *Rediscovering institutions*, p. 22.
18 March and Olsen, *Rediscovering institutions*, p. 23.
19 March and Olsen, *The logic of appropriateness*, p. 5
20 March and Olsen, *The logic of appropriateness*, p. 11.
21 March and Olsen, *The logic of appropriateness*, pp. 9, 13.
22 March and Olsen, *The logic of appropriateness*, pp. 14–15. See also Schmidt, 'Taking ideas and discourse seriously' for a discussion on how ideas and discourse are important aspects of explaining change and continuity in relation to institutions (and policy).
23 Lakoff (1966) referenced in March and Olsen, *Rediscovering institutions*, p. 31.
24 Fairclough, *Discourse and social change*, p. 64.
25 Fairclough, *Discourse and social change*, p. 9.

26 Drawing on the earlier works by Foucault, Fairclough argues that applying critical discourse analysis is viable for a wider context than that of the sciences. *'Foucault is concerned with the discursive practices as constitutive of knowledge, and with the conditions of transformation of the knowledge associated with a discursive formation into a science. . . . Although the focus of Foucault (1972) is upon the discursive formations of the human sciences, his insights are transferable to all types of discourse.'* Fairclough, Discourse and social change, p. 40.

27 Fairclough, *Discourse and social change*, p. 3.

28 Fairclough, *Discourse and social change*, p. 42.

29 Fairclough, *Discourse and social change*, p. 4.

30 Fairclough, *Discourse and social change*, p. 72.

31 Fairclough argues that *text* should be broadly defined, including all types of written documents, for instance transcribed interviews.

32 Fairclough, *Discourse and social change*, p. 75.

33 Here the intelligence analysts could be considered both as consumer of text – information and data presented to them in the form of incoming reports – and as producers of text because they produce the intelligence assessments that are disseminated to external intelligence consumers. For an excellent study that uses Fairclough's model for showing the relation of both relation of consumer and producer of texts, see Gustafsson, *Pamfletter! En diskursiv praktik och dess strategi i tidig svensk politisk offentlighet*.

34 I am grateful to Professor Mats Lindberg's creative and insightful comments and ideas on this point.

35 Fairclough argues that the discursive practice in play is the result of previous struggles over discourse that may be seen as temporarily institutionalised but may be changed over time. Hence, Fairclough interrupts a structuralist take on the relation between structure and agent, acknowledging that the members of a discursive practice may change the practice. This is stressed by emphasising a top-down and bottom-up understanding of the constitution of a discursive practice (Fairclough, *Discourse and social change*, pp. 80–1).

36 Fairclough, *Discourse and social change*, p. 81.

37 Fairclough, *Discourse and social change*, p. 85.

38 Fairclough, *Discourse and social change*, p. 85.

39 Kuhn, *The structure of scientific revolutions*.

40 Meyer, 'Review essay visiting relatives'.

41 Meyer, 'Review essay visiting relatives'.

42 Berger and Luckmann, *The social construction of reality*.

43 Millstone, 'A framework for the sociology of knowledge', p. 111.

44 Fleck, *Uppkomsten och utvecklingen av ett vetenskapligt faktum*.

Framework 37

45 Fleck, *Genesis and development of a scientific fact*, p. 27.
46 Fleck, *Uppkomsten och utvecklingen av ett vetenskapligt faktum*, p. 100.
47 Wesely, 'Philosophy of science and sociology of knowledge'. The constraining effect, although still holding a contingent element, is discussed by Kuhn (Kuhn, *The structure of scientific revolutions*). See also Bloor and Edge who argue that the social character of knowledge is a necessity for scientific research, although encompassing a constraining feature for the new knowledge and research (Bloor and Edge, 'For the record').
48 Kuhn, *The structure of scientific revolutions*, p. 37.
49 Törnebohm, *Inquiring systems and paradigms*, p. 14.
50 Fleck, *Uppkomsten och utvecklingen av ett vetenskapligt faktum*, p. 39.
51 However, Törnebohm says that if the findings are argued and proven in such a manner that they are considered to conform to an appreciated literary style, they are more likely to win favour (Törnebohm, *Inquiring systems and paradigms*). Kuhn on the other hand (although discussing conceptualisation more thoroughly) only briefly mentions the absence of a neutral scientific language to for communicating scientific research. However, he argues that the differences (in meaning) of the concepts are one of the important difficulties for inter-paradigm dialogue (Kuhn, *The structure of scientific revolutions*, pp. 125–6, 129).
52 Kuhn defines normal science as the scientific endeavour of *'an actualization [being] achieved by extending the knowledge of those facts that the paradigm displays as particularly revealing, by increasing the extent of the match between those facts and the paradigm's predictions, and by further articulation of the paradigm itself'* (Kuhn, *The structure of scientific revolutions*, p. 24). Hence, the purpose of scientific work is not to evaluate or challenge the paradigm (or its assumptions), but rather to verify the same. He elaborates the prerequisites for formulating new theories and argues that as the theories accepted within scientific community during an era of *normal science* display decreasing explanatory power of observations (anomalies occur and increase), the theories experience a crisis. As a result, the paradigmatic power of science unravels and new science and theories are sought and formed. To respond to a paradigmatic crisis, the scientific community formulates *'numerous articulations and ad hoc modifications of their theory in order to eliminate any apparent conflict'* (Kuhn, *The structure of scientific revolutions*, p. 78). Eventually, the modifications and ad hoc responses have difficulty in forming a coherent theoretical framework and a paradigmatic shift (a scientific revolution) takes place (Kuhn, *The structure of scientific revolutions*, pp. 90–1).
53 Fleck, *Uppkomsten och utvecklingen av ett vetenskapligt faktum*, pp. 41–42.
54 Kuhn, *The structure of scientific revolutions*, p. 26.
55 Fleck, *Uppkomsten och utvecklingen av ett vetenskapligt faktum*, p. 47.

56 Fleck, *Uppkomsten och utvecklingen av ett vetenskapligt faktum*, p. 49.
57 An ethical approach must be applied to research when, for instance, a researcher uses results from other researchers. Here Törnebohm distinguishes between internal and external ethics of research. Internal ethics involve a responsibility toward other researchers, and its primary concern is the possibility of using the results for further research. External ethics concerns the responsibilities towards recipients outside the community of researchers. The primary concern here is that the result of the research may affect policy and society. Törnebohm argues that a researcher might have to consider the language used while disseminating the research results, suggesting that the language used within the inquiry community might not be easily accessible to outsiders (Törnebohm, *Inquiring systems and paradigms*, p. 17).
58 Fleck, *Uppkomsten och utvecklingen av ett vetenskapligt faktum*, pp. 50–3.
59 Fleck, *Uppkomsten och utvecklingen av ett vetenskapligt faktum*, p. 55.
60 Fleck, *Uppkomsten och utvecklingen av ett vetenskapligt faktum*, p. 28.
61 Fleck, *Uppkomsten och utvecklingen av ett vetenskapligt faktum*, p. 102.
62 Fleck, *Uppkomsten och utvecklingen av ett vetenskapligt faktum*, p. 102.
63 Fleck, *Uppkomsten och utvecklingen av ett vetenskapligt faktum*, p. 100.
64 Fleck, *Uppkomsten och utvecklingen av ett vetenskapligt faktum*, p. 109.
65 Fleck argues that the *Denkkollektivs* are not mutually exclusive. One individual may be a member of several *Denkkollektivs* concerning different aspects of life. One can be a member of a specific religious group – one *Denkkollektiv* – and still be a part of political group – another *Denkkollektiv* – simultaneously. In the same manner one individual may be a part of an esoteric part of a *Denkkollektiv* and a part of an exoteric in yet another (Fleck, *Uppkomsten och utvecklingen av ett vetenskapligt faktum*, p. 105).
66 To uncover the 'structured meaning in use' in the text of the estimates, this study is inspired by predicate analysis in particular. Predicate analysis implies an empirical study of language practice to *'draw out a more general structure of relational disjunctions and hierarchies that orders persons' knowledge about the things defined by the discourse'* (Weldes and Saco cited in Milliken, 'The study of discourses in international relations', p. 231). Hence, in the context of this study, this view suggests that the subjects (here the intelligence analysts) are formulating and maintaining the dominant discourse and are endowed with authority for articulation and re-articulation. The predicate analysis suggests that subjects are constructed through predications within the language practice in texts by attributing specific features and characteristics to them. Milliken argues that a predicative analysis *'is suitable for the study of language practices on texts (e.g. diplomatic documents, theory articles, transcripts of interviews), the main research materials for International Relations discourse analysis'*. Predicate

analysis, Milliken further argues, is suitable both for analysing the subjects articulating discourses and for reasoning within a specific context. 'Predicate analysis focuses on the language practice of predication – the verbs, adverbs and adjectives that attach to nouns. Predications of a noun construct the thing(s) named as a particular sort of thing, with particular features and capacities. Among the objects so constituted may be subjects, defined through being assigned capacities for and modes of acting and interacting' (Milliken, 'The study of discourses in international relations', p. 232). The idea is that predicate analysis (as one form of discourse analysis) should not only establish the objects, but should also define the objects and their relational spaces and, thereby, order this into a frame for *'defining certain subject identities'* (Milliken, 'The study of discourses in international relations', p. 233). See also Peräkylä, 'Analyzing text and talk' (2008), pp. 354–8 for a discussion (drawing on Foucault and discourse analysis) on the implication and power vested in description and how that may be uncovered through various types of discourse analysis. Hence, through predicate analysis of language practices, it is possible to uncover a discourse and in this study a specific 'style of thought'. I argue that predicate analysis is one technique for analytically uncovering the assumptions (and possibly the valuations) underlying the intelligence analysis made in the estimates. In the context of the estimates, the use of predicate analysis is extended to identifying what 'name the things are named' within the given construct (i.e. what concepts and terms are used for the societal phenomena described in the text). Sartori argues that what is not named risks remaining unnoticed and the naming choice implies an extensive process of interpretation (Sartori, *Social science concepts*, p. 16). Sartori is working under assumption that *'Clear thinking requires clear language. In turn, a clear language requires that its terms be explicitly defined'* (Sartori, *Social science concepts*, p. 22). He argues that it is a necessity because concepts are the *'meaning-centered units'* in our construction and are used for whatever we are trying to describe. Sartori further argues that when there is ambiguity over how concepts are defined or confusions of the meanings of a concept, this ambiguity may occur on an individual and on a collective level. If there is a collective ambiguity about the use of a concept in a context (or discipline), the ascribed meaning to the concept become an individual meaning. Thus, such a situation may risk undermining the body of knowledge created within that context. (Sartori, *Social science concepts*, pp. 27–35) Sartori outlines a methodological framework for achieving (and constructing) a consistent use of concepts (within specific contexts), expressed in *'practiced oriented rule form'* (Sartori, *Social science concepts*, p. 28). In this study, I have used the parts of this framework for unfolding the conceptual use within the intelligence knowledge production.

Analysing the concepts and terms is intended to include an examination of 1) what concepts are used, whether they are defined, and if these definitions are unambiguous and consistent in the declared meaning; 2) whether these concepts remain consistent throughout the texts; and 3) if other words are used as synonyms, what requirements were used for attributing the different meanings to justify the inconsistent use of words. The set of rules further suggests significant questions (of how definition of concepts should be constructed) and strategies for obtaining such concepts. However, in this study, the ideas suggested by Sartori primarily function as a guide for the aspects of conceptual construction and the applied concepts that are important to examine the impact it might have on the knowledge produced. The rules are discussed at length and presented in a condensed form (Sartori, *Social science concepts*, pp. 63–4). This methodological approach is used to further the uncovering of the textual discursive practice within the intelligence knowledge production process.

Chapter 3

INTELLIGENCE IN SWEDISH POLITICAL CULTURE

THE SPECIFICITIES OF SWEDISH POLITICAL CULTURE

As stated above, intelligence literature tends to centre on states with extensive intelligence presence throughout the political establishment (for example the US and the UK).[1] In contrast, this case study of intelligence is situated within a small state, where intelligence holds a more modest institutional position. Intelligence in general, and the MUST in particular, is a rather unusual topic within both contemporary Swedish political debate and research in the social sciences.[2] Correspondingly, the specific traits of the Swedish political culture and political institutional arrangement for intelligence cannot be assumed to be common knowledge. Therefore, this chapter begins with a brief reflection on the particularities of the Swedish political culture that effect the intelligence community itself, and the role of the intelligence community within the institutional setting. It merely serves as general overview of a selection of specificities in the political culture – a background for the following chapters describing the intelligence responsibilities and directions within the institutional setting, and a brief overview of the MUST.

A CULTURE OF COMPROMISE AND CONSENSUS

The function of and role for intelligence has a reclusive existence in societal and political life in Sweden. The character of societal and political life – like in any state – has a number of specificities, thus constituting the unique Swedish political culture. Drawing on such a wide and contested concept as political culture should be seen as a most humble attempt to create some sort of flavour for the Swedish political context, rather than intending a thorough analysis of the same. First, the political system is a unitary parliamentary constitutional monarchy. Even though the latest thoroughgoing constitutional amendments date as late as 1976, the roots of the Swedish democracy go back as far as the seventeenth century.[3] However, this chapter aims at displaying the culture within that system.

In the Swedish political context the presence of established constitutive principles for ruling (usually found in constitutional texts) does not hold the same precedence as, for instance, the constitution in the US. Nevertheless, an institutionalised overarching idea in the Swedish political context is that of division of power. That is, between the legislative, judicial and the executive power laid down in the constitution (The Instrument of Government (the principal content of the fundamental laws), the Riksdag Act (*Riksdagsordningen*) and the Electoral Law). In Sweden, this division of power is particularly evident in the long tradition of extensive autonomy for government agencies. Also, the board of the government agencies contains representation from the parliamentary parties. Further, multi-party participation is practiced in parliamentary inquiries. The fundamental laws guiding political processes tend to be more descriptive of how the processes work rather than normative and guiding principles.[4]

As a consequence, Swedish political culture is characterised in general by the concept of 'the Swedish model'. The Swedish political culture has been described as *'deliberative, rationalistic, open, and consensual.'*[5] This description from 1969 is supplemented with a later description of the Swedish political culture as pragmatic. In this sense pragmatism implies that decisions are reached through negotiating and 'muddling through' rather than guidance from founding principles.

Compromise and consensus is vital for the Swedish political system. The absence of comprehensive reliance on constitutional guidance for the principles and processes for political decision making implies a political culture characterised by negotiation and compromise with the aspiration of reaching consensus. This aspiration within the political process for decision making might therefore be more time-consuming – hence the negotiating between political parties and diverse interests – and is sought through dialogue across party boundaries and interests, with modest open political conflict. In order to make compromise and consensus possible, alliances are every so often reached across party boundaries and within conflictual policy areas.[6]

For example, one policy area where compromise and consensus is the hallmark is corporatism between conflicting societal interest groups. Corporatism, mostly argued within the policy area of economics, the relations within the labour market and in relation to the welfare state, implies that compromise is sought between conflicting interests in decision making. In this context a defining feature of corporatism is seeking consensus between seemingly disparate interests, such as trade unions and industry.[7]

Such compromise and consensus are also sought in regard to the policy areas of security, defence and foreign policy. Within international relations it is often argued that seeking national consensus for security and foreign policy is a common objective for states, although in the Swedish context such consensus is often argued to be explicitly sought. The praxis within decision making in these policy areas also bears witness to consensus across party lines being an objective for the political actors.

Deliberation, as a consequence of the political culture of negotiation and compromise and consensus seeking, might be argued to be a necessity. That is, the process of policymaking includes various societal actors with vested interests in the policy area. As a consequence the process of compromising between differing interests and possible objections raised are dealt with before a decision is reached.[8] The policymaking process, which might be considered as comprehensive in terms of participants, is therefore more time-consuming in its initial phase – before an actual decision is made. However, the time and effort spent on implementing the policy is shortened (since the actors involved have already voiced their possible objections).[9] In short, the political culture may be characterised as deliberative as the decision relies on the idea that the best solution possible may be reached through a rationalistic dialogue between the interested actors. The characteristic of deliberation also holds a notion of inclusiveness towards the general public and the idea of rationalistic argument as the foundation for decision making, rather than ideological viewpoints or normative principles guiding the policy outcome.

Therefore, the Swedish political culture also entails the concept of openness. Through one of the fundamental laws – the principle of freedom of information – the general public is able to access all public records (classified information being the exception). The freedom of information is of great significance for scrutiny and transparency of political decision making. However, in the policy areas of security, defence and foreign policy, openness is rather restricted.

Yet another characteristic of the Swedish political culture is a long tradition and founding idea of independent government agencies. The government implements the policy decision through independent government agencies. These agencies are directed through laws, administrative and budgetary means, and government decrees, and indirectly through appointments. Hence, the Swedish political culture is not accustomed to direct instructions from the government (or ministers). Therefore, government agencies enjoy a high degree of freedom in how to exercise their executive power through implementation. On such government agency is the Armed Forces, within which the intelligence service is embedded (see Chapter 4).

In sum, the Swedish political culture, of importance for the intelligence community, may be characterised by an effort to seek compromise and consensus. Therefore the political dialogue holds traits of deliberation, openness and pragmatism.

Notes

1 There are recent exemptions to the Anglo-Saxon centrism. See, for example, Davies and Gustafson, *Intelligence elsewhere*. Also de Graaf and Nyce, *Handbook of European intelligence culture*.
2 There has been a series of books written concerning the legacy of the MUST, referred to as the 'MUST-program' within Swedish social science. The research has primarily been focused on military intelligence and security services in Sweden from the early 1900s until the 1980s. The programme includes the titles: Bjereld and Demker, *Främlingskap: Svensk säkerhetstjänst och konflikterna i Nordafrika och Mellanöstern*; Ekengren and Oscarsson, *Det röda hotet: De militära och polisiära säkerhetstjänsternas hotbilder i samband med övervakningen av svenska medborgare 1945–1960*; Eliasson, *I försvarets intresse: Säkerhetspolisens övervakning och registrering av ytterlighetspartier 1917–1945*; Lundberg, *Ryssligan: Flyktingarna från öst och morden i Bollstanäs 1919*; Oredsson, *Svensk oro: Offentlig fruktan i Sverige under 1900-talets senare hälft*; Schmidt, *Antikommunism och kommunism under det korta 1900-tale*. The academic focus for Swedish intelligence also includes Fägersten, *Sharing Secrets*. However, this research does not engage with the character or conditions for intelligence analysis.
3 For an excellent account on the emergence of the Swedish political system see Petersson, *The government and politics of the Nordic countries*.

4 See, for instance, Heclo and Madsen, *Policy and politics in Sweden* and Petersson, *The government and politics of the Nordic countries*.
5 Anton, 'Policy-making and political culture in Sweden'. For a later account see also Anton, *Administered politics*.
6 Heclo and Madsen, *Policy and politics in Sweden* and Anton, *Administered politics*.
7 Ruin, *Att komma överens och tänka efter före*.
8 Heclo and Madsen, *Policy and politics in Sweden*.
9 Lundquist, *The hare and the tortoise: Clean air policies in the United States and Sweden*. Lundquist argues, through a comparison between the political decision making and implementation processes in Sweden and the US, that while the Swedish decision-making process is far more time-consuming the implementation process is more efficient. In the Swedish context compromise and consensus between competing interests groups is sought before the decision is made, making the implementation process free from substantial political conflict. In the US political context, decision making may be quicker, but the competing interests and political conflicts tends to surface during the implementation process.

Chapter 4

THE INSTITUTIONAL SETTING

This chapter discusses the legal framework within which the MUST conducts its activities. This framework partly defines the formal context within which the MUST operates. The legal framework and formal instructions from the political level define the responsibilities and constraints of the MUST and define the MUST's formal external relations with other government agencies. The institutional setting also constitutes the overall structure of the MUST and specifies its functions. Thus, the institutional setting structures the overall processes and thereby the MUST's actions and through that what constitutes social practice for the MUST.

TASK AND LEGAL FRAMEWORK

The Swedish government directs the MUST and the overall focus of the military intelligence.[1] The government uses different kinds of policy instruments to direct and control the activities of the MUST.[2] These policy instruments provide, among other things, the legal framework, budgetary means and the ability to direct the focus of the MUST through annual appropriation directions.[3] There are several legal paragraphs concerned with intelligence activities, although the vast majority are not directly concerned with the task and focus for the MUST. The primary legal paragraph concerned with an overall focus for the MUST is expressed in the Defence Intelligence Act (Försvarsunderrättelselagen).[4] One paragraph of the Defence Intelligence Act describes the responsibility of the MUST:

> Military Intelligence will be conducted in support of the Swedish foreign, security, and defence policy, with the aim of identifying

Institutional Setting

external threats to the nation. Activities include participation in international security cooperation. Military Intelligence is only to be concerned with foreign relations. The Government will direct the activities of military intelligence. Within the framework of this direction, authorities appointed by the Government may give more detailed instructions.[5]

The Defence Intelligence Act states that the intelligence objectives are to serve decision making in regard to issues of relevance to foreign and security policy and to external military threats. The government further directs the efforts of the intelligence service to focus its analytical capabilities on areas that play a significant role for Swedish foreign and security policymaking. Other government decrees provide further information about the task and focus of the intelligence agencies: 'At the policy level intelligence activities primarily serve to provide a continuous build-up of knowledge, competence and the ability to confirm or deny public information or other actors' actions or statements.'[6]

Government decrees and public inquires had indicated that, in their view, the intelligence activities are even more important today than in the past. This has happened because the globalised world makes international relations more difficult to interpret and distant security-related situations and conflicts may have an impact on Sweden and Swedish security. Because MUST's primary responsibility is *'to identify foreign states' military and political conditions and opportunities'*,[7] intelligence is needed to provide a vital contribution to the basic understanding of world events and to assess possible security and military risks of relevance for Sweden. This view is further underlined by the government:

> The purpose of the military intelligence activities is to provide support for assessments and decisions in support of the Swedish foreign, security and defence policy, to contribute to the Swedish participation in international security cooperation and to assist with intelligence to strengthen the civil society during severe situations during peace-time. (. . .) In addition to providing a basis for decisions about Swedish operations and support personnel in theatre, the intelligence services also have the ability to provide the government with the information necessary for Sweden to be able to make independent assessments of the security policy issues and to critically examine other actors' arguments and actions.[8]

Although the primary intelligence focus is on the political, security and military developments in the near abroad, this should not prevent military intelligence from simultaneously analysing security and military issues in a broader context.[9] After the end of the Cold War, government decrees indicated that the intelligence service needed to understand new risks and threats such as terrorism, the proliferation of weapons of mass destruction and international organised crime (weapons smuggling, drugs and trafficking).[10] Further, according to its formal instructions the MUST was to provide information about other possible security threats of relevance to Swedish policymakers: 'be further conducted in support of Swedish foreign, defence and security. . . . timely identification and reporting or providing early warning of such changes in world events that require a political decision about the total defence posture.'[11] The military intelligence was to also identify trends and situations that might mean a need for adaptation concerning defence and security preparedness with an extended timeframe.[12] In addition to these rather general instructions, the MUST (and the other intelligence agencies) receive annual instructions covering the government's priorities for intelligence collection and intelligence analysis.[13]

THE PROCESS OF TASKING AND DIRECTING

For a long time, intelligence issues were formally managed by one of the departments at the Ministry of Defence and seemed uncoordinated.[14] Today, the government's, and the Defence and Foreign Affairs departments' intelligence coordination and requirements are further specified in a process lead by Enheten för samordning av försvarsunderrättelsefrågor (SUND). SUND was created in 2000 as a direct result of an increased need for coordination and a more formalised dialogue between the intelligence service and government.[15] Its primary task is to coordinate, evaluate, task and develop the defence intelligence agencies. In addition to the MUST, three other government agencies receive assignments from the government and are coordinated via SUND.[16] The formalised structure for managing and directing the focus and priorities to the MUST is illustrated in Figure 4.1.

Figure 4.1 displays the institutional setting for the MUST in relation to SUND and to the Armed Forces. SUND coordinates the intelligence requests from within the government and tasks the appropriate intelligence agency. Coordination includes an attempt to bridge the 'stove-

Institutional Setting

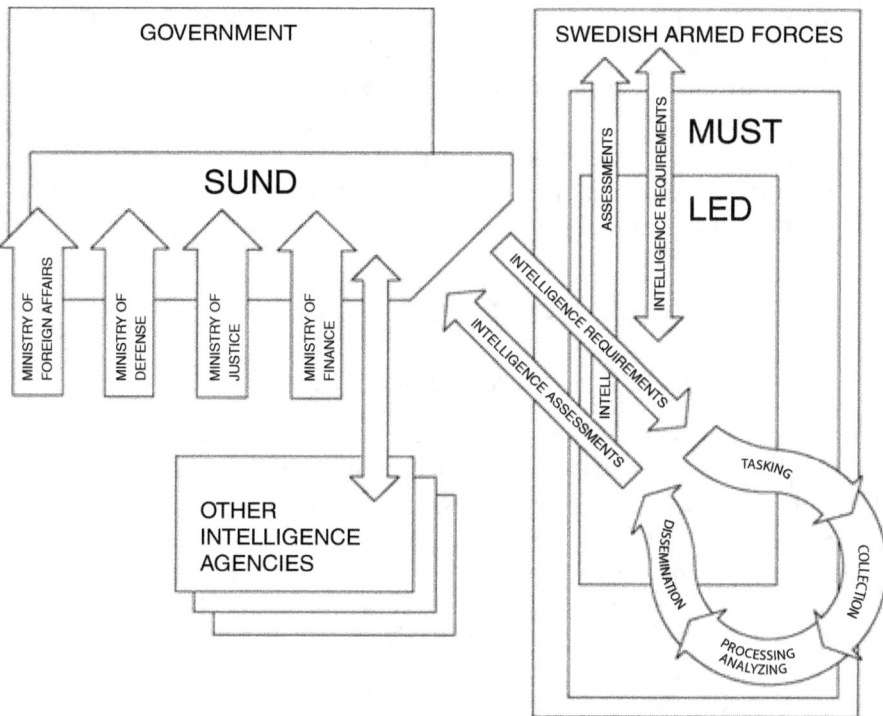

Figure 4.1 The institutional setting

pipes' within the intelligence community (by, among other things, arranging cross-agency current intelligence groups). SUND also plays a role in the more traditional government policy instruments through budgets, decrees and management.[17] In 2009, a new law established a new state body, the State Inspection for Military Intelligence (Statens Inspektion för försvarsunderrättelseverksamhet – SIUN). The role of SIUN is to review the practice of the military intelligence agencies. For instance, SIUN is to review how the intelligence agencies observe the integrity of citizens and whether they conduct their activities (especially signal intelligence and human intelligence practices) according to established laws.[18]

The tasking and control function of the defence intelligence is carried out through general policies, annual appropriation directions and a classified government prioritisation of intelligence requirements and priorities.[19] These documents instruct the defence intelligence agencies on areas of focus and identify which government agencies are entitled to further specify the intelligence priorities. The list of priorities is decided by government departments in discussion with the intelligence agencies through a process managed by SUND.[20]

In addition, the Armed Forces task the MUST with intelligence requests for military purposes. These requests are sent directly to the MUST and become part of the issues to be considered in the organisation's internal process of prioritisation.

THE FORMALISED INTELLIGENCE WORK PROCESS

The Process Guiding Intelligence Work

The direction provided by the government via SUND and by the Armed Forces is processed and further prioritised within the MUST. This process is part of the MUST's formalised work process. The MUST view on how the work process is organised is found within the organisational view of what intelligence is and what it should contribute. It is also founded on the concept of 'the intelligence cycle', a widely accepted schematic model of how the intelligence production is understood to work.[21] The intelligence cycle is most often considered a normative ideal of how the intelligence process should be organised.

The MUST defines intelligence as a form of product from the (intelligence) process as well as the process itself. Further, the definition states that intelligence consists of data, information and knowledge: 'Intelligence is those products created by the intelligence process that describe, explain and predict external phenomena ... Intelligence consists of data, information or knowledge that has been analysed by the intelligence community.'[22]

The organisation states that the aim of intelligence is to describe, explain and predict issues of relevance for the state's policymaking. As the definition turns to focus on the process of intelligence, it states: 'Intelligence is the activity that produces intelligence through planning, collection, analysis and dissemination. Intelligence is also the name of the organisation engaged in such activities.'[23] The activities listed in the definition, 'planning, collection, analysis and dissemination' correspond to the components of what is usually described as the intelligence cycle.[24]

Institutional Setting 51

The Ideal of the Intelligence Cycle

The guiding documents from the government and the intelligence service describe the intelligence process in terms of the widely used intelligence cycle. The basic idea of the intelligence cycle is that the intelligence is produced through a work process consisting of *planning/ directing*, *collection*, *systemising*,[25] *analysis* and *dissemination*.

The general idea is that the intelligence is directed, collected, analysed and disseminated in an iterative process. The concept in the model of the intelligence cycle is that the process is guided by a demand from intelligence consumers posing questions or intelligence requests. The intelligence service then identifies whether the information needed to answer the intelligence requests is available or if further information is required. If further information is required questions are, in turn, sent (*tasking*) to the parts of the organisation (or other organisations) engaged in collecting the information. The *collection* process is thought of as seeking information through various channels and delivering the required information. If necessary, the information is processed (e.g. translated) and systemised (*processing*). Thereafter, the analytical process begins and an assessment is prepared for release (*analysis*). Finally, the assessment is disseminated to the intelligence consumer who raised the initial request (*dissemination*).[26]

The Work Process of the MUST

The intelligence cycle model provides a basic idea of how the intelligence work process within the MUST is conceptualised, within the community of intelligence consumers and the intelligence service itself. The planning and directing is done by the Ledningsavdelningen (LED) Department. Figure 4.2 illustrates the formalised process of producing intelligence analysis within the MUST, from intelligence requests to finished intelligence product being disseminated to the intelligence consumer.

LED communicates with SUND and the various departments within the Armed Forces, and channels the intelligence requests and questions to the intelligence collection and analytical departments. Even though the LED is responsible for planning the intelligence production, decisions over prioritisation and schedules are decided between the LED, collection and analytical departments.[27] Within the analytical

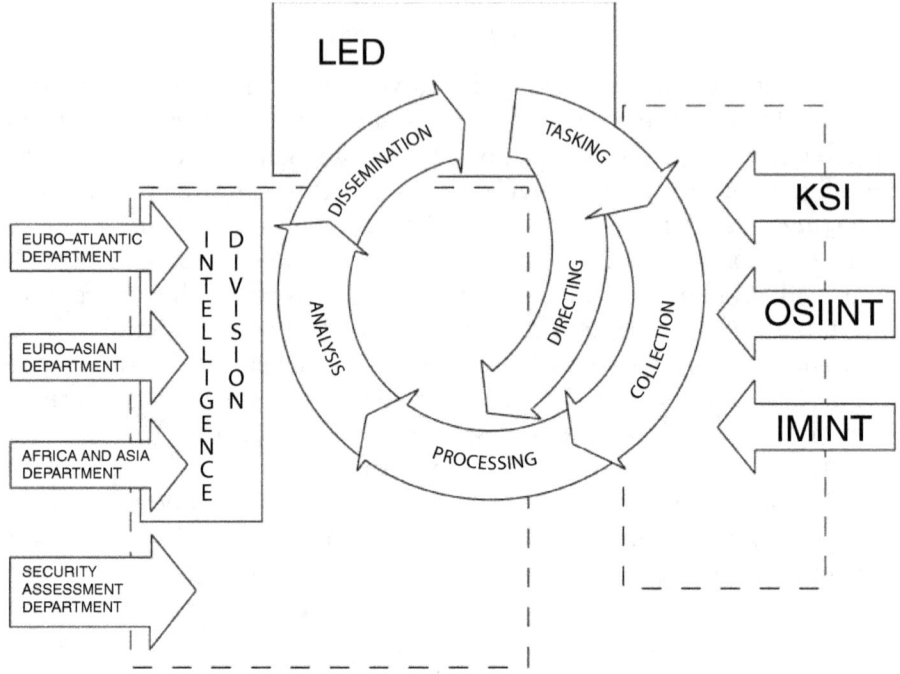

Figure 4.2 The work process for the MUST

Note: KSI = Kontoret för särskild inhämtning; OSINT = Open Source Intelligence; IMINT = Imagery Intelligence

departments, the intelligence requests are answered through the production of intelligence analysis (written assessments). Thereafter, the assessments are communicated, released and disseminated by the LED to the intended intelligence consumers.

Notes

1 Regeringens Proposition 2006/07:63, p. 19
2 Governmental transparency and control of the intelligence service is mainly exercised through the Defence Intelligence Board (Försvarsunderrättelsenämnd – FUN) created in 1976 shortly after the Informations Byrå (IB) affair (a political scandal). The FUN exercises control over intelligence activities regularly and continuously. Its jurisdiction includes the central military intelligence (the MUST), the regional military intelligence offices and the other defence intelligence agencies (such as the Försvarets Radio Anstalt – FRA, the Försvarets Forskningsinstitu

Institutional Setting

 – FOI and the Försvarets Materielverk – FMV). It exercises control over intelligence production, international intelligence cooperation, intelligence collection methods, personnel recruitment issues and the establishment and structure of records/databases (Statens Offentliga Utredningar, *Underrättelsetjänsten – en översyn*, pp. 75–6). See also Gustavsson, 'Hemliga tjänster och det öppna samhället'.
3 The budget, the appropriation directions and any further specific instructions to the MUST are confidential and therefore cannot be used in this study.
4 Alongside the Defence Intelligence Act, other legal frameworks ensure transparency and the ability for government authorities and committees to audit the activities and conduct of the intelligence agencies. Other Swedish intelligence agencies subject to the Defence Intelligence Act are the FRA, FOI and FMV (MUST Årsöversikt för verksamhetsåret 2000).
5 Lag (2000:130) om Försvarsunderrättelseverksamhet, § 1.
6 The government document further states that the intelligence service should have the ability to analytically provide a critical perspective on world events. Regeringens Proposition 2006/07:63, p. 17.
7 Statens Offentliga Utredningar, *Underrättelsetjänsten – en översyn*, p. 64.
8 Regeringens Proposition 2006/07:63, p. 16. Security policy in this context includes political actions that might come to influence the risk of conflict and international diplomatic situations. See also Statens Offentliga Utredningar, *Underrättelsetjänsten – en översyn*, p. 68.
9 Statens Offentliga Utredningar, *Underrättelsetjänsten – en översyn*, p. 56.
10 Regeringens Proposition 2006/07:63, p. 33.
11 Regeringens Proposition 2006/07:63, p. 18.
12 Regeringens Proposition 2006/07:63, p. 18.
13 The more specific instructions for the focus of the MUST are classified.
14 Statens Offentliga Utredningar, *Den militära underrättelsetjänsten*, p. 81.
15 In the 1999 public inquiry, the Intelligence Committee raised a concern about the lack of coordination between the intelligence agencies and argued for the need to create a department responsible for coordination, tasking, evaluation and development within the Swedish intelligence community (Statens Offentliga Utredningar, *Underrättelsetjänsten – en översyn*, pp. 26, 57, 226).
16 These agencies are FRA, FOI and FMV and all are subject to the Defence Intelligence Act (Lag (2000:13) om Försvarsunderrättelseverksamhet).
17 Regeringens styrning av Försvarsunderrättelseverksamheten, pp. 4–5.
18 Förordning (2009:969).
19 Regeringens styrning av Försvarsunderrättelseverksamheten, pp. 9–11.
20 Regeringens styrning av Försvarsunderrättelseverksamheten, pp. 15–17.
21 The MUST and other intelligence functions within the Armed Forces

hold that the intelligence cycle is the fundamental process of intelligence. This is expressed in founding documents such as Försvarsmakten, *Försvarsmaktens grundsyn underrättelsetjänst 08*, pp. 13–14 and in Försvarsmakten, *Försvarsmaktens underrättelsereglemente 2010*, p. 23ff. The intelligence cycle is an important concept in intelligence research, where it is most often considered as an ideal model of how intelligence work may be conceptualised. The intelligence cycle is the most common approach used to illustrate the work process of intelligence production. However, the intelligence cycle has been criticised within intelligence research because of the lack of relevance to how intelligence work is actually done. Some critics say the model is too ideal and has little relevance to the practical work of intelligence. Related research also critiques the intelligence cycle's relevance as a normative ideal of how intelligence should be organised. Among other things, arguments have been raised about the inefficiency of separating, for example, the collection and analysis functions. For a more elaborate discussion of the intelligence cycle, see, for example, Clark, *Intelligence analysis*. However, the concept of the intelligence cycle continues to play an important role in conceptualising intelligence work.

22 Försvarsmakten, *Försvarsmaktens grundsyn underrättelsetjänst 08*, p. 13.
23 Försvarsmakten, *Försvarsmaktens grundsyn underrättelsetjänst 08*, p. 13.
24 Many references are made in intelligence-related public inquiries to the intelligence cycle to describe the work process within the intelligence service. Försvarsmakten, *Försvarsmaktens underrättelsereglemente 2010* and Försvarsmakten, *Försvarsmaktens grundsyn underrättelsetjänst 08*. These components are widely accepted as the vital parts of the intelligence cycle within intelligence-related research.
25 One part of the intelligence cycle is to process and systemise the information collected, which includes translation, editing or deciphering of the collected information (Statens Offentliga Utredningar, *Underrättelsetjänsten – en översyn*, p. 65).
26 In the dialogue between the intelligence consumer and the intelligence, the model of the intelligence cycle sometimes involves an element of evaluation.
27 Besides the work process for the intelligence production illustrated with the schematic model, intelligence products may be initialised by the analysts themselves.

Chapter 5

THE SWEDISH MILITARY INTELLIGENCE DIRECTORATE

This chapter provides a brief overview of the growth of the organisation from its formation until today. It includes details of the organisational structure and the institutional structure within which it is situated. The aim is to provide sufficient information for readers to orientate themselves in the context of the MUST.

BEFORE 1945

The history of the intelligence service in a Swedish context[1] dates as far back as the fifteenth century, although intelligence and more specifically military intelligence appeared in an organised form in the early years of the previous century. In the early years of 1900 an intelligence department was created in both the army headquarters and the navy headquarters. During the period between the First and Second World War interest for intelligence decreased and it was not until 1937 that interest in intelligence surfaced again. The intelligence function within the Defence Staff grew during the early years of the Second World War.[2] The primary task for the intelligence function during the Second World War was to detect any signs of German (or other) preparations for hostile action toward Sweden.[3]

FROM 1945 UNTIL 1989

After the end of the Second World War the intelligence department was reorganised and renamed T-Bureau (Tekniska Kontoret – T-kontoret). The scope of its primary task changed somewhat and the focus became a 'near-abroad perspective', although with a clear emphasis on the Soviet bloc and the Warsaw Pact.[4] Its organisation and the institutional position remained more or less static until the mid-1960s, when the intelligence organisation, the Information Bureau (Informations Byrån - IB), was formed.[5]

The IB era has significantly influenced the institutional arrangements for the intelligence as well as the public recollection of Swedish intelligence. The IB became known to the public through a series of articles revealing that the IB had been used for collecting information on the political opposition within Sweden and conducting operational work, which was in sharp contrast with the Swedish government's official political agenda.[6] The government had to investigate the circumstances surrounding the conduct of the intelligence services, and in 1974 formed the intelligence committee to do it. The committee presented its results in a public inquiry in 1976.[7] In response, the government formalised and increased control and transparency mechanisms through creation of the Defence Intelligence Board (Försvarets Underrättelsenämnd – FUN; see Chapter 4).[8]

After the IB affair, the various intelligence collections units were brought together in the Joint Intelligence Bureau (Gemensamma byrån för Underrättelser – GBU). The continuation of reforms focused mainly on management and institutional restructuring. The GBU became a part of the General Staff and changed its name again to the Section for Operations 5 (Operativ Sektion 5 – Op 5) and the collection unit was reorganised and became the Special Collections Unit (Kontoret för Särskild Inhämtning – KSI).[9]

In 1989 the General Staff and, thereby the intelligence service, was reorganised and renamed Intelligence and Security Management (Underrättelse- och Säkerhetsledningen – USL).[10]

FROM THE COLD WAR UNTIL TODAY

During the early 1990s, the General Staff was again reorganised and the intelligence service became a part of the Supreme Commander's headquarters, although with a special organisational position (of increased independence). The KSI was merged into the USL structure and together they formed the Military Intelligence and Security Directorate (Militära Underrättelse och Säkerhetstjänsten – MUST).[11]

In 2002, yet another reorganisation was initiated and as a result the internal organisation of the MUST was restructured. The coordination and management of the intelligence production was operated by the section for Plans (Planeringssektionen – PLAN). PLAN had the responsibility to coordinate and task the collection and dissemination of intelligence, within the Armed Forces and with other government institutions and agencies. PLAN also led the dialogue concerning the government intelligence needs through the Division for Coordination of Defence Intelligence Requirements (Enheten för samordning av försvarsunderrättelsefrågor – SUND).[12] Furthermore, the organisation of the MUST contained: the Situation Centre, Analytical Department, Intelligence Department, Security Department, Department for Information Security and the Department for Support of International Missions.[13]

The analytical tasks were distributed to three departments: the Intelligence Department,[14] the Analytical Department[15] and the Department for Support of the International Missions.[16] There was a slight difference in the intended intelligence customers for each department. The intended customer for the intelligence products from the Analytical Department was foremost considered to be the government (i.e. Ministry of Foreign Affairs and Ministry of Defence) and the Armed Forces Headquarters. Hence, the focal point of the intelligence products being security, political, economic and military strategic issues. The Intelligence Department and the Department for Support of International Missions had, to a greater extent, intelligence customers within the Armed Forces. Hence their products had more of an operational purpose, namely providing intelligence to the international missions abroad and the Armed Forces as grounds for operational decisions.[17]

Today, after yet another restructuring, MUST has six divisions/ departments: the Command and Planning Department (Ledningsavdelningen – LED), Intelligence Division (Underrättelsekontoret – UNDK), Security Division (Säkerhetskontoret – SÄKK), Special Collections Division (Kontoret för Särskild Inhämtning – KSI), Administrative Division (Stödkontoret – StödK) and Development and Long-Term Policy Department (Utvecklingsavdelning – UTV).[18]

Figure 5.1 illustrates the organisation of the MUST. The Collection Coordination Intelligence Requirements Management (CCIRM) function is responsible for planning, prioritising, tasking and disseminating the intelligence production. The analytical work done resides mainly within the Intelligence Division, which is organised primarily according to geographical regions: Euro–Atlantic Department,

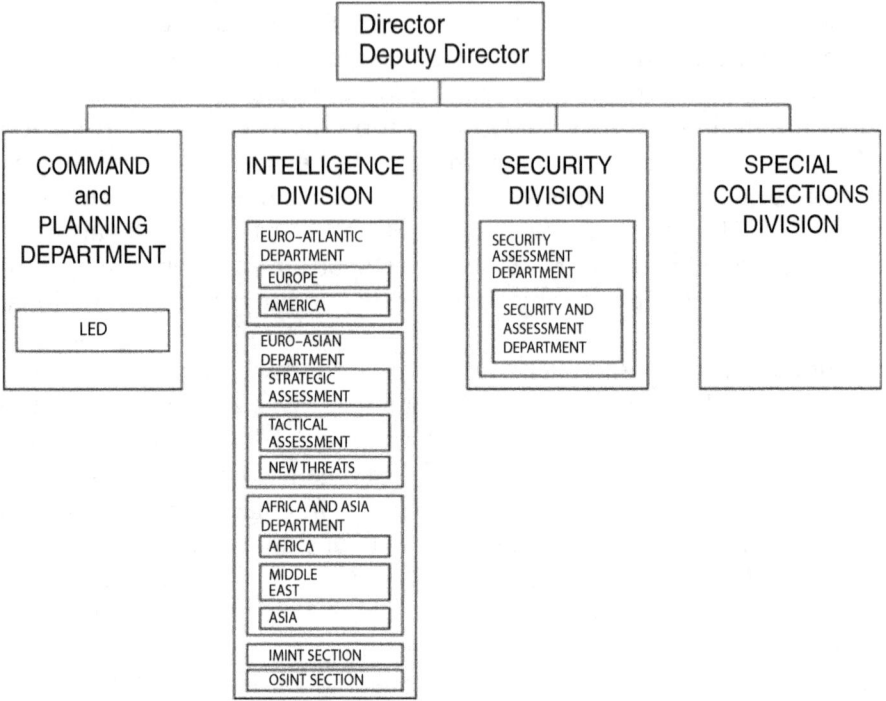

Figure 5.1 Overview of the MUST organisation

Note: OSINT = Open Source Intelligence; IMINT = Imagery Intelligence

Euro–Asian Department, Africa and Asia Department, Imagery Intelligence Department and Open Source Intelligence Section.[19]

SUMMARY

The actions of the intelligence service are directed by government laws and by decrees. These laws and decrees allow for controlling and managing the intelligence services' actions through policy decisions (budgetary and other means) and prioritise the overall intelligence focus. The intelligence focus is further decided by annual instructions issued by the government and the Armed Forces. Further, specific prioritisation and procedures are developed within the intelligence service itself. The laws and decrees also outline the external and formal institutional setting for the overall processes and relationships to intelligence consumers (policymakers) and other government agencies. The dialogue and overall structure, within and between the functions outlined in the formal social practice, seem to suggest a hierarchical order between the intelligence consumer and the intelligence service.

The institutional setting also makes a clear distinction between MUST's responsibility to provide expert knowledge on issues of importance to Swedish foreign and security policy and the role of policymaking being reserved for designated policymakers. However, there are few indications of how intelligence knowledge is incorporated into policy; rather it is stated that intelligence knowledge is of the utmost importance within foreign and security policy.

The ideal context for conceptualising the work process of the intelligence service is found primarily in the model of the intelligence cycle. This is, for instance, visible in the strong resemblance between the ideal model of the intelligence cycle and the general work process within the MUST. Further, the institutionalisation of the intelligence cycle into the MUST process seems to suggest that important roles within the intelligence analytical process may be found in the handover between the various functions defined by the intelligence cycle, that is, between the collection and the analysis and between the analysis and the dissemination. However, there are no indications of how the interplay between this function works in formal social practice. The intelligence cycle might work as a schematic overview of the intelligence process, although a more refined view on what is embodied in the practices for producing intelligence knowledge is required to understand and critically examine what directs and characterises that knowledge.

Notes

1 For a richer exposé of the history of Swedish military intelligence, see Frick and Rosander, *Bakom hemligstämpeln* or Ottosson and Magnusson, *Hemliga makter: svensk hemlig militär underrättelsetjänst från unionstid till det kalla kriget*.
2 Statens Offentliga Utredningar, *Underrättelsetjänsten – en översyn*, pp. 62–3. During the Second World War, the G-section (specialising in intelligence collection) was separated from the intelligence unit to form an

autonomous department called the C-Bureau (C-byrån; Statens Offentliga Utredningar, *Den militära underrättelsetjänsten*, p. 68). For a detailed description of Swedish intelligence during the Second World War see Carlgren, *Svensk underrättelsetjänst 1939–1945*.
3 Statens Offentliga Utredningar, *Den militära underrättelsetjänsten*, pp. 68–9. Also see Palm, *T-kontoret några studier i T-kontorets historia*, p. 39.
4 Statens Offentliga Utredningar, *Den militära underrättelsetjänsten*, pp. 62–3.
5 In 1961 the Foreign Division changed its name to Intelligence Division (Underrättelseavdelning) and the Internal Division (Inrikesavdelningen) became the Security Division (Säkerhetsavdelningen) in 1965. Then institutional status of the Defence Staff changed in 1968 from being an independent government agency to an integrated part of the Supreme Commander's staff, and thereby the IB was formally headed by the chief of the Defence Command (Chefen för Försvarsstaben; Statens Offentliga Utredningar, *Den militära underrättelsetjänsten*, pp. 63–9).
6 This became known as the IB affair in the public mind. The IB affair is covered in public inquiries, research literature and biographies. For instance, see Ottosson and Magnusson, *Hemliga makter: svensk hemlig militär underrättelsetjänst från unionstid till det kalla kriget* and Statens Offentliga Utredningar, *Den militära underrättelsetjänsten*.
7 Statens Offentliga Utredningar, *Den militära underrättelsetjänsten*, pp. 119ff, 151–4.
8 Statens Offentliga Utredningar, *Underrättelsetjänsten – en översyn*, pp. 75–6, 120.
9 Statens Offentliga Utredningar, *Underrättelsetjänsten – en översyn*, pp. 80–2.
10 Statens Offentliga Utredningar, *Underrättelsetjänsten – en översyn*, pp. 81–2.
11 After being reorganised (in 1993/1994), the MUST then consisted of five departments focusing on: management, analysis, operations, military forces, security and collection (Statens Offentliga Utredningar, *Underrättelsetjänsten – en översyn*).
12 Statens Offentliga Utredningar, *Försvarets underrättelseverksamhet och säkerhetstjänst integritet – effektivtet*, p. 53.
13 Statens Offentliga Utredningar, *Försvarets underrättelseverksamhet och säkerhetstjänst integritet – effektivtet*, p. 53.
14 The Intelligence Department was structured in five sections: Operations, Army Intelligence, Naval Intelligence, Air Force Intelligence and the Section for Transnational Threats. The overall assignment was to process and analyse intelligence on military forces and capabilities. The Intelligence Department was also responsible for collecting, processing and dissemi-

nating intelligence on weapons of mass destruction (WMD), terrorism, information warfare and biographical intelligence (Statens Offentliga Utredningar, *Försvarets underrättelseverksamhet och säkerhetstjänst integritet – effektivtet*, p. 55).
15 The Analytical Department was structured into four sections: Section East, Section West, Section Sout, and The Section for Global Issues. The Analytical Department (in contrast to the Intelligence Department) provides intelligence with a focus on political issues, mainly concerning conflicts where there is the possibility of the need for international interventions (Statens Offentliga Utredningar, *Försvarets underrättelseverksamhet och säkerhetstjänst integritet – effektivtet*, pp. 54–5).
16 The Department for Support of International Missions was structured in two sections: Potential Operations and Ongoing Operations. This analytical department has a clear operational focus, with the primary task of providing military leadership with information and threat assessments with direct relevance to the military units (Statens Offentliga Utredningar, *Försvarets underrättelseverksamhet och säkerhetstjänst integritet – effektivtet*, pp. 54–5).
17 Statens Offentliga Utredningar, *Försvarets underrättelseverksamhet och säkerhetstjänst integritet – effektivtet*, pp. 53–5.
18 Policy Documents on the Military Intelligence and Security Directorate – MUST (unclassified).
19 Policy Documents on the Military Intelligence and Security Directorate – MUST (unclassified). Any further changes in the organisational structure have not been possible to identify from unclassified information.

Chapter 6

PRACTICE FOR PRODUCING KNOWLEDGE

This chapter's focus is on uncovering the social discursive practice in terms of informal procedures, routines and roles that influence actions for the intelligence analyst. This social discursive practice creates a specific logic of appropriateness within the social context of the intelligence service. In this chapter, I argue that the social discursive practice contains features that suggest a specific logic of appropriateness within the 'collective of thought' of the intelligence collective.

MAKING INTELLIGENCE ANALYSIS

The intelligence analysts express their view on what intelligence analysis should contribute, by emphasising that the analysis should be customer friendly and easily accessible, the customer should be able to make decisions based upon it,[1] and it should describe and draw attention to new information and/or new events. It should also contextualise the events from reality and thus bring meaning to an unorganised world and in turn make decision making easier.[2] Although these characteristics are the normal features of any kind of analysis, the intelligence analysts underline the special features that are unique to intelligence analysis.

> The core of intelligence analysis is to process the information you get through covert intelligence collection and make something of it, put it in the right context, and make sure it is usable. (. . .) The distinction between intelligence analysis and ordinary analysis, where all the relevant information is available, is that you need an intuitive feeling for the conclusions that might be drawn on the information available, without taking it too far.[3]

Producing Knowledge

The quotation above underlines two commonly mentioned characteristics of intelligence analysis. First, it needs to be based on secret information. That the analysis should be based on, or at least contain secret information, is a common feature for defining intelligence analysis as something specific and something different from other kinds of analysis.[4] Second, that the nature of intelligence analysis requires an element of indecipherable analytic tradecraft mostly referred to as 'gut feeling' or 'intuitive feeling'. The need for this intuitive feeling is argued by the analysts partly because of the intention of intelligence analysis to make predictions, and partly because the analysis most often is made on scarce information. This 'gut feeling' is commonly referred to, and sometimes described as, *'the courage to take a leap'*,[5] *'to trust your intuition'*[6] or *'to trust the feeling of where the information takes you'*.[7] The analysts themselves express difficulties in pointing out what exactly it is that they do, and explaining how they *'do their magic'*.[8] However, analysts tend to view this tacit event of relying on their 'gut feeling' as an individual action. In the interviews the analysts describe this ability by stating that *'some analysts have it, some don't'*.[9]

Imagine instead that this intangible act of 'gut feeling', among other things, is dependent on the social context and the discursive practice of how the analytical process is conducted. The description the analysts provide of this aspect of the intelligence analysis is an intertwined picture of the dual processes of writing and thinking. I would argue that this 'gut feeling' that the analysts refer to, though have trouble describing, is the 'thinking part' of producing knowledge, of making predictions and of 'connecting the dots'. Therefore a better understanding of this social context, the discursive practice of producing knowledge – the routines, procedures and codes guiding the analytical intelligence work – brings a new and more explicit perspective to the thinking tradecraft of intelligence analysts. Hence, in pursuit of a better understanding of the intelligence analysis, I will examine here how these analysts go about answering a question or a request for information, and try to uncover their analysis by closely dissecting the knowledge production process, step by step.

Being well aware that the formal production process is strictly regulated through memos and formal procedures, the analytical process is portrayed slightly differently here: from the analysts' point of view and aimed at the thinking and writing part of the process. The chapter is divided in five different phases of the knowledge production process that will function as a structure for uncovering and discussing the thinking and writing part of intelligence knowledge production; getting the question right; reading up; thinking and writing it down; aligning and creating support; and releasing the assessment. These five analytical phases will structure the depiction and (to some extent) the understanding of the intelligence analysis in this particular study.

PHASE ONE: GETTING THE QUESTION RIGHT

The first phase of the intelligence analytical process is about getting the question right – about the analyst understanding the intended purpose of the requested assessment. The overall direction of the intelligence analysis is decided through a formal dialogue between the intelligence service and the intelligence customer. From the analyst point of view, this dialogue is in general insufficient to gain specific understanding of what the customers 'are really after'. Therefore the analysts need to make choices about the scope and the focus of their assessments.

> The key is to understand the purpose of the question. Almost all questions can be answered in a thousand ways. But if you understand the purpose of the question, you can eliminate half the possibilities. (. . .) Sometimes, I understand the purpose of the question, mostly because I've had it [the same kind of question] before, sometimes not.[10]

A deeper understanding on the part of the analyst is achieved in different ways, depending on the sort of topics the analyst works with and the type of relation and dialogue they have as individuals with the customers. If the assignment is a specific question, the analysts underline the necessity of understanding the intended use of the answer, to make sure that the assessment is formulated in such a manner that the intelligence customer can make the most out of it.[11]

The relation between the analysts and the intelligence consumers varies. Some of the analysts have no dialogue at all with the intelligence consumers. Some analysts consider the formal annual organisational dialogue sufficient for understanding the needs of the intelligence customer, while others emphasise the necessity of having a frequent and lively dialogue on almost a daily basis.

Although I thought I had a pretty good idea of what was needed when I was new, I realised after a while that it was important to have a close dialogue with the customers. Wherever they were. And so my output gradually became more dependent on my dialogue with the Department of Foreign Affairs. (...) So, after I'd had a dialogue with the customers to find out what they were really after, it was time to start collecting information.[12]

The dialogue with the customers affects what the analysts do, in terms of choices of scope and focus for the intelligence analysis. It is important to clarify that the influence is not what is commonly referred to as the politicisation of intelligence;[13] rather the analysts consider it as guidance to make analytical work and direction effective.

If the assignment is of a more long-term nature, the intended use seems to be of less importance, and the analysts work more independently from the need of the intelligence customer: 'The second reason I started writing was when I could see for myself that something was of interest, and then it was often not as time critical. (...) So much of the long-term work I had control of myself.'[14]

The quotation illustrates that the analysts, when working on more long-term analysis, deem themselves capable of appreciating what the consumers need. This could be an effect of the analyst's impression that long-term assessments are generally initiated by the analysts themselves rather than being ordered in advance with a specific use in mind. Still, the analysts have a preconceived view of what the intelligence consumer usually wants, and also have a fairly good idea of what the intended use will be; they are therefore prone to adjust how they structure and express their assessments depending on who the intended consumer is.

Thus, the analysts find it of importance to fully understand the context and the intended use of the assigned question, in order to provide a useful assessment. The wide possibility of intended use and the broad spectrum of intelligence consumers imply to most of the intelligence analysts that further instructions or contextualisation are needed if they are to feel assured that their assessment will be valuable to the consumers. These further specifications are needed for the analysts to be able to initiate the analytical process. However, it is not an institutionalised routine or procedure for further dialogue between the analysts and the consumers to take place. Therefore gaining this insight becomes highly individualised based on, among other things, the analysts' initiative and the involvement of the consumers. In many cases the analysts are left without further specifications of the intended use of the assessment. In those cases the analysts usually tend to either rely on their preconceived idea of the need of the consumer or to rewrite previously produced assessments by *'just adding the new information available'*.[15] In these latter cases, where the dialogue is absent or no further specifications are given, the risk of the intelligence analyst relying heavily on the already existing body of knowledge without critical reflection, is vast.

PHASE TWO: READING UP

The process of reading up on the information available and orienting themselves in the narratives of the topic is usually done by the analysts within the existing body of knowledge (previous assessments) and the information already available within the intelligence organisation. Once the analyst feels confident of what the question or task actually is, the next step is to orient themselves within the question and its context. The subsequent reading up is both the process of the analyst orienting themselves and contextualising the topic, and also a sort of inventory of the information that is available.

> I started by looking at what was in the computer [the intelligence information system] and then asked questions of the collection elements [of the organisation] and then I talked to people who worked with the same geographical region as I did ... or those who had knowledge about that area. I started to read everything available on the subject. That we had already written.[16]

The material and information the analyst quoted above searches for and will use mainly originates from within their own organisation. While reading up on the topic the analyst starts with the information already at hand, what has already been written, and inquires of other analysts their thoughts concerning the same region. Although the approach described above is the prevailing one, variations on this theme do exist between analysts, where information and narratives external to the intelligence organisation are incorporated. This is done not for the explicit reason of contrast and contestation, but rather because it is easier to come across; it is not used as a basis for contextualising and deepening the understanding of the issue, but rather comprises part of the search for new pieces of information.

> Well, the next step is to sit down and start reading. I read a lot of open source material. Not just because I think it's good, but because I can find it myself. And I don't only mean the Internet and news reporting, but also books and articles. And policy magazines. They usually have some good information. (. . .) Sometimes I read what we [MUST] have written previously. If it is relevant. Sometimes I've just stored old reports and updated them. It differs a bit from report to report. Sometimes, of course, I have relied on previous reports.[17]

Even though this quotation illustrates that there are possibilities for contrasting discourses to enter into the analytical process through the vast use of unclassified material, this is not done by recognising that the external search might bring new perspectives to the analysis, but rather it is viewed as another form of collecting pieces of information. The last part of the quotation illustrates the habit of recycling old intelligence assessments if possible, with possible new information being added to the existing assessment. This also suggests (discussed further below) that it is considered preferable if the assessments are cohesive: that the knowledge in one assessment relies on the information and the conclusion of previous assessments.

In this process there is no apparent ambition to systematically contrast the organisation's own established knowledge or information with analysis or information from other perspectives. The analysts repeatedly referred to the explicit ambition of making sure that newer assessments remained within *'the same line of argument'* as the previously written ones, allowing little room for appreciation or awareness of the possible downsides of relying heavily on *'in-house information'*.[18] The quotation also mentions what the analysts consider as an upside of using open source information: the argument that they *'can get it by myself'*. It is a reoccurring view among the analysts that information from within the organisation (for instance intelligence reporting) is considered as valid and reliable.

However, although there is no explicit acknowledgement of a critical perspective and reflection on the established knowledge within the reading-up process, there are some indications of an ambition to critically examine the information incorporated in the analysis.

> I read through all the material I have. I usually try to collect as much information as possible and then I research the material as much as I can and then I think for a while about what I want to include in the report.[19]

The quotation illustrates an analyst who seems to be aware that the information needs further assessment and evaluation before being used as part of an analysis.

Thus, the analysts focus their reading up on various topics in the previously established body of knowledge within the organisation. The analysts primarily rely on the previous assessments and on the information already available within the organisation. In this process there is no explicit aim of evaluating or reflecting on the accuracy of the previous assessments or the information at hand. As the analysts read up and gather information before writing an assessment, they seek not only information related to their topic, but information that acceptable as a continuum of the established body of knowledge. During the process of reading up, the analysts chooses to highlight and use information that is compatible with the previous assessments yet new. Hence, the general tendency to rely extensively on the established and accepted body of knowledge, with a lack of reflection or critical examination of the arguments and conclusion, imply a risk of merely reproducing that specific knowledge. Once the analysts have oriented themselves within a specific topic and identified the information available, the process of thinking and writing starts.

PHASE THREE: THINKING AND WRITING IT DOWN

The thinking process of the intelligence analysis is an unrecognised and unarticulated practice. Rather, the 'thinking' is reduced to systemising pieces of information and facts, and where the added value of the intelligence analysis is created in making the information available to the decision makers through contextualising the intelligence information and providing conclusions. The analysts' thinking is unarticulated, and referred to as 'seeing', 'feeling' and 'just knowing what it means'.

The analysts consider the thinking process as an individual action not influenced by the social context.

Analysis without Interpretation

In general the intelligence analysts describe the thinking process in terms of systemising information.

> I usually start off by brainstorming a bit with myself so I can write good RFIs [requests for information] and then initiate a dialogue with collection. I use the Internet and 'Google' . . . Then I let them [the questions] go back and forth a few times [between] me and collection until I get the relevant information. (. . .) But when I have all the material, I go through it systematically and carefully, trying to extract as much material as I possibly can, to put into the system.[20]

The quotation above primarily illustrates three aspects relevant to the thinking and writing process of the intelligence analysis. First and foremost what should be an assessment followed by some sort of thought process or an analytical process seems to be possible by just processing pieces of information available through the different collection channels, without any need for interpretation. Here the analyst underlines that the aim is to make as much new information as possible available and that the analytical added value is reached by sorting and systemising the information. It also suggests that it is the analyst's choice as to what information to use for further processing.

The second aspect also emphasises the focus on information rather than on analysis. The quotation above illustrates the idea that a new assignment or question from the intelligence customer calls for new input in terms of new information. In turn, the need for new information usually implies the need for new covert intelligence collection. This suggests that the idea that the new knowledge created demands new pieces of information, and that the idea of analysis is primarily concerned with systemising the incoming information rather than providing added analytical value through contextualisation and interpretation.

Thirdly, it is also worth noting that the analysts consider their analytical work as an individual action. It is definitely difficult to brainstorm on your own, although this might be just an expression for a creative phase in which the analyst is trying to think freely. However, there is also a recurring reflection made by the analysts: that they are alone when working within their specific field. That would also imply additional difficulties in creating the dynamic and reflection needed as a basis for thorough analysis, considering different perspectives and grounds of analysis. The analysts say that their work is characterised by individuality, both in terms of being alone in their expert fields of knowledge but also that the thinking and analytical process is defined by them as individuals. This might be illustrated by the analysts' acknowledgement that it often takes a change of personnel for the organisation to change its opinion on specific issues.[21] The description of the thinking and writing process of yet another analyst illustrates the emphasis on the systemising of information rather than interpretation and of making the assessment cohesive with previous writings:

> I don't know exactly what others do . . . But I'm very much guided by where it [the information] comes from. If it comes from a Defence Attaché, then I go with it because then we have our own source that says so. (. . .) But that's an individual preference . . . I stay pretty close to what they say. Otherwise, I think it is the arguments that guide me. (. . .) And I don't follow any textbook model or anything like that . . . I would probably like to use that sort of thing more . . . But often we are probably too pressed for time to use them [models and schedules]. Instead I try to let the argument speak for itself. And when you find a line of argument and then see what it can be connected to, so to speak. But usually there is of course some starting point. What we [the MUST] think about something and then I usually just try to stick with that.[22]

The abovementioned hesitancy to acknowledge the thinking part of the analytical process is also present in this quotation. Again the analyst expresses a hesitation to move the analysis beyond the stated information, saying that '*I let them [the facts] speak for themselves.*'[23] It is striking that the analysts limit the possibilities of the analysis and assessment to merely producing an aggregated form of the incoming reports. When asked to clarify a number of issues, the analysts never seem to discuss the analytical possibilities that might be worked out to provide tentative answers. Rather, they limit their own role as analytical knowledge providers by constantly emphasising that '*We don't know that yet. We will not know for sure until they actually have started to...'*[24] Another way of arguing for the written arguments in the assessments is to refer to the text of previous assessments: *'I got most of the text from last year's document and just rewrote it a little bit.'*[25] Hence, the reoccurring view of the analysts seems to suggest that knowledge in the assessments is built by accumulation of information, like building blocks placed one on top of each other. In this context the analysts express an uncertainty over what kind of information constitutes these building blocks.

> Not arguments. But more facts, or, well not the facts, but information ... More descriptions about what someone has thought or said or so on ... So well, that's a kind of fact. Or basis of some kind. But I use different inputs ... but I often have to combine several strands in order to be able to say that 'in general it seems that ...' (...) which means that the customer must trust that I have a basis for what I say. It becomes a matter of conscientiousness, to ensure that there is information backing up all reports.[26]

The quotation above illustrates the view that the bricks of knowledge, the information and facts, may be put together (without implying any need for reflection) and then presented even with little concern paid to the origins and possible contexts. However, there is hesitation over what these pieces of information really are. As the analyst makes choices about what information to use as building blocks for new knowledge, there is little reflection about what kind of information, facts or just a 'basis of some kind'. Instead the analysts seem to be accepting the information as valid by being *'the organisations own information'*.[27] The prevailing point of view seems to be that the facts speak for themselves and so analysis is not recognised, thus again failing to acknowledge any thinking (besides systemising and presenting), analysis or interpretation.

There are two more aspects of relevance to the thinking and writing process revealed in the interviews. First, the information that is collected within the organisation is to be considered more reliable or in some other way better than other kind of sources of information. That view is perhaps only to be expected given the opinion that the defining characteristic of intelligence analysis is precisely the ingredient of secret information, which can only be created within the organisation itself. Yet, it is important to recognise that the secret information is considered as more important by the analysts, thereby downgrading other possible sources of information. Second, the analysts tend to primarily rely on the secret information already available in the organisation or by tasking the collection units to gather new information, although both have been or are collected with the aim of keeping the previous line of argument intact, making the new assessments cohesive with the established knowledge. Third, by not incorporating other possible sources of information on the same terms, there is a risk of the building blocks of information to just be reproduced. Which raises the second concern: the analysts seem to be making an active choice to try to adhere to the previous line of assessment. The analysts also underline that they make active choices of what information to incorporate in the assessment.[28] Therefore the analysts risk choosing the building blocks of information that will make the assessment remain cohesive with the established body of knowledge. The view of the intelligence analysis as an accumulation of systemised information, staying within the established discourse, might imply that in some cases it seems as if the incoming reporting is more or less the same as the refined assessment disseminated by the MUST.

Thinking within a Continuum

The importance of the continuity of the assessments is underlined by the analysts and by the managers, among other situations, in regard to how the assessment should be characterised in order to gain the trust of the intelligence customers.[29] The analysts make clear that it is important that the assessment is a part of a continuum. The assessments should, as far as possible, be consistent with those of previous years and in line with previous arguments and assessments. It is preferable that the same sort of language, terms and concepts are used. Otherwise, the analysts argue, the intelligence consumer might be confused.[30] However, this line is taken not only out of concern for the possible confusion on the part of the intelligence customer; an equally prominent motivation is the internal reluctance to change and confusion over how to handle change. Another opinion in this matter is that the text should give little room for the consumer to make their own analysis. The analysis provided should be expressed in such a manner that it should seem to be the only possible answer.[31]

Producing Knowledge

> The report I'm working on now . . . Then you always have to check what we have written before and decide what it is that you want to say. (. . .) Then I start with the report that's the most important input, and I've retained the same structure. (. . .) And the report template states that the conclusions will be on the first page, so I know that. Then I've tried to be fairly neutral and only some minor comments in the margin, so to speak. Then I've got a feel for it . . . And then I probably start writing almost immediately. (. . .) I've always started writing very early in the process. Not just reading. Actually they are overlapping processes; collection, processing and dissemination. I hope that's an answer. That's the way I work.[32]

The same analyst continues later: 'By that I mean that you more or less have the subconscious ability to weigh up everything that you have heard and seen in new inputs etc. until the answer itself appears: "*this is actually the case*".'[33] Again there is an attempt to keep the information as intact as possible, and the analyses seem to consist of simply commenting on the incoming information. There is also a reference to neutrality, which this quotation suggests might be achieved through an avoidance of interpretation. Thus, the analysts seem to consider the analysis to be almost the same thing as writing; and when the analytical process is verbalised, words such as 'feel' and 'sense' are used to describe what the analysts do with the information.[34] As the analysts present their assessments and conclusions, they often refer to facts from incoming reports as their basis for assessment and analysis. However, the statements they make while doing this during the seminars usually start with phrases such as '*I believe . . .*', '*I don't know, but I think . . .*' and '*It feels unlikely that they would do such a thing.*'[35] Second, the analyst's description of the components of the intelligence process entirely omits the analysis itself. This would actually be a quite coherent description of their own working process, which literally seems to consists of 'collection, processing and dissemination', thus leaving out the analysis altogether. These aspects are again present in other analysts' reflections on their own work and thought processes.

> The question is what are the facts and has been confirmed. We [the organisation] should actually evaluate the accuracy of the information and the credibility of the source. (. . .) But that was not the case there [at the MUST] at all. I would say they approached

> the problem from more of a journalistic perspective. (...) I mean you read a number of reports from various sources and combine them into some sort of conclusion, without references to sources, and you use whatever methodology you knew from elsewhere. (...) And I mean, if you employ analysts from the academic world, and don't give them any intelligence training ... Then assessments and criteria ... Standards of quality are completely up to the individual and there is no system.[36]

The quotation illustrates not just one analyst's discontent with how the analysis is conducted; it also illustrates that the thinking and analytical part of the intelligence process is unarticulated. Without judging whether the discontent is valid, there is at least one aspect relevant to this study: there again seems to be an indication that how the analysis is performed is a choice made by the individual, or perhaps not even a conscious choice but rather a combination of who the person is, what they know from before and how they are used to working with analysis. The approaches used for systemising or for structuring the analytical process (analytical methods or techniques) are unarticulated, not explicitly expressed or discussed. When asked to reflect on what guides their analytical work, the analysts state that after a while they *'just know what the information means'*,[37] instead of possibly mentioning some sort of analytical frame (for instance, testing hypothesis) for interpretation and making conclusions.

> Gut feeling really should go via your head. (...) But I don't think it's possible to break it down into various sources or specific incoming reports. You see a trend, then you need some way of showing where you got the indication from. You must be able to show how you derived it [the trend], perhaps not in an academic fashion, but still. It's a way of working.[38]

In the quotation it is acknowledged again that the analytical process is a process of the mind, however difficult this is to pinpoint or verbalise. Still, the analysis is still referred to by the analysts using verbs like 'see' and 'feel'. When the analysts are asked to reflect on what arguments or evidence they use to argue or prove their analysis or conclusion, they tend to answer that they use the facts or information that they find in the incoming reports. In this context the analysts also answer that they tend to work with the same kind of arguments and facts that they 'know work' from previous assessments. During formalised discussions of the estimates, there is nearly no reflections made or questions raised of how the analysts have come to one conclusion over another nor do the discussions reveal what arguments or what type of information or facts are put forward to strengthen a specific conclusion or assessment.

Thus, the thinking element of the analytical process seems to be closely related to the existing information and assessments and also to the incoming reports. This would actually imply that the intelligence analysis is reduced to merely systemising a rather narrow range of collected information, without adding any analytical value to the assessment. The prevailing idea seems to be to stay close to the facts and information in the incoming reporting – let the facts speak for themselves. Thereby, the contextualisation, the interpretation and the arguments for specific conclusions are situated in the background. The analysts also underline that the information collected by the organisation is more valid or 'better'. Not because it is better suited for the analytical task or contains more details, but because it is the organisation's information.

Moreover, the analysts perceive the thinking element of the analytical process as an individual action. The analytical choices of both what information to use for the assessment as well as the approach to systemising and analysing are considered individual choices. Furthermore, the thinking element within the analytical process is unarticulated in terms of analytical methods and techniques. The analysts refer to the thinking and arguing for specific assessments and conclusions in terms of 'gut feeling', 'just knowing what it means',[39] and 'seeing trends'.[40] Although the analysts consider the thinking element and the choices made within the analytical process as individualised, once the assessment is written they acknowledge the need to create alignment and support for the conclusions made.

PHASE FOUR: ALIGNING AND CREATING SUPPORT

The analysts express that there is a need to get support and consensus for their assessments – the assessment need to be 'reasonable'. What is considered as reasonable is an implicit norm of writing about topics in specific ways. The norm seems to be to write the assessment without being controversial, preferably not to evoke change, and in such a manner that it does not contradict assessments and conclusions made within other parts of the organisation.

The analysts recognise that they need to have support or consensus for their assessments from the organisation. The support for the assessments needs to come both from fellow analysts and from management.

> If the product is to be released, then it is good [to have the manager's support for the assessment]. I guess it is a good thing if you're able to persuade your colleagues that you're right and if you can't persuade them then it is a good thing to have considered their counter-arguments. It's actually a requirement. It's really important to be able to agree on the product so it can be released. And then once it has been released it is important that the organisation can stand united behind the product.[41]

In this passage the analyst expresses the perception that there needs to be an agreement or consensus over the assessments and conclusions made. In this quote the analyst expresses it in terms of 'requirement'. Even though this requirement is not formally expressed the analyst acknowledges that it is expected within the organisation. The analysts' perception of the search for consensus is in general rather uncomplicated. Through discussion with fellow analysts they seek to anchor the assessment and to proactively respond to possible critique and counter-arguments.[42] However, there are conditions for and situations within the process of seeking consensus that constitute implications for the analysts' work.

The search for alignment and consensus are problematic when the same or similar issues and topics are dealt with in different parts of the organisation.

> It probably varies a lot from one analyst to another. For some it is very important and for others totally irrelevant. For me it isn't particularly important anymore. But there may be a problem if one topic is handled by two different departments . . . then the reality is that one department will decide what the others think. (. . .) It probably affects the younger analysts a great deal and they are very afraid to go against this norm. It becomes a bit of a norm, and it applies to both the political and military sides.[43]

The analyst in the quotation illustrates the view of how the search for agreement on assessments affects the writing of an assessment when one issue or topic is dealt with in different parts of the organisation. One department has the opportunity (and apparently this is the case) to decide what another department should think and write on a specific topic; the organisational need for consensus overrides the possibility of diversity. Further, the quote illustrates a continuous feature expressed by analysts in different situations – that there seems to be a norm of how to think and write about specific questions. The analysts have a two-fold perception of this norm. First, there is a norm of how to think, conceptualise and write about specific issues and topics.

> The sort of group-think that appears is completely crazy, and the scope for thinking differently is very limited. (...) In these environments there are always some analysts who set the norm for which analyses will be completed. Everything else falls by the wayside. It is all about thinking alike. If you asked me why we aren't bold in the conclusions we come to, my answer would be because the organisation doesn't allow it.[44]

The analyst in this quotation illustrates the general perception that there is a norm of thought present throughout the organisation. This analyst refers to the concept of group-think. Even though that might not need to be the case, it is clear that there are specific ways of how analysts are expected to think about specific issues. The analysts do not perceive or refer to any explicit instructions of how to think. Instead the analysts seem to consider the situation as some unfortunate state of being that has occurred.

Second, this norm relates not to what you write as analyst, rather how you write. The analysts state that it is preferable for the assessment to be written in such a manner that they seem uncontroversial and *stays within the box* of how they are expected to write and express the assessments.

> You are not really used to discussing and putting your arguments forward. That's because you haven't been trained to express your opinion on an issue. They never really ask how you have interpreted the situation. (...) There is a fear of not 'having the right opinion'. Not because it is something that the organisation has

explicitly said, it's more of a social issue. And maybe this means it is difficult to deal with things that are out of the ordinary . . .[45]

The analyst in this situation expresses a fear of not having the right opinion in regard to a specific set of questions. This is a prevailing wisdom among the analysts and is noticeable, for example, when the analysts reflect on how they relate to previous established knowledge and the opinions of other analysts. The quotation above is an excellent example of how the analysts perceive what they occasionally refer to as *'the company policy'* for specific topics.[46] This company policy is not explicitly stated by the organisation nor its managers. There are only rare examples of analysts given instruction on what to write (or what not to write). Yet, the analysts are well aware of what the organisation will consider as reasonable (within company policy) and what will be considered as controversial. Getting support for the former is easy; getting support for the latter is difficult and, therefore, as the analysts expresses it, it is easier to stay within *'company policy'*.[47] This is illustrated again by one of the analysts stating that:

> I don't think there are unwritten laws about what to think or write. But the more controversial you are the better you need to be at backing up your ideas. But as long as you do that, then I don't think so. (. . .) I have never seen anybody present anything controversial. Then of course we might miss a few things because people don't want to stick their neck out, I don't know. Maybe that's the case.[48]

The quotation above illustrates that writing assessments that are considered controversial would imply more and better arguments, in order for fellow analysts to render their support. It is also worth noting that the analysts are reluctant to write assessments and analysis that are controversial or at least outside *'the company policy'*. This is, for instance, illustrated in the quotation above, by the analyst that, despite all the years spent working within the intelligence service, claims never to have seen a controversial assessment. The analysts attach the idea of a controversial analysis or assessment with three risks that make life in the intelligence service harder: being wrong, having to promote a change of opinion and exposing themselves of criticism. These three features are considered as risks by the analysts, risks that in the end will make them less of an analyst (discussed further below). The difficulties of changing opinion in the assessments are voiced by one analyst:

> I think that depends very much on what topic you're dealing with. If there is a basic viewpoint or not. That everything should be based on previous assessments, we can't change our assessments any old way we like. (. . .) I would like to clarify though, if we had a negative view about, say, Russia, just to get an increase in defence spending, that is *not* the case. Of course, it's good that there is integrity in our assessments and that we're able to stand by them.[49]

The quotation above illustrates the prevailing idea that it is important, for what appears to be credibility reasons, to formulate assessments that the organisation can 'stand by' (have consensus about) and that need not to be easily changed. But the need for agreement and consensus on the assessments are occasionally recognised as something that might be problematic 'But, to me it is important that everyone thinks together. The products will be better if more than one person has thought about the problem. On the other hand, it is dangerous if you end up in group-think situations.'[50]

Some analysts do not seem to care about achieving consensus per se, although it seems important not to stray too far from what the rest of the analysts consider a reasonable analysis. At the same time, there seems to be an awareness of the risk of group-think situations. Several other analysts also reflect on the risk of becoming a victim of group-think and other similar phenomena.

The analysts in different ways underline the desirability to seek agreement and consensus for their analysis and assessments from fellow analysts and by the organisation. As the analysts describe this process they refer to an established way of thinking about and expressing themselves about specific topics. While describing this process they refer to this established way of thinking and expression in terms of the norm, the company policy and thinking inside the box, for instance making the analysts reluctant to thinking and writing in ways that they perceive as controversial. This raises the question of what happens in the unlikely event of analysts that write controversial assessments – when they break the norm.

Breaking the Norm

As described above the analysts perceive that there is an established way to think and write about specific topics – what the analysts refer to as 'the norm'. Breaking away from this this norm of how to think and write is uncommon. In the unlikely event of an analyst thinking and writing about topics differently, the demands for arguments and proof are greater. The analysts also perceive that breaking the norm would mean less credibility in the organisation: 'I really don't know what would happen [if somebody broke the norm]. I really don't know how to answer that question. I don't know. But it would have been cool if it happened.'[51] The quoted analyst represents the general perception that the breaking this norm is exceptionally rare. Although the norm of how to think and write is commonly an unwritten and implicit expectation imposed on the analysts, there are situations where there have been explicit instructions to stay within a certain line of argument for an assessment. Such an example is expressed in the quotation below, where a preventive order to ensure that the accepted way to write about a specific topic of one of the partner organisations was not questioned.

> Sometimes it was very clear. I received a direct order that I wasn't allowed to think differently from SÄPO [Swedish Security Police] on a specific issue. It was clearly stated. I can't remember now if this happened several times or if this was only the time. (. . .) Their argument was that they [SÄPO] had the lead on this issue and they were the ones entitled to have an opinion.[52]

The situation described above, with the explicit order not to write an assessment that might conflict with the view of another intelligence organisation, was perceived by the analyst as one way to make sure that the norm of what to think and write was not questioned. This particular case might also be partly explained by interagency politics, although in general there does seem to be an objective for some sort of norm or homogenisation of the analysis to try to prevent analysts from breaking the norm.

The analysts describe being controversial and being wrong in the analysis as grounds for decreased credibility as an analyst in the organisation. The analysts describe that the credibility in the organisation is affected negatively by being considered as controversial or being

Producing Knowledge 81

wrong. Although it is accepted to be controversial or wrong on occasions with what could be considered a viable explanation, it will affect the analyst negatively if it happens repeatedly.[53]

If the analysts do break away from the accepted way to think and write, the assessment is more critically examined and greater demands concerning facts, arguments and proof are required.

> I remember once, an analyst who was pretty bold in his reports wanted to write a report on the link and corruption between criminals and politicians in a particular geographic area. But he didn't get to write the report because he couldn't *prove* that the connections existed. (. . .) I mean that our [the intelligence service] purpose is not to *prove* things. (. . .) But suddenly it became an insurmountable restriction, we couldn't produce evidence. (. . .) We should be an organisation that thinks. But we were not allowed to.[54]

The analyst quoted above illustrates the ambition to write something new and maybe a bit controversial, but it is the organisation that increases the requirements by arguing that there is a lack of evidence. The quote above also highlights the aspect of criticism. In this particular case the assessment was criticised for not presenting proof or evidence in support of the conclusion and the analyst perceives this as due to the controversial nature of the assessment. This raises the issue of what is being criticised and how this critique is being voiced.

Criticism and Status

In the process of creating support for their assessment, the analysts perceive it to be difficult both to accept and to propose criticism. Criticism voiced in this process is primarily concerned with textual issues, such as minor changes in wording, structure of text or requests for further specification of information used. It is exceptionally rare that the criticism contains comments on how the conclusions of the assessments are derived or the interpretation of the information used.

In general, the analysts describe that the comments provided are more of a formal nature, focusing on minor language issues.

> Personally, I think comments about language are quite nice. All comments are good if they are put across well. (. . .) But if they [the

comments] introduce a new way of thinking about things . . . then it would be seen as difficult. (. . .) Of course it would be difficult if somebody thought I should include lots of things that I would rather leave out.[55]

The comments (or, if the term may be used, criticism) seem to be well received if they are primarily focused on language and structure. This was also displayed during the seminars, when the moderator encouraged the attending analysts to comment and critique the texts at hand, although the instruction to do so was conditional – *'the critique put forward should be within your own area of expertise'*[56] – and it was made clear that the comments and critique should revolve around 1) facts, 2) language and 3) structure.[57] Hence, comments concerning the analytical 'tradecraft', the line of reasoning and the actual basis of assessment are almost entirely absent. On occasions when analysts were asked to validate the assessment, they usually referred to the lack of incoming reports or stated that the issue at hand was not included in their area of expertise. The analysts use expressions such as *'I haven't seen anything in the incoming reports.'*[58] On a few occasions, the analysts used similarity between the written text and newspaper articles as affirmation of the strength of the analysis.[59]

The criticisms that seem uncontroversial to offer are those regarding formalities, structure and other language issues. In some cases it might be acceptable to comment on the (amount or access to) information used for the analysis, but it seems to be both very sensitive and very rare to comment on other aspects, such as the interpretation, the analysis and methodological issues. If the comments are of more substance, they seem harder for the analyst to accept, but if they are of the easily received kind, focusing on language only, they seem to be included in the assessment.

> Often I just paste them [the comments] straight into the document. If the comments provide additional information, you can just paste them right in. I mean, if it is stuff you didn't know before. When there is a difference of opinion I usually talk to the person who wrote the comment and ask what their case is built on. (. . .) If they have some other kind of reports or information. And then you have to think about why there is a difference.[60]

The quoted analyst illustrates that the comments regarding minor criticism are easily accepted and just pasted into the assessment. Criticism that includes a more substantial difference apparently leads to some sort of negotiation over which view should be the one to prevail (see above on the need for consensus). The quote above also illustrate that the difference in conclusion could only happen if the two parties have different access to information.

The analysts' perception of criticism containing comments on substance or of an analytical character is visible during the discussions prior to realising the estimates. On a few occasions comments were raised concerning more analytical and substantial aspects, and in all of these cases the comments were noted, sometimes nodded at but never argued or countered. The original assessment is never validated or defended by the author, and it is unclear how the comments actually come to have an effect on the written text. There have been cases where attendees have raised issues about what topics to cover in the document,[61] comments about the negative effect of using specifically agreed upon concepts,[62] and limits and possible uses for this kind of intelligence assessments.[63] During the seminars, some issues were passed over or corrected by the moderator as not appropriate for the seminar. This is in line with the general description by the analysts that providing comment, feedback and criticism is difficult,[64] both because an idea that criticism can only be provided by an analyst within their own area of expertise and because there are groupings within the analysts that are *'above criticism'*.[65]

> I think it's a result of respect for each other's area of expertise. There is a whole group of people working on an issue. So, if you're going to question such expertise, then you really must have good grounds and not just some analytical gut feeling. But that is the way we work.[66]

In this quote the analyst illustrates the idea that criticism only may be raised within an analyst's own area of expertise. The analysts refer to the importance of having access to the relevant information, rather than acknowledging that another analysis may be possible, an analysis perhaps made from a different viewpoint or using different analytical methods. The analysts are also described as sensitive to criticism in general.

> The analysts are very, very, very sensitive to criticism and if you're going to criticise them you have to choose your words very carefully. Otherwise they could lash out. (. . .) It is much easier to comment on the facts. As soon as you start to mix in opinions it gets so much more personal, even if that would be more relevant on most occasions. People get upset. (. . .) Sometimes we discuss questions of method when facts are at issue.[67]

According to the quotation above, the analysts are very sensitive to criticism in general and in particular in regard to opinions (which, in this case, I understand as analysis and interpretation).

The analysts also underline that there are differences as to which analysts can be critiqued. The analysts perceive that some analysts or groups of analysts have gained such a status within the organisation that it makes them impossible to critique. If the analyst has already achieved a certain status within the organisation, it seems as if this will cause their analysis be viewed as more credible from the start. Increased status for an analyst could possibly also make it more difficult for fellow analysts to comment on the assessment. That is, status provides the analyst with a better chance of convincing the managers of the assessments and thereby increasing the chances of releasing the assessments.

> It is a form of intellectual snobbery. It's all about how you fit into your niche or how you are perceived to fit into your niche. You have to be an expert in your field to be entitled to an opinion. If you're not 100 % into your subject, anything you say is completely irrelevant.[68]

Again, the increase in status means that an analyst both receives less criticism and gets to hand out more criticism. The analyst continues:

> It was OK to comment on some analysts, but others seem to be above comment, and everything that they said was simply the truth. So you didn't comment on those [reports]. (. . .) these analysts were somehow untouchable. They had put themselves on a pedestal and then the managers had done so too. This made it impossible to have a fruitful discussion about the content of the reports.[69]

Producing Knowledge

The quotation illustrates how some analysts have gained a status in the organisation, making it difficult to criticise their analysis and assessments. When the analysts describe this situation they depict it as that these analysts, immune to criticism, have gained a status within the organisation. Status seems to create a division over what may be commented on and who might be informally allowed to do the commenting.

To achieve this desirable status, one needs to work within a productive topic – a topic where the organisation generates a substantial amount of collected intelligence information – and one needs to be right.

> You need to have written a report that is timely, that is a bit exciting, that has a little bit of an *edge* that makes people notice you. And then I think it depends on whether or not a person is ambitious and thorough and is really looking to succeed. (. . .) And you have to be a good writer as well. And be able to give good presentations, be able to handle discussion and give a sound impression (. . .) to have shown solid production and are able to explain if things go wrong. Because you are allowed to make mistakes, but you have to be able to explain why and pick yourself up again.[70]

The quotation describes that the status in the organisation comes from working on a high profile topic using timely information, which makes it possible to have the edge needed. However, other necessary characteristics are that the analyst needs to write well and give good briefings, and must have a solid production of assessments. This solid production refers to both good quality of the assessments (being right) and it also refers to a solid stream of assessments. This is illustrated again by another analyst stating that:

> There are basically two ways. Either you are recruited from outside and have already proven yourself. Or you have worked for a very long time and have done good work [assessments]. You have shown yourself to be competent. You have to have written a couple of solid pieces. (. . .) At least done some well-substantiated assessments. But I suspect you don't get to be a senior analyst if you're wrong.[71]

An analyst may achieve status through having a long career, and by being right. Status might also be gained more or less by reputation, from having proved oneself in another intelligence (or other) environment. Status affects more than just the situation surrounding critique and criticism; as we will come to see, it also affects the process of releasing assessments. Nevertheless status means credibility in the organisation and this will affect the critique received and given: 'Credibility is also dependent on what your bosses think of you, if they consider you to be a good analyst or an experienced analyst. Then the report will be considered more credible.'[72] The analyst quoted illustrates the relationship between status in the organisation and the credibility assigned to the assessments. The quote also highlights the importance of being perceived as credible to the managers. The effect of being perceived as credible is described by one of the analysts:

> But sometimes in this process [of giving criticism], it is very much about politics. Internal politics that is, not party politics. And that means perhaps it's more about taking a position, in certain circumstances, rather than giving constructive criticism on various issues. Sometimes you hear opinions, often from someone with a little authority. Such as a middle manager, who completely dismisses something that someone has written. Without any arguments, apart from 'they feel this or that'. (. . .) Then you understand that the whole process is politicised and that there is no point in going on.[73]

In this quote by one of the analysts, it is highlighted once again that the risk of getting criticised for the assessment is dependent on the attitude of managers, and not only on an evaluation of the facts and arguments in the assessment.

Thus, the analysts consider the need to create alignment and support for their assessments as vital. Although there is no explicit requirement for getting support for assessments from fellow analysts, there is an expectation that the products should be part of a continuum of thought and not make possible alternative interpretations. However, management approval is required.

Within the process of writing an assessment, there is a norm for what and how the analysts are expected to write. The norm is twofold. First, the analysts perceive that the norm encompasses what the assessments include and concludes (staying close to the previously written assessments). Second, the norm implies a specific way of writing and expressing the assessments. Breaking the norm of what and how to write is highly unusual, and in doing so the analysts perceive that they make themselves vulnerable to criticism and risk decreasing their status of being 'good analysts'.

PHASE FIVE: RELEASING THE ASSESSMENT

The last part of the process is getting the assessment released. This seems to be of little concern to the analysts; they seem to consider it mainly as a formality filled with technicalities. However, there are two aspects that are relevant to this inquiry: stylistic questions of the written language consent from managers and production managers, and the lack of context for the finished assessment.

Within the formal process of releasing assessments, the style of the written language is harmonised. The analysts consider releasing the assessment as a matter for the production managers who process the assessments through the administrative process. The process may be described as highly formalised, and once the writing part of the assessment is done and the conclusion has been approved at the production board meeting, then the assessment is out of the analyst's hands. Thereafter, the assessment undergoes proofreading to harmonise the language and the style of the assessments released from the organisation. Besides the function of grammatically correcting the written text, proofreading also includes harmonising the use of concepts and terms in the assessment.

Most of the analysts consider the proofreader to be a very important asset and of great assistance correcting the language grammatically, although a few of them view proofreading as a time-consuming process with little added value. A few analysts consider proofreading as critique, which leads to them not wanting to change anything about their text in the assessment. The analysts also express the importance of making sure that the assessment is expressed in the right 'style' – that the text of the assessment conforms to 'how an assessment should be written'. One analyst describes it as:

That we agree on our approach to how we write. That we explain and show new recruits at an early stage that 'this is the way we write here'. That it should be clear that it is your job in the early years to write about this issue, in this way, for these customers, using this language. If you have a problem with that then maybe this is not quite the right job.[74]

The quoted analyst specifies that it is important that all the assessments are written in a specific style. Proofreading is generally thought of as one tool to make that happen. Furthermore, the analysts do not seem concerned about the possible effect of using specific concepts and terms when describing different topics. The harmonisation of the use of terms and concepts are referred to as an issue for the proofreader. This gives quite a powerful impact to the actual proofreading in terms of framing, through words and language.

The second aspect of the process of releasing the assessment is the need to get consent and support from the managers and the production managers: 'Everything goes via the manager, who puts his stamp on the product and also takes responsibility for it. And if I don't succeed in convincing him about the product, it will never be disseminated.'[75] This quote illustrates the importance of the managers and the production managers, although the analysts question the role of managers as the ultimate decision maker of whether the assessment should be disseminated or not. In general the analysts perceive the managers not as experts, and with little or no experience of the topic in the assessment. The process leaves it to managers to give the go-ahead or not, or they may even *'give the analysis a last touch'*.[76] If the managers make changes to the assessment, it leaves the analysts feeling left out and ultimately perceiving that their expertise is second-guessed.

> Somehow the MUST functions by all experts working on thematic and geographic lines. At the same time it is a strictly hierarchical organisation. But there has to be a releasing officer, a production manager, who is ultimately responsible for the quality of the assessment. And he will never put his name on something before he is reasonably sure that it [the assessment] is right, that it is the best that we can produce. And if there is a conflict between the experts then he [the production manager] will force the system to resolve that conflict, by making a decision one way or the other.[77]

Producing Knowledge 89

The quote illustrates that the production manager will decide what way to go with the analysis, and thereby make a decision on the organisation's assessment in specific issues and topics. The analysts underline that it is therefore necessary to get the consent of the managers to get the assessments released, although they have reservations about the arguments raised by the managers in these kinds of decisions.[78] The analysts perceive that the managers seldom argue the required changes in the assessments based on different facts or information. Nor are they argued in terms of analysis and conclusions; rather, the changes in the assessments are justified by *'how managers feel about this and that'*.[79] However, the analysts stress that the official position of the manager gives them a greater insight into the customers' perspective, which in their viewpoint creates acceptance for managers providing the final touches to the assessment.

The third aspect of the process of releasing assessments is how well received by the intelligence consumers the analysts perceive the assessments to be. In general the assessments are disseminated in writing to the intelligence consumers. At times the written assessments are supplemented and explained with briefs. These occasional intelligence briefs provide the opportunity to engage with the intelligence consumers with a further explanation and a chance to get to feedback.

Nevertheless, the analysts say that there is seldom any effort put into explaining the context of the assessment, either in detail or to cover such issues as the definitions used or the limits of the intelligence analysis.[80] The analysts underline that they believe that the assessments being communicated only in writing as insufficient for explaining the reasoning behind the conclusions made and that they do not enable the answering of any possible questions that might be raised by the consumer.

Yet another downside, underlined by the analysts, is that the instrument for feedback from the intelligence consumer is thereby very limited. The analysts express dissatisfaction over this, and regret being left without what could be an instrument of improvement: 'Throughout my entire time here, I must say that the weakest link has probably been the relationship between us (the intelligence service) and the consumers.'[81] The analyst later continues by describing the dissatisfaction of being left without the possibility of feedback from the intelligence consumer, a dissatisfaction that is a reoccurring issue throughout the interviews. The analyst perception of the assessment *'being sent into a big black hole'* leaves them without knowing whether the initial intelligence need from the consumer was met, if the scope and depth of the assessment was sufficient for the decision maker to form an opinion or if the assessment actually contributed to the decisions made.[82]

Thus, the process of releasing the assessment may be characterised by, firstly, aesthetic harmonisation by the proofreading focusing on 'the intelligence style' and the language and concepts used. This implies that the analytical process invests little significance on the possible effect of the language used, and how issues and topics may be understood by the intelligence consumer. Secondly, that before the release of an assessment there is a need to get support and consent from the managers. Thirdly, when the assessments are released to the intelligence consumer the dialogue is limited, leaving little room for further explanation of the conclusions made and for the possible limits of the assessments. The limited dialogue between the analysts and the intelligence consumers also imply restricted opportunities for feedback.

SUMMARY

The social discursive practice of the intelligence service may, on the one hand, be characterised by a 'collective of thought'. The importance of collectiveness is disclosed in the search for producing knowledge within a continuum, in line with the previously established and accepted knowledge. The collectiveness is also visible in the analysts' reluctance to produce controversial assessments – breaking the norm of what conclusions to draw and how to express the assessments. Furthermore, the collectiveness is visible in the disinclination to critically discuss the assumptions for and the substance of the analysis.

However, within this collective thought, individuality is, on the other hand, equally important. The individual analysts make important analytical choices (from initiating assessments, selecting what information to use, to how the analysis is conducted). The analysis itself is considered as an individual action. The individuality of the analytical process also reinforces the difficulty of discussing, reflecting and critiquing the analysis itself, thereby allowing the analytical assumptions and process to remain unarticulated and being described as a 'gut feeling'.

Notes

1. Interview 1. In the intelligence sphere, this is most often referred to as actionable intelligence.
2. Interviews 3 and 4
3. Interview 10.
4. The idea that the intelligence analysis is defined by the element of containing secret information is also a common view within intelligence-related research.
5. Interview 10.
6. Interview 2.
7. Interview 5.
8. Interview 8.
9. Interview 2.
10. Interview 1.
11. Here it is important to clarify that is not the substance of the assessment that is debated, but rather the length, depth and scope of the assessment must be decided to fit the need of the customer.
12. Interview 4.
13. The concept of 'politicisation of intelligence' indicates that the policy-maker influences the intelligence analyst or intelligence organisation to write assessments that fit with the planned policy choices. See the vast intelligence research on both the US and UK intelligence service assessments before the Iraq War. For example Bar-Joseph, 'The politicization of intelligence'; Hastedt, 'The politics of intelligence and the politicization of intelligence'.
14. Interview 4.
15. Interview 11.
16. Interview 2.
17. Interview 7.
18. Interviews 7, 9 and 3.
19. Interview 10.
20. Interview 4.
21. Interviews 7 and 5.
22. Interview 7.
23. Interview 7.
24. Observation 2.
25. Observation 3.
26. Interview 10.
27. For example, interviews 4, 8 and 11.
28. Interview 10.
29. Observation 6.

30 Observations 4 and 3.
31 Observations 4 and 5.
32 Interview 9.
33 Interview 9.
34 For example, Observations 2, 3, and 4.
35 Observation 1.
36 Interview 6.
37 Interviews 4 and 1 and Observation 1.
38 Interview 8.
39 Observation 6.
40 Observation 2.
41 Interview 7.
42 Interview 3.
43 Interview 4.
44 Interview 2.
45 Interview 7.
46 Interview 6.
47 Interview 6.
48 Interview 9.
49 Interview 8.
50 Interview 2.
51 Interview 5.
52 Interview 6.
53 Interviews 4 and 10.
54 Interview 2.
55 Interview 7.
56 Observation 1.
57 Observations 1, 2 and 4.
58 Observation 2.
59 Observation 2.
60 Interview 9.
61 Observation 3.
62 Observation 3.
63 Observation 2.
64 Although one respondent felt he was free to give any comment, and felt that the atmosphere was quite open-minded (Interview 5).
65 See for instance Interviews 2, 8, 9 and 10.
66 Interview 8.
67 Interview 4.
68 Interview 2.
69 Interview 2.
70 Interview 10.

71 Interview 3.
72 Interview 6.
73 Interview 7.
74 Interview 9.
75 Interview 5.
76 Interview 11
77 Interview 1.
78 See above for a more elaborated discussion of getting support for an assessment. The argument made there concerning norms, criticism and status is also valid for getting support and consent from managers.
79 Interview 6.
80 Interviews 6 and 2.
81 Interview 4.
82 Interview 5.

Chapter 7

PRACTICE FOR CREATING KNOWLEDGE

DIRECTING THE INTELLIGENCE KNOWLEDGE

The analytical work of the intelligence service is directed based on the previously accepted knowledge. Even though parts of the analytical work are directed by the need of the intelligence consumer, many of the choices of prioritising and the scope of the analysis are made by the individual analysts. The chapter examines which facts and arguments are used, how the analysts argue when conceptualising the issues in focus and how choices are made regarding what information to relay for the intelligence analysis. The information and facts used for the assessments are primarily dependent on previous analytical work and therefore are also constrained by the accepted knowledge. Additionally, the chapter examines the literary style of the estimates by investigating how conclusions are presented and substantiated in those estimates. That is, it examines how analysts relate to the possibility of objectivity and value neutrality.

Direction and Prioritisation

There are three different ways for a specific assessment to be written: first through the annually revised production plan, second as a result of something that has happened and direct tasking coming from the intelligence consumers, and third through initiation by the analysts themselves motivated by their insight into changes within their area of expertise.

The first of the ways to initiate an assessment begins with the established production plan of general issues and topics that the intelligence consumers have expressed interest in. Next follows organisa-

Creating Knowledge

tional decision making and prioritisation over how and when different assessments should be written. The general topics to which the intelligence service should pay attention are decided by the intelligence consumer,[1] but prioritisation between the different needs is conducted within the intelligence service. The prioritisation choices are usually made after preparation by a specific planning management team and thereafter through a decision made at an organisation-wide weekly production board meeting at which all departmental management is represented. Following this, the question is distributed to the analyst or group of analysts.[2]

The analytical management in combination with the analysts themselves decide the internal prioritisation within this overarching production plan on what and when intelligence requirements are turned into assessments, or as one analyst expressed it:

> There are certain topics that are a bit closer to your heart. (. . .) So that's what guides you and it also makes you more attentive to issues around these topics. So, you read more about these topics and accumulate more [information] about them.[3]

The quotation above illustrates that the analysts themselves have a vital influence on prioritisation, and also gives recognition to the risk of subjectivity when prioritising. There is also a tendency to strive for continuity in the topics that are frequently covered, also partly illustrated in the quotation, as the analyst described how they tend to read and accumulate more information on specific topics. Although the knowledge production process revolves around analytical management and the production board meeting, it would appear that quite a large proportion of the responsibility falls on the analysts themselves in regard to prioritising and directing the analytical work. This is illustrated again by another analyst underlining the impact of the individual analyst.

> It can never be a manager's task to decide which reports should be written. They can be added to at the management level, but it is the individual's [the analyst's] responsibility to say that we have this understanding. That's the way it is.[4]

The annual production plan is thereby prioritised via the production board meeting, and the individual analysts play a significant role in this prioritisation based on their own unique expertise.[5] The opinions of the analyst, being an expert on a specific topic within the organisation, have a substantial impact on the choices of when and how a topic should be written about in an assessment. The analysts also have the most detailed knowledge on what information is available and what has been written before: if there is enough information and facts in order to make an assessment possible and whether there is 'something new' to write about. Both what has been written before as well as the information available in the organisation are vital in the analysts' choice of what, how and when to write.

The second way that assessments are initiated is when something happens. Usually, when something extraordinary happens in the world, the intelligence consumers will pose a direct question and ask for an explanation and an assessment. These more direct and more short-term questions are also distributed via planning management to the analyst responsible, who will then prepare or write an assessment.[6] A similar situation arises if some sort of action is about to be undertaken by the Swedish Armed Forces or the international mission that the Armed Forces are a part of; this again might call for a new assessment.

> Sometimes you can see that an issue is of interest . . . I can assess that it is of interest to someone. (. . .) If, for example, we [the Armed Forces] are about to undertake some action of some kind and you know that there is an organisation that has said they will disrupt that action. So, of course that is something you would like to inform somebody about.[7]

In this situation the analyst is partly responsible for directing and prioritising what assessments should be written, although it is the direct need for the intelligence consumer that initiates the assessment. The analyst nevertheless directs attention to what is considered to be problematic in the specific situation, that is, the analyst has the knowledge of the region and thereby makes the analytical choices of what might be problematic for the intelligence consumer.

The third circumstance under which an assessment may be initiated is through the intelligence analysts themselves. The analysts have the opportunity (and responsibility) to initiate an assessment if through their expertise they have found something new that they feel is about to happen. One example of this could be that there is something changing regarding the issue or area that is their analytical responsibility. When this occurs, an analyst may feel the need to make an assessment, without being directly tasked.

> And the other reason I started writing a report was when I could see for myself . . . and then it wasn't as acute [as when given specific questions], but I could see that something was beginning to happen often before the media paid any attention to it. (. . .) So, much of the long-term assessments I ran myself. And my view of what was important and relevant [prevailed].[8]

The idea here is that as analysts pay close attention to a specific region or issue, their expertise will make it possible for them to react and draw attention to new trends and tendencies through prediction. A slightly different focus is the distinction between changes that take place in the world and changes in the incoming information, as illustrated by the quotation below.

> And partly [you begin to write] because you find something in the material that you'd like to bring out. That it seems to indicate something . . . When I saw interesting things begin to appear in the material we gathered . . . trends, tendencies, connections . . . I wrote about it.[9]

Both of the quotations above illustrate how assessments may be initialised by the analysts themselves, motivated by changes or events in the areas and issues that are within the intelligence focus. It should be noted, though, that the nuances of the second quotation emphasises that it is what is in the material (the incoming reports) that makes the analyst react. Within this third and final way to initiate assessments is the analysts' own choices that call for spontaneous reporting.

This last way to initiate an assessment is considered as one of the basic intelligence tasks, as the 'alarm bell function'.[10] Depending on the topic that the analyst works with, the ratio between these three types of initialisation of assessments differs greatly between different parts of the organisation.[11] If the analyst works within a topic that is currently in focus, for example international missions, then the number of direct (and usually short-term) questions increase. Conversely, other topics have more of a long-term perspective, and within these topics the production plan tends to be given greater significance in prioritising which assessments to write.

Facts and Arguments

The analysts play a significant role in directing the analytical prioritisation of what assessments should be written. In the choices of what should be written the analysts are guided by what has been written before and also by what information is available. The next issue in the knowledge production process is how to choose which pieces of information and reporting should be included in the assessment. The selection of the incoming reports is influenced by what kind of information has been used in previous assessments and also by an established idea that continuity of opinion is desirable.

The analysts describe that the choices of what information to use are not methodologically systemised; rather they are made subjectively and are motivated by the previously described 'gut feeling' and previous experience. The analysts make their choices of what information to use based on their pre-understanding of the question at hand, and the assessments already in place.

> There was no method or system for how such things were decided. . . . And deciding what information you went with or what information was missing, you used your intuition all the way. (. . .) The more you got to know an area, the better you were at saying 'this piece of information is not credible and we can ignore that'. This is probable and plausible. (. . .) But it's mostly gut feeling.[12]

The quotation exemplifies the intuitive character of the choices for what information to use made by the analysts. The analysts' choices of what information to use for their assessments are also partly decided by what is deemed reasonable. What is deemed as reasonable is dependent on the analysts' pre-understanding of the topic or region. Also illustrated by the quote above, as the analyst argues, the more you get to know an area the better the analyst gets at assessing what information is credible.

The organisational ambition for continuity and coherence together with the ad hoc approach for selecting what information to use as

Creating Knowledge

grounds for the assessment will likely make it much more difficult to incorporate information contesting the established way of thinking. The overall aim to make the new assessments match up to previous statements made by the organisation also has an effect on the selection of information and incoming reports, making the selection less likely to include information that opposes the established line of assessments. There seems to be no established method or technique for making this selection, nor any requirements for determining the information chosen.

> Then you actually have to go back and look . . . it's part experience. . . . I think it's very seldom that it [the information] is contradictory. I mean diametrically. Often there is more or less contradiction, but the indications usually point in the same direction. But then we actually have a pretty good knowledge base about many important issues [in the organisation]. Indeed, there are issues where we haven't had to change our opinion at all. Time has shown that we have been right, and I think this allows us to rely pretty much on what we have written previously and our bank of experience. When you have to pick things out.[13]

The quotation above represents the ambition of continuity for the assessments, influencing the choices of what information is used in the assessments. Also absent is an articulated consciousness or discussion of what might affect this selection, or an approach that might help the analysts to sustain a critical perspective throughout the selection process. Instead, the general approach is that the analysts seek compatibility for the incoming reports and information both to each other and to the previously established knowledge and assessments. The incoming information is considered as pieces of information that may be used for answering different needs and questions, without being conditioned to a specific context or under any sort of restriction. The choice of which pieces to include and which to leave out is up to the individual analyst. Not all of the pieces of information at hand will be included, but rather specific types of information and specific pieces of information will be chosen for describing and assessing issues or events. The analysts' understanding of the choices as intuitive are represented again by yet another analyst.

> Often it depends on how the report is written, to be completely honest. If it feels like it is good information . . . I think that we can quite often be fooled . . . If the person who writes to me, if that person is like me and they express themselves like me, then I'll think that the report's better.[14]

Besides illustrating the analysts' perception of the choices of information as intuitive, the quote also represents another aspect of dependency on pre-established knowledge: the relationship between the previously written assessments and the information from intelligence collection. Illustrated here is a relationship between the analyst and collection, where the analyst gives positive feedback to the information provided from collection only as long as it is compatible with established ideas and knowledge. This in turn motivates collection to actively search for more information of a similar kind, which again narrows the span of information to that compatible with established knowledge, thus making contradictory or contrasting information less likely. This is a general feature of the relationship between the analysts and the collected information that strengthens the reliance on previously established opinions and knowledge

If the process of selecting the incoming information and reports occurs primarily through a reliance on previous reports and old habits, there is a greatly decreased chance of finding information that might indicate something other than the established assessment and opinion. Even if the selection at first glance might appear to be left to the individual analyst, the absence of structure or an articulated approach could imply that the socialisation of the individual analyst risks becoming even stronger, making the choices even more predictable and risk reproducing the same knowledge.

Hence, there are three primary different ways that assessments are initiated: according to the production plan, due to world events (directly tasked by intelligence consumers), and on the analysts' initiative. The individual analyst plays a significant role in directing what assessments should be written. What the analysts find relevant and feasible has a decisive impact on the focus and scope of the assessments. These choices by the analysts are directed by what is usually written, topics frequently covered and what the individual analyst finds interesting. It is only in the case of being directly tasked by the intelligence consumer that the impact of the analyst decreases.

THE LITERARY STYLE

In the process of producing knowledge, the contexts under which specific issues are framed are of great importance with regard to both how the issues are thought about and how the assessments are perceived by the policymakers. Ultimately, the framing of different topics might have an impact on the policies made. This raises the question of what affects the decision about the concepts and terms used when portraying societal phenomena appearing in the assessments.

The choice of terms and concepts in the intelligence analysis is made by the analysts. The choice is made with the idea of coherency to the established way of thinking and writing about a specific topic or issue. The concepts used by the analysts for depicting, contextualising and explaining the issues at hand are seldom explicitly defined. Rather, it seems as if the analysts are reluctant to produce explicit definitions, with the argument that it would make the analysis more difficult. There is no deliberate discussion or forum for reflecting on the choices of the terms and concepts used. Nor are the concepts used consistently in the assessments. The analysts want continuity in the use of concepts, creating resistance towards change in the use of terms and concepts.

Choosing Concepts

Generally, the choice of terms and concepts is a deliberate one, aimed at conforming to the established use in previously written assessments.

> I prefer to use accepted concepts and definitions. And by that I mean those already used within the Armed Forces. But then sometimes you have to define a concept yourself. But it's not . . . I did that once, and I got yelled at, but even so it's up to the analyst to put his foot down and use the definition he wants. (. . .) Instead, I think it [the definition] should be apparent in the reports you write, then there wouldn't need to be so much arguing.[15]

This analyst's experience underlines how the analysts choose what concepts are used. The decision of what concepts to use seems to be an individual decision made by the analysts themselves. In general the analysts also seek conformity to the concepts already used within the organisation.

> We had a country that used a specific expression for the neighbouring region. It was an expression that reflected the previous historic relationship between the two countries. And then it was suggested that we should use another expression that was a little bit more customer-friendly, an expression with a bit more of a security political nuance. But this was outvoted because we had a tradition of using another word in that context.[16]

The quote illustrate that changes in the use of concepts are generally not desired in the organisation. Hence, there seems to be resistance in the organisation towards using new concepts. The analysts' perception of the individuality in the choice of concepts is displayed by another analyst stating that:

> Everyone is free to make their own definitions. Maybe there's a consensus further up in the hierarchy, but there's none horizontally. (. . .) It is up to the writer of a report to clarify what she or he means by a particular term. Then it is of course up to the reader to try and understand the writer's perspective.[17]

This quotation again illustrates that it is up to the individual analyst to formulate, define and stand by the chosen concepts in the specific contexts.

The analysts also acknowledge that the organisation is aiming for consensus with regard to the understanding and use of concepts. The need for consensus over concepts is argued by the analysts to be an important part of ensuring that the assessment can be understood by the intelligence consumer, although this consensus is not easily achieved considering the individuality in the choices made. The analysts perceive that there is no internal consensus on how to use these concepts.[18]

Inconsistent use of terms of concept might risk creating a conflict of concepts when, for example, there are two different departments in the organisation both engaged in the same field (for instance, issues relating to ethnic conflict). The organisation's intention is that they should both use the same concept for comparable situations, though since the choices of understanding and use of concepts are individually decided and without a forum for discussion of concepts this consensus is not easily achieved.[19] The organisation's strive for consensus is also

Creating Knowledge

illustrated during seminars where management underlines the necessity of coherence in the use of concepts, and simultaneously stresses the importance of *'sticking with the concepts we already use'*.[20] However, the process of establishing this consensus is not necessarily a negotiation between the departments, but rather the decision is a result of the formal hierarchical structure. This is also visible during seminars, where during the meeting management decides how certain concepts should be understood and what concepts should be used for a specific region.[21]

The Use of Language

In the process of knowledge production in general, and in regard to the framing issues and topics in particular, it is apparent that concepts are thought of in an instrumental way by the analysts. The analysts' view on the use of these concepts and terms is that they are only a way (imperfect but the only media available) to communicate a snapshot of reality. Hence, in the assessments, the choices of words, terms and concepts are 'just language', without associations to any specific meaning, value or political implication.

> I think the viewpoint you have to remember is that of the customer, their language style. But when the number of people on the distribution list increases, as an expert there is a temptation to develop complicated language with your own definitions, which I think is a completely useless. You have to start with the language that the customer understands and stick to it. (. . .) [You have] to say that 'we use these expressions that deal with these phenomena, which are specifically like this. And we have decided that this term is closest to the truth and is the term used by the customer himself.'[22]

The possibility that there may be power and meaning invested in a specific use of language and that different concepts might imply different understandings of the same specific question is not recognised. The same analyst continues, and describes a situation where the organisation's tradition of using one concept clashes with the ambition of adapting to the customer's narrative. There also seems to be an idea of adjustment to the expected language of the intended customer.

The view of language as a mediator for portraying the world, without internal meaning and power, becomes prevalent through the eyes of the analyst. There is also a tendency to work within what is viewed as the conventional language, without contesting the conventionality of the language. In regard to decisions on what concepts to use, there is also compliance with established collectives of experts. These groups contain those analysts who consider themselves and are considered to be experts on specific topics, and not just within their own organisation. These expert collectives may contain members from academia as well as different kinds of partner organisations and also the corresponding collectors. Still, within this collective, the space and ambition for reflection and contestation of concepts used seems rather modest. When discussing the choices of concepts in assessments, the analyst argues that:

> It is better to have a proofreader who is not so familiar with the issues. I think it is much better to a have a person who's really good with language and not too familiar with the regions, terrorism and aircraft. Instead they just look at the language and at what message is being communicated.[23]

Here again the quotation reveals a rather naïve view of the function of language itself, overlooking the role that it can play as a producer of both values and political connotations. There seems to be a view that the language per se may be used without implying specific understanding, while at the same time there seems to be an understanding that the assessment 'communicates a message'. There are, however, exceptions to this, and even occasionally recognition of how influential the language is both in the way we express ourselves (and thereby how we are understood) and also in the way we think.

> I write quite differently from how I think. Or you know when you're having lunch and talking about your area of interest ... then you use jargon and crack jokes about it. But then, after a couple of years the jokes aren't that funny anymore. You become so accustomed at the end that you are *it* [the language]. This language has become the way I think. There is always a difference between the language of our thoughts, and our written language. But they have actually become more and more alike over the years. There used to be a much bigger difference.[24]

Defining Concepts

The estimates contain quite vague formulations of concepts that usually (in other public or policy documents) would be accompanied by some sort of definition or list of defining characteristics (see also Chapter 11 – The Representation of Terrorism). The defining characteristics of terms and concepts are not explicitly stated in the assessments. Nor are they explicitly discussed between analysts or elsewhere in the organisation, although the analyst clearly states that they are affected in the way they write (and think) about their topics by the concepts (and the literary style) accepted within the organisation: 'I don't think [about my subject] in the words I use when I write. But then when I write, I translate what I think into the words and terminology used in intelligence jargon.'[25] The quote illustrates the influence that the words and concepts accepted within the organisation have over how the analysts write and think about their topics.

The analysts also describe their own reluctance to define the concepts that they use in their assessments. It almost seems as if there is a strategy of not being explicit about what the intelligence service means by specific concepts and terms.[26] The analysts justify this reluctance by arguing that it would make it much more difficult to express their assessments and conclusions. Another argument raised by the analysts is that striving for continuity and the disinclination to change make explicit definitions even harder to use in their analytical work. Once a concept has been defined in a specific manner, then if conditions change, changing the concept is too difficult to process in the organisation. Then, the analysts argue, it is much easier to either use another concept for the new situation or to constantly use wide definitions.

Incidentally, during one of the observations of a working seminar, as one of the authors tried to clarify what he meant by a specific wording, one of the intelligence analysts turned to me and quietly let me in on a secret of his. In his view:

> As an intelligence analyst, you should never define any term that you use in an assessment, because that would mean you could

only use that word in that specific context, and then you would also have to make sure you get consensus for the new term when you have to use it in the next context.[27]

This analyst's solution was to never define anything and to be imprecise in the use of conflicting concepts. This expressed ambition, of keeping concepts as wide as possible and with as little definition as possible, seems like a conscious strategy used by the analysts to ensure that concepts can be used in a variety of contexts and to avoid bickering over concepts themselves.

Changes of Concepts

As already discussed, there is a reluctance towards the use of new concepts, and there is the possibility of conflicting ideas on how a specific concept should be understood, or differing opinions over which concept should be used for a specific event or happening. This raises the question of what happens when there is no consensus on how a concept should be used, or when a situation might need the infusion of a new concept or term. The disinclination to change concepts or to change the use of concepts is general argued on behalf of the intelligence customer: 'I wouldn't be surprised if we spend too much effort into being supposedly consistent, while the consumer pays much more attention to the arguments and assessments.'[28]

There is a worry within the organisation that the intelligence customer would be confused if the changes are too frequent. This worry of being perceived as indecisive by the intelligence consumer is explicit and well known to the analysts, and thus also amplifies the expectation that the analysts will comply with the conventional use of language and concepts. This general idea that the consumer might perceive the intelligence service as indecisive is illustrated by statements made during the seminars by several of the managers present. They stated that *'If we [the intelligence service] have used this term before, you will have to give me very good reasons for changing it'*[29] and *'The costumers are going to think that we can't make up our minds if we keep changing the way we write.'*[30] These quotes illustrate both the general reluctance to change itself and also the idea that the consumers would be confused if the intelligence service changed the concepts used in the assessments.

If changes of concepts or the use of concepts are needed, it is not clear to the analysts how these changes are made and who decides or affects the circumstances of change. The whole process of a possible change of concept is unarticulated and almost perceived as a matter of proofreading or adjusting to changes made by somebody else (a consumer or partner organisation).

> Then I'm afraid the writing is vague, and if anyone raises an issue with the use of a term, it would be sent to the proofreader and then the production manager, who in true military style, decides and says 'from now on, the MUST mean this when using the term conflict'. And it's final. Once it's done we can't take it up for discussion again. Then you just have to abide by it.[31]

The quotation above illustrates that the reflection and discussion about what concepts are used, and how these might be defined and changed are not really a question of the substance of the concepts but rather an issue of being consistent.

If change is needed, the analysts almost seem to assume that this is due to a change of reality, and then the concepts will be changed for them by someone else. What initially seemed like a choice (of concepts) by the individual analyst now seems like an acceptance of the established discourse of language, within a sort of broadly defined security policy sphere. The role of the individual analysts then tends to become that of a spectator, accepting and adjusting to common practice or to the language discourse of another party (often the intelligence customer and policymakers).

The overall view of concepts and their function within the intelligence knowledge process imply that concepts are individually decided. Concepts are generally not explicitly defined nor are they discussed within the organisation. The analysts seem to apply a practise of wide definitions in order to avoid having to change them or the definitions of concepts. There is a general disinclination towards change in the use of concepts, argued by not wanting to confuse the intelligence consumers. In general the analysts do not seem to acknowledge the possibility of specific meaning being attached to the use of language (terms and concepts) per se. Rather, language does not matter that much ('it's just language') and is considered language as value free and neutral – it is just used to describe reality.

CONSISTENCY AND CONTRADICTIONS

In their analytical work the analysts generally seek consistency with the previously written assessments. The search for consistency impacts both the analytical work in producing the assessment and the choices made by the analysts of what information to use. The analysts acknowledge that the aim of consistency affects how they approach contradictory information. The organisation's strive for consistency also implies that analytically only one single interpretation of the information may be understood as the accurate one and only that assessment is disseminated to intelligence consumers.

The analysts disclose an awareness of the organisation's strive for consistency in the analytical work and in the assessments produced. The explicit aim of the organisation for consistency was displayed, for instance, on several occasions during the seminars. To exemplify this, during one of the seminars one of the managers stated that: 'In this case we say something that we have not said before. Just so that we are aware of it. . . . Everything said in estimates must be a logical consequence of previous estimates.'[32] The quote illustrates the organisation's aim of consistency in the assessments. The analysts also acknowledge that the strive for consistency forms an explicit goal for themselves in their analytical work.[33] The analysts are affected by the expectation of consistency within several of the parts of their analytical process. The analysts describe situations concerning when they systemise and select the information they use for their assessments, when they choose what terms and concepts they use for describing their respective topics, the language they adjust to in expressing their assessments, and how they understand and explain issues and topics in their assessments. In general the analysts perceive the strive for consistency as a constraint.

> We [the intelligence services] have missed all the major upheavals in the world. There isn't much that we have managed to get right! Is there? It's like we didn't even see the changes. We have our sights set on one thing, and if something doesn't fit in, we don't even see it.[34]

The quote illustrates that the analysts perceive that a predetermined focus to the analytical work make them less attentive to new phenomena, and cause them to miss important changes in world affairs. This difficulty is expressed by another analyst:

> For focused or specialised reports I base a lot on what I've written before. (...) In that way I think you can just continue to build [knowledge] like a pyramid of bricks. (...) A reasonable analysis can only be a normal, solid, steady analysis and can only have so many variations. The fact is that it can sometimes be difficult to be innovative and see trends before anyone else does.[35]

The difficulties with relying on previous estimates and the constraining effect that the idea of consistency has on the analytical process for the analysts was again described by one of the analysts by an example from the Balkans.

> When things started to happen in Serbia at the end of the 90s, our assessment was, on a number of occasions, that Milosevic would remain in power. We looked at the resources he had, his motives, and what options he had if he had resigned. None of these things changed and we stuck with our assessment – which he would remain in office. When we briefed the Supreme Commander the day after Milosevic's resignation we were told: 'That's nice, now let's hear all the reasons for Milosevic to remain in power.' But the analysis was genuine and one we had made on three different occasions. And the analysis was actually correct the last occasion too, but something had changed that made the analysis turn out wrong. And really, how the hell do you make that judgement? Then you have to understand that some basic factors have come to changed and therefore the outcome will be different.[36]

The striving for consistency also affects the analysts' approach to contradictory information. One of the choices that are left to the individual analyst is what information to use for the assessments. When making these choices the analysts refer to whether the information appears reasonable or accurate. The analysts say that with experience comes the ability to determine what information is reasonable and accurate,[37] although they also say that information that *'seems to be compatible'* with the previous opinion and assessments is more often determined as relevant.[38] The analysts say that the information needs to be reasonable to be used in the assessments and what is deemed as reasonable is the previously written assessments. Information that is of a significantly different kind or deemed as unreasonable is simply not incorporated.[39]

There are of course exceptions and nuances. Some analysts argue that although the information is contradictory, it should not be dismissed instantly. Rather, it could be an indication that something is about to change in the area or regarding the topic, although the information still need to be perceived as reasonable.[40]

If the information on a topic or an issue or if there is an assessment written that is too contradictory to the predetermined view and previously written assessments, it is ignored.

> We generally have difficulty in accepting change because we become set in our ways. I think that we do not dare [to think differently]. If you try to think outside the box you risk being laughed at by the managers. You're expected to write along the same lines of reasoning as before. (. . .) The question is whether we are mentally prepared to think about the next step; for example, how will terrorism develop in the future? To dare to think about the unlikely.[41]

The quoted analyst illustrates that striving for consistency affects the analysts in how controversial an analysis they are encouraged to write. The analysts describe it in terms of it being safer to write in line with the previous assessments than to try out new ideas. The analysts argue that it is this encouragement to be consistent and 'staying inside the box' that makes them unlikely to identify new trends, making them less successful in their predictions.

Thus, there is a strong inclination towards seeking consistency within the intelligence analytical process. This consistency is sought over accepting and trying to explain contradictions in, for example, information. The striving for consistency also impacts the analysis in the assessments, making them less sensitive towards change and making it more difficult to recognise new trends. The aim of consistency also implies that there is an expectation that only one analytical answer is possible.

THE ETHIC COMPONENT

The analysts emphasise that the primary purpose of the assessments (hence also the knowledge) produced is to make a difference for decision makers, aiding them to make informed decisions: 'I think as an intelligence analyst you should be neutral. My job is not evaluating what is happening. It is more about reporting on what is actually happening.'[42]

According to the intelligence analysts the assessments should bring an added value to the decision makers in terms of explaining world events, reaching conclusions and aiming to predict future events. However, the analysts' description of the analytical work conducted reduces this added value to accumulating and systemising information. While doing this the analysts aim at impartiality and objectivity. In doing so the analysts want to make further analysis possible, as well as communicating the conditions for the assessments to consumers.

The Value of Intelligence Analysis

In general, the intelligence analysts underline the importance of the usefulness of intelligence analysis. If the assessments are not put into use by various kinds of decision makers, the knowledge is irrelevant. The use might be of various kinds, and need not be grounds for direct action or policymaking; the use is also justifiable if the assessments might contribute to background knowledge or a greater understanding on behalf of the intelligence customer.

The analysts see the analysis as a process of refining the incoming information (see below), bringing both order and systematisation to this sea of rather disparate information, and in different ways explaining its underlying meaning and context to the decision maker. The primary contributions of the intelligence analysis are systemising information and facts, to a certain extent contextualising it, and if possible make assessments or predictions.

> The analyst at this level should provide a comprehensive view of the information collected. You see, a strategic analysis should take into account many different kinds of information. Then it should be compiled and made accessible to decision makers. And to some extent it should be forward-looking. That's the way I think it should be . . . But that's not exactly how we usually work.[43]

The quotation underlines three key aspects of what the analysts in general consider good intelligence knowledge. First, the intelligence analysts should base their assessments on different kinds of information, not just the (secret) information collected within the organisation itself. Second, the assessment should be forward-looking (instead of just describing), which incorporates the idea that intelligence analysis should prepare the decision makers for future decisions and events. Third, this forward-looking analysis should be easily accessible to the decision makers, the designated customers of the intelligence analysis. The quotation above also illustrates that the analysts believe there is a discrepancy between what the intelligence analysis should contribute (described above) and what they actually do.

> Of course the MUST suffers from these problems, as all Swedish authorities do ... That you alone should arrive at the accepted truth, because there really is such a thing, instead of having your own opinion and standing by it. We are expected to find that single truth that everyone can agree on. This often means we get it completely wrong.[44]

The quotation above illustrates the notion that there is 'one truth out there' and that it is the job of the intelligence analysts to find it. The analysts perceive that they are expected to reveal the only way that an event may be understood, and to depict and describe the way things really are. At the same time, the analysts themselves are sceptical of the possibility of the 'one truth', yet it is this single possibility of interpretation that is the ideal end result of their analysis. They seem to adapt to the expectation of finding the one truth by suppressing their analytical contribution and presenting analysed and interpreted materials as accumulated information and facts, rather than interpretations. Within the organisation, there is an explicit ambition to have coherence within the assessments, and to be extremely careful with changing the current assessment. This makes explicit the positive connotation to the idea of rationality, stability and coherence.

The analysts consider the analytical work they do as guided by principles of objectivity and impartiality. The analysts frequently underline the necessity of being value neutral in their assessments. At the same time, the analysts' own understanding of the added value they create is combined with the idea of bringing as much 'new material' into the intelligence process as they possibly can.[45] This raises the question of how the analysts understand this 'new material' in terms of what is information, facts and viewpoints, and conclusions formed through interpretation.

Information, Facts and Valuations

The analysts make no clear distinction between information, facts and viewpoints in their systematisation of what 'material' they use in the assessments. The ambiguity between these concepts is also reflected in their own analysis. The analysts also disclose that there is no discussion over these issues within the organisation.

The ambiguity over how the analysts consider the distinction between facts and information is, for example, displayed as one analyst describes the situation.

> Within the organisation, and it's probably the same for all organisations that are doing this kind of thing [intelligence], it [information] becomes facts over time. Although it [the information] has not been substantiated or confirmed, it sort of gains a life of its own and then finally becomes facts. As long as nobody questions it. And then we'll add some new information that has not had time to become facts yet . . . We make some sort of distinction even if we are not that clear about how. There are many assumptions that have become facts.[46]

The quote illustrates that the analysts sense that there is some sort of distinction between information and facts, although the defining features are not clear to them. In general the analysts (also illustrated in the quote above) refer to the distinction between information and facts to whether the information has been confirmed or not. The analysts acknowledge the idea that in order to be considered as a fact, the information should be confirmed by two independent sources, although they also disclose that this is rarely the case.[47] The difficulty of confirming the information used for intelligence analysis is illustrated by another analyst stating that:

> For the most part, the things that I'm looking for, I cannot get them verified as being true. So I would say that I think about them more as information than facts. Actually, I rarely look for facts, because I work mostly with people and their behaviour, there are seldom facts. . . Therefore it is mostly interpretations and the like and that makes it difficult . . . It's not really facts, it's more information.[48]

The quote illustrated the difficulty of confirming the information used by the analysts. The analysts argue that this difficulty of confirming information in search of 'getting facts' implies that the best they can do is to try and apply a critical perspective and evaluate the credibility of the source and the accuracy of the information.[49] The analysts in general describe that the information is considered more likely to be accurate if it confirms the already accepted assessment or line of reasoning within the organisation. There is a wide acceptance among the analysts that their pre-understanding of what is reasonable will affect their valuation of the accuracy of the information. Also, the analysts acknowledge that information collected by the organisation from its own sources (secret information) is in general considered to have more credibility than open source information.[50]

The analysts consider viewpoints as something undesirable and something that makes the analysis subjective and less substantiated. The analysts describe that they try not to express viewpoints in their analysis, in order to remain value neutral and objective. They primarily try to avoid that by using a language that does not contain evaluative words, such as 'good', 'bad' and so on. Some analysts again underline the process of proofreading as one way of correcting the language not to include viewpoints. Nevertheless, the analysts disclose that it is difficult not include viewpoints in the analytical process including interpretation. As discussed above one strategy used by analysts to avoid subjectivity and thereby viewpoints is *'to stay as close to the information as possible'*,[51] that is, by avoiding interpretation they also avoid viewpoints.

Thus, the analysts perceive that the primary purpose of intelligence analysis is to aid decision makers in making informed decisions. When conducting intelligence analysis the analysts aim at impartiality and objectivity (being value neutral). In the opinion of the analysts their contribution through the assessments is to accumulate and systemise information about world events, with the aim of contextualising and explaining 'how things really are'.

SUMMARY

The writing of assessments are directed by the three primary different ways of assessment initiation: according to production plan, due to world events (direct tasking by intelligence consumers) and analyst initiative. The individual analyst plays a significant role in directing what assessments should be written. What the analysts find relevant and feasible has a decisive impact on the focus and scope of the assessments. These choices by the analysts are directed by what is usually written, topics frequently covered and what the individual analyst finds interesting. It is only in the case of direct tasking by the intelligence consumer that the impact of the analyst decreases.

The overall view of concepts and their function within the intelligence knowledge process implies that concepts are individually decided. Concepts are generally not explicitly defined nor are they discussed within the organisation. The analysts seem to apply a practice of wide definitions in order to avoid having to change them or the definitions of concepts. There is a general disinclination towards change in the use of concepts, argued by not wanting to confuse the intelligence consumers. In general the analysts do not seem to acknowledge the possibility of a specific meaning being attached to the use of language (terms and concepts) per se. Rather, language does not matter that much ('it's just language') and it is considered value free and neutral – it is just used to describe reality.

There is a strong inclination towards seeking consistency within the intelligence analytical process. This consistency is sought rather than accepting and trying to explain contradictions in, for example, information. The striving for consistency also impacts analysis in the assessments, making them less sensitive towards change and making it more difficult to recognise new trends. The aim of consistency also implies that there is an expectation that only one analytical answer is possible.

The analysts perceive that the primary purpose of intelligence analysis is to aid decision makers in making informed decisions (the ethic component). When conducting intelligence analysis the analysts aim at impartiality and objectivity (being value neutral). In the opinion of the analysts their contribution through the assessments is to accumulate and systemise information about world events, to contextualise and explain 'how things really are'.

Nevertheless, the analysts have not formed a clear distinction and idea between information, facts, arguments and viewpoints. As the analysts sort and use the incoming reports for assessments they do not apply a reflective and systemised thinking to discern what information from facts or arguments and viewpoints. Nor are such distinctions explicitly made in the assessments produced, thus making the overall aim of the intelligence analysts of objectivity and impartiality difficult.

Within the organisation, there is a tendency towards only writing and producing assessments on matters that are new or that have changed,[52] while at the same time having to comply with the explicit ambition of continuity within the assessments. As the analysts manoeuvre within a sort of paradox – producing news within a continuum – the structural incentive is to use established concepts, to seek consistency rather than new interpretations and to look for similar conclusions in comparable situations.

Notes

1. The intelligence consumers come from within the armed forces, the government and other the government agencies. These intelligence requirements are distributed through a division at the Department of Defence – SUND (for more details see Chapter 5).
2. Interviews 1 and 2.
3. Interview 7.
4. Interview 8.
5. This raises the question of how the analysts perform this prioritisation. This issue will be discussed further in relation to how the information that is included is selected.
6. Interviews 6 and 5.
7. Interview 5.
8. Interview 4.
9. Interview 2.
10. See also Chapter 5 for the internal view of the different functions for intelligence.
11. Interview 8.
12. Interview 2.
13. Interview 9.
14. Interview 10.
15. Interview 1.
16. Interview 7.
17. Interview 5.
18. Interview 2.
19. Interviews 6, 2 and 4.
20. Observation 6.
21. Observation 6.
22. Interview 7.

23 Interview 9.
24 Interview 10.
25 Interview 2.
26 See Chapter 11 for a more elaborated discussion of defining the concept of terrorism.
27 Observation 5. Intelligence analyst at one of the seminars held during the production process of the estimate.
28 Interview 7.
29 Observation 6.
30 Observation 5.
31 Interview 4.
32 Observation 4.
33 The impact of consistency is present and visible throughout the discussion on the knowledge production process in Chapter 6.
34 Interview 2.
35 Interview 10.
36 Interview 8.
37 Interviews 2, 4 and 10.
38 Interview 10.
39 Interviews 9 and 7.
40 Interview 2.
41 Interview 6.
42 Interview 10.
43 Interview 6.
44 Interview 7.
45 Interviews 3, 4 and 11.
46 Interview 2.
47 Interview 6.
48 Interview 10.
49 Interview 6.
50 Interviews 3, 4 and 6.
51 Interview 7.
52 This also overlooks those issues that might be of relevance through their character of not changing.

Chapter 8

THE INTELLIGENCE WORLDVIEW

Chapter 8 aims at uncovering the intelligence worldview, the way that worldview directs the analytical choices made by the analysts, and what that worldview implies for the framing of concepts, terms and that which it is important to create knowledge about. In this chapter I argue that the intelligence worldview is rooted within the ontological position of political realism. Therefore the first section of the chapter provides a short overview of the general characteristics of a political realism. Thereafter the following sections of the chapter provide argue and expose that the realist perspective is imbued in the estimates. The chapter concludes with a discussion of what the intelligence realist position implies for intelligence knowledge – what is viewed as problematic, what it implies for the process of articulation, and what this position implies for how the knowledge should be argued and proved.

POLITICAL REALISM

It is widely accepted that intelligence analysis is located within an overall frame of international political realism.[1] I agree with this position, and argue that realism is the general frame of reference for intelligence analysis. The theoretical tradition of realism is perhaps the most influential theory in international relations and over its long and rich history has come to encompass a variety of theoretical variations and positions. The early ideas of realism originate in what is referred to as 'classical realism', dating as far back as the ancient Greek, Thucydides. Since then, realism has been challenged and refined (with new approaches through structural realism, modern realism and neo-realism),[2] although for the purpose of this study it is sufficient to outline the core assumptions of classical realism, which still remains vital to the understanding of realism today. I have no ambition to cover the overall evolution of realist thought, but merely to sketch the core assumption of it in order to be able to identify traces of realist thought in the estimates.

Statism

From classical realism and onwards, the central actor is the state. The characteristics and functions for the state are considered to differ deeply between the domestic and the international arena. Domestically, the state is considered as the supreme power in a hierarchical system. To the realist, power in a state means *'man's control over the minds and actions of other men. By political power we refer to the mutual relations of control among the holders of public authority and between the latter and the people at large.'*[3] A state is considered by realists to be a societal system that is usually ordered, rational and characterised by the supremacy of the state authority. Domestically, the state is an arena for power struggle which leaves open the possibility for a diversity of political interests; however, projected externally in the international arena the state is considered as a coherent actor with one unified political will. This unified political will is expressed by states and is referred to by realists as 'national interests'. The state is considered as the only legitimate societal actor formulating the collective will of individuals.[4]

International Relations

One central realist assumption is based on the view that *'[p]olitics, like society in general, is governed by objective laws that have their roots in human nature'*.[5] The international arena is characterised by the lack of a central overriding power, and thus the actors – the states – are entities which actively compete for power. Therefore realism claims that the primary priority of the state is its survival. As the states seek power in the international arena, realist assumptions imply that the primary target for a state is to promote its national interests. The national interests of states are seen as unified, coherent and rational and thereby as creating logic for the actions taken. The national interests are therefore a means to achieve competitive advantages against other states. As states seek to create such advantages, they seek to increase their power and the ability to exercise power.[6]

Power

For realists, international politics – like all politics – is a struggle for power. In *Politics among Nations*, Morgenthau argues that power and the elements of power are the most vital factors for states.[7] The elements that constitute power for states in the international arena according to modern realists are geography, natural resources, industrial capacity, military preparedness, popultion, national character, national morale and the quality of diplomacy.[8]

The realist perspective on the international arena distinctly relates the concept of power to geography, or rather to geographic quantity and character. In Morgenthau's view, the mass of land and its geophysical attributes serve as power enhancers or reducers. Another facet of national power is comprised of the natural resources and industrial capacity; the idea is that the nation needs to be self-sufficient in terms of food and commodities needed for industry (both for economic prosperity and for a possible need to increase armament). Morgenthau argues that it is *'inevitable that the leading nations have been identical with the great powers. . .'*[9] In this sense, Morgenthau seems to have the potential for military armament in mind, rather than the need for economic prosperity, and closely relates the need for industrial capacity to the fourth element of national power – military preparedness. The need for military preparedness for national power *'is too obvious to need much elaboration'*.[10] The effect of military preparedness on national power is, in Morgenthau's argument, dependent both on the military's capacity to use technology and on the numeraire of men.

In the realist assumption there are elements of national power of an intangible character. Bridging to these intangible power characteristics is the fifth element of national power – population. The impact of population size on national power is related to the nation's ability for large-scale industry and military preparedness. The sixth element of national power is national character. National character and national morale are thought to *'stand out both for their elusiveness from the point of view of rationale prognosis and for their permanent and often decisive influence upon the weight which a nation is able to put into the scales of international politics'*.[11] Morgenthau continues by arguing that certain nationalities are more prone to certain characteristics, and that this influences the possibility of that nation exercising power in the international arena.[12] Closely related to this is the seventh element of power, national morale. In the realist approach, national morale is *'the degree of determination with which a nation supports the foreign policies of its government in peace and war'*.[13] National morale is the intangible quality of the governability of a state, the unity and obedience to and by the state. By creating strength and weakness, it indirectly influences a nation's ability to harvest from the remaining elements of national power (natural resources, military preparedness and so on). The eighth and final element of national power is the quality of diplomacy, which is described thus: *'Diplomacy, one might say, is the brains of national power, as national morale is its soul.'*[14] The quality of diplomacy is an integrated element of national power that is vital to a nation's chances of succeeding at promoting its national interest in the international arena.[15]

More contemporary realist ideas of the concept of power in both domestic and international relations claim that state leaders play a significant role in determining the impact of the distribution of power. Realists argue that rather than the objective evaluation of the distribution of power between states, what matters is the state leaders' perception of the relative power distribution.[16] This position also underlines the distinction between the ambitions of states in the international arena, where some states are prone to the status quo while others will actively seek to gain power over others. Also, realists argue that states differ in their ability to make use of the power resources at hand, which in turn affects the strength of the state. State strength is considered as the ability to make use of these power resources to gain in the specific national interest. States therefore have differing abilities to translate capabilities into elements of power and thus into state power, making the states unequal units in international relations.[17]

Balance of Power and State Security

Based on the realist assumption that the primary ambition of all states is to ensure survival, it is necessary for the state to be responsible for its own security. Realists argue that a state should not be dependent on other institutions for its own survival – hence the constant pursuit of increased power. However, it may be the case that a number of smaller states need to join forces to make certain that they are not dominated by the will of a greater (or hegemonic) state. In forming an alliance or formal collaboration, they thus increase their power but decrease their independence. The balance of power is considered to be the result of deliberate action taken by states; hence it is not a natural process but rather a construct of man.[18] In contrast to this, structural realists argue that a balance of power will be reached irrespective of any intentions by any particular state. In this view, the balance of power is created through a natural process of forming and dispersing state collaborations and alliances until eventually a balance between powers is reached.[19]

Structural realists do not rely on human nature to explain power-seeking behaviour. Instead, they argue that there is a distribution of capabilities of power in international relations that affect stability, peace and war. Waltz argues that power is when states have the possibility to gain security, and that *'in crucial situations, however, the ultimate concern of states is not for power but for security'*.[20] Waltz and other structural realists thus argue that states tend to act accordingly to maximise their security rather than to maximise their power. States are therefore thought to seek enough power to ensure their own survival and security. Other structural realists claim that the presence of uncertainty and anarchy in the international arena implies that states seek to maximise their relative power position. The overall logic is therefore to try to increase the state's own power position at the expense of other states, and the desired end status (although virtually impossible) is to have accumulated more power than any other state, hence hegemony.[21]

Summary

The above brief sketch of the basic ideas of realism covers the traits that are expected to be found in the framing of world events used in estimates. One can analyse and debate whether estimates are articulated through the realist components of national power, but one can also try to find whether and where there are gaps in the text. Even if one expects to find that the estimates tend to be framed from a realist worldview, there is the question of which of these core components of societal actors, the international arena, national power and security reflections, are present in the intelligence analysis. These elements have in many ways become the ontological framework within which intelligence analysis is situated.[22] If it is realist presuppositions and assumptions that underlie the estimates and analysis, what is it that the intelligence analysts see?

REALISM IN THE ESTIMATES

The estimates aim to provide a background for how world events are to be understood and interpreted as a basis for strategic and operational management and for long-term planning.[23] These estimates are aimed at describing, explaining, assessing and predicting national political and military settings, international relations and threats. In the framing of different national settings and international relations, the most important societal actor is the state and the most central concepts are power, power relations and national interests. Power and power relations are framed in a specific set of circumstances in the estimates, where the focus on national interests and national power are portrayed through the lens of possible scenarios for security political complications and threats.

> They say that the intelligence services are very good at predicting war, but really bad at predicting peace. But most people are looking for peace while we're looking for war. And then I think if you're sitting here working with intelligence information, you should be looking for threats and risks.[24]

The interview excerpt above illustrates the specific mindset of intelligence analysis in terms of possible interpretation of political actions and intentions. Since the estimates provide an understanding for interpreting world events, it is important to investigate further what connotations and relations the intelligence analysis gives to these actors (states) and to the central concepts (power, power relations and national interest).

Statism

The most central type of societal actor in the estimates is the state. Throughout the estimates, the states are referred to and considered to be the main possessors of political and military power. The states are considered the articulators of political will and ambition in the international arena, and the main actor around which all international relations form and conform.[25]

Further, different states are referred to interchangeably as *nations*, *countries* and *states*. The references to states (used for all kind of statehoods) are made without specifying the assumed characteristics needed for a precise use of such a wide and undecided concept as a nation state. The relation between the state actor and the idea of the nation (the nation state) as the bearer of political will and political meaning is evident through the frequent reference to national interest.[26]

National interest is seen as the inner drive for political positions and decisions in the international arena. The following quotation is typical, and its essence can be found in any of the estimates under study: 'National interests and national will are by far the most crucial aspect in deciding whether or not the international community should become involved in various crises and conflicts.'[27] Or in other words from another passage in the estimate; 'Vital interests are defined by the President and specifically include: the people, the territory and the freedom to be sovereign. Vital interests also include France's strategic global interests.'[28]

Another estimate, while discussing important political actors in international relations, states: 'National interests continue to dictate the development of security policy in Europe.'[29] As well as illustrating the assumption that national interest is the inner drive for political decision making, this also shows that the states are assumed to have one unified view on international issues and relations. Again, this position overlooks the possibility of a plurality of international politic viewpoints within states.

Throughout the intelligence analysis in the estimates, the states are represented as unified power-maximising rational actors. While discussing international relations and issues, the state is referred to as a univocal actor. The state is described and assumed to represent one unified political viewpoint in international issues and relations.[30]

The states are portrayed as rational actors in the international arena in the estimates. The viewpoints, decisions and actions of states are described and referred to as being calculated and rational. In the analysis, arguments for strengthening the assessment for the course of action for states are expressed in terms of '*[that] it is the logic course of action*'.[31] The assumed rationality of the state as a unified actor is represented through the assumption that the states will rationalise how to prioritise political power. This assumed rationality is also related to the assumption of a unified national interest founded on the inner drive for increased power. Therefore, the logical course of action for states in more or less all situations in the international arena is the course of action in which power is increased.

In the estimates, the inner drive for the state actors in the international realm is power, as well as increased power in relation to other states. The power of the state might be sought through deterrence, political influence, economical influence, and some sort of military power and capability. In the international arena, the power of the nation state is projected in different contexts and through different means by the states, with the purpose of increasing power. In the context of international relations, the states are determined by their power relations in a zero-sum game where increased real power seems to be the ultimate goal itself.[32]

State Collaborations

Although the main actors in the international realm are states, there are other types of actors in the estimates. The primary group of non-state actors represented in these estimates are the bilateral and multilateral collaborations with states as members; these state collaborations are considered to hold and exercise power in the international arena.

It is assumed that the comprehensive logic for states to enter into collaborations is to increase the political power of the nation state or to promote national interest through an alliance. The state collaborations are not primarily considered to be bearers of their own ideology, ideas or political agenda, but rather are thought of as an aggregation of national interests and ideas. State collaborations themselves are thereby also vulnerable to conflicting national interests among their member states.

> Despite the fact that political and economic cooperation within the European Union (EU) often faces crises and various sorts of setbacks, the European integration process has moved forward slowly, but surely. Although it is reasonably safe to assume that this trend will continue, politically motivated and politically driven processes, such as those in the EU, are by nature very sensitive to conflicts between member states.[33]

As illustrated in the quotation above, a state collaboration (here represented by the EU) might be threatened by conflicting national interests between its member states.

The estimates also acknowledge that state collaboration entails a certain amount of international dependence (especially economic dependence). International dependence is presumed to weaken the states, as it decreases the possibility of independent decision making. The decreased sovereignty thereby implied is considered to be a contributor to conflict between states. This can be seen as a contrast to the previously assumed logic for nations to engage in interstate collaboration, where the reason for engagement is to seek to increase power.

International dependence in turn is assumed in the estimates to have a dual and perhaps paradoxical effect on the wellbeing of states. To some degree, state collaboration is assumed to create international dependence, and in turn, international dependence is assumed to weaken the position of the nation state (through decreased independence) and thereby to increase the risk of conflict between the states. On the other hand, it is also assumed that state collaborations function as a mediator of diverse national interests, and may therefore be viewed as a contributor to stability.

> The EU has long had an important long-term stabilising role through its process of political and economic integration in Europe. Of no small importance are the candidate countries' aspirations to membership, where the suppression of international and internal conflicts is a prerequisite.[34]

The quotation above illustrates how a state collaboration (in this case the EU) is assumed to contribute to stability through integration of states and to be an actor in the international arena that decreases the risk of crises and conflict. Hence, the state collaboration is assumed to represent a benign common social institution in the international arena contributing to long-term stability.

Though the estimates recognise the existence of these state collaborations as actors that influence politics in the international arena, they are still actors that consist of states and they are still framed and thought of in a *nation state fashion*. It is assumed that the state collaborations are subject to the idea that hierarchy and order are desirable characteristics of societal actors. It is also held that state collaborations are weakened in comparison to states, because of the absence of a designated leader and the lack of a clear hierarchy.

The increasing convergence in memberships of NATO and the EU could simplify the development of the EU security policy dimension and the future division of roles in Europe. . . . In comparison to NATO, one fundamental weakness of the EU is that the organisation lacks a clear leader. This is a crucial weakness in dynamic situations that require strategic flexibility.[35]

The quotation above illustrates the idea that societal actors are likely to be more effective and more able to exercise power if subjugated to a hierarchical structure. The assumption in the estimates is that effective exercise of power does not come from lateral decision making, but rather it would seem that the MUST as an organisation holds a desire for a hierarchical top-down idea as grounds for leadership.

Non-state Actors

In the estimates, the articulation of international relations is dominated by states and state collaborations (see below). Political action and the evolution of international relations are constantly articulated within a frame of statism. Other potentially relevant societal actors in international relations, such as multinational or global organisations and corporations, are not included as potential holders of power and capabilities of power. However, such organisations and corporations are included in the domestic spheres of different states.

There are rare exceptions where other societal actors are ascribed an influential role in international politics. The most obvious of these is al-Qaida. Al-Qaida is attributed with political power (although undefined in terms of the elements of power) and the ambition of promoting interests.[36] These interests are considered in the same logic as traditional realist national interest, although lacking formal statehood as an actor. There are repeated attempts in the estimates to link and relate the organisation to different states. The interests ascribed to al-Qaida are thought of as a coherent and unified political goal projected in the international arena. The interest of al-Qaida is rationalised through an argument of seeking to increase the organisation's power position, through decreasing the power of 'Western interests'.[37]

Despite being an exception as an influential non-state actor in international relations, the rationale of al-Qaida is still attributed with the logic of realism. The logic of realism for al Qaeda is noticeable through the assumed coherency of political will and the unification of political goals, as well as through the assumption of seeking to maximise power rather than to achieve specific political goals.

International Relations

The competition between states for power is what characterises international relations in the estimates. This competition is recognised as a struggle for states to gain power in relation to other units (states) through their promotion of national interests: 'The initiative [from Russia] is seen as a balance against US and NATO influence in Europe, but also one way to driving a wedge between the US and Europe.'[38] The quotation illustrates the assumption that the rationale for Russia's action is its inner drive to gain power over the US. Like the ideas in realism, the thought is that Russia seeks to increase its power in a competitive situation with US, and if Russia succeeds then the US will automatically lose power.

The assumed incentive for states to seek involvement in international relations is to promote national interests and through that seek increased power. There is also a void in the estimates when it comes to alternative explanations for state actions. Such alternative explanations could include ideas, ideology, belief system or religion, and ethical or moral considerations. This may be illustrated through, for example, the discussion in the aftermath of the presidential elections in the US in 2001.

> The difference between the Clinton and Bush administrations in terms of defence and security policy is to be found in the definition and perception of where (and what) might constitute a threat to vital US global interests and what might be expected to happen in the future.[39]

While the estimates are seeking to address the possible changes the newly elected president might have, the reference is not attributed to a difference in political party affiliation or ideological viewpoint. Instead, the only reference of difference is in the persona.

The assumed rationale of seeking increased power is also reflected in the politicians and leaders portrayed in the estimates. The actions and viewpoints of state leaders are rationalised through an assumption of power-seeking behaviour, and lack any reference to ideas, ideology and ethics.

Power

The estimates use references to power and striving for power as *the* momentum for the imperative actors in international relations – the states. Although no explicit definition is given of the estimates' take on power (discussed at greater length below), in international relations there are a few characteristics that will give us some indication of the substance of the concept. There are several references to different kinds of power: military power, political power, economic power, influential power and personal (influential) power; the concept of 'power' is closely related to geostrategic conditions.

Politics and power

In the estimates, the terms 'politics' and 'political' are equivalent to power. The assumed reason for any actor (the political party in the domestic arena and the state in international relations) to take part in politics is to increase its own possibility of power. In this sense, the 'political' is reduced to a struggle for influence without ascribing the strive for power or basis for political action to any particular political programme ideas or ideology.

> The new President has a difficult balancing act between, on the one hand, listening to the old guard that still constitutes a dominant element of the power elite and its interests, and on the other, responding to an increased demand for economic and political liberalisation from large sectors of the population.[40]

This illustrates an assumption that reduces politics and the political to the struggle over power, without recognising their possibility as bearers of ideas.

The terms 'politics' and 'political' are also used in the estimates in the sense of representing something as *'just politics'*,[41] as if the expressed view or intention is not a genuine viewpoint. The political in society is assumed to be a rationalisation, a cover that is needed for creating legitimacy, while in reality it is merely one way of seeking power. Politics becomes an act: 'Reforms are nevertheless important in the short term because they boost confidence in positive development by making it clear that the nation's leadership understand the problems Russia is facing and has the ambition to deal with them.'[42] The quotation illustrates the view that although political reforms are initiated they may not even be intended to succeed. Yet the reforms are assumed to have a short-term effect, creating an impression among the population that the politicians really do understand that there are problems in society, while the motive of the politicians is to hold on to power.

Geography and power
Geography and geopolitics are closely related to the perception of power in the estimates, although again there is no explicit definition of what geographic power is regarded as. Throughout the estimates, the geographical position of states in relation to other states is expressed as affecting the possibility of power. This is, for example, visible in the description of the situation of Turkey. 'Turkey remains an important actor in the region due to its geographical position, military strength and its large population.'[43] The assumed effects of the geographical position of the states are referred as geopolitical facts in the estimates. This view may also be exemplified in a different setting.

> Military power has lost its geopolitical importance when compared with political and economic power. However, it [military power] is still an important geopolitical instrument for both influencing and ultimately ending a conflict through the threat or use of military force (including crisis management).[44]

The quotation above illustrates the prevailing view in the estimates that the geographic situation is of vital importance to different aspects of power. In this particular quotation, geography is assumed to be a factor affecting the possibility of military power. On the other hand, there is rather limited attention paid to the geographical issues within the states (issues of climate, topography and so on), even though these issues are traditionally of importance in a military operational perspective.

The physical location of the nation state is seen as important both in terms of possibilities of alignments between states, and for the risk of facing different threats.

Although Russia and the US share the anti-Islamist agenda, Moscow sees the increasing US involvement in Central Asia as a threat to its strategic interests in the region. This is especially true if the US military presence in Uzbekistan becomes prolonged and threatens the security structures that Russia has built up over a long period of time.[45]

The quotation above illustrates the reoccurring view on power related to geopolitical conditions and aspirations. This physical aspect of power also seems to be interpreted in a zero-sum manner. If one actor (State A) has established a presence in a particular geographic area, its geographic power will decrease if another actor (State B) also establishes a physical presence in that same area.

Economic power
Economic power and the power of economics are ascribed vital importance in the estimates. The importance of economic prosperity for states is seen as an increasingly important factor of power for states in international relations. To gain economic power, a state's economy must possess specific characteristics: 'The primary means for long-term stability are political democracy and economic development through a market economy.'[46] The view expressed in the estimates is that economic power may be reached only through a liberal market economy characterised by free trade. Furthermore, a strong economy (a state with economic power) is denoted in terms of high economic growth, sound trade balance and the relation between unemployment and the inflation rate. Other possible characteristics of an economy, such as economic distribution within the state, are not considered as factors influencing the possibility of economic power.

The estimates tie a number of other effects to the role of an economy as described above. Economic power is described both as an enabler for elements of power and as being necessary for other desirable societal characteristics. Economic power is assumed to create possibilities for expanding other elements of power. In the estimates, a strong and vital economy is regarded as an enabler for an increase in military expenditure and for the possibility of a state to engage in international power projections (war). In the same manner, a weak economy is considered to be a disabler of projecting power internationally.[47]

The estimates state that *'the primary means for stability is political democracy and economic development through market economy*.[48] Further it is stated that a market economy fosters democracy. The estimates thus assign a strong liberal market economy to democratic growth and thereby also to stability. This is expressed in several contexts: 'The most important crisis prevention measures lie in a long-term effort to spread and strengthen development towards democracy and economic development through market economy and free trade.'[49] The quotation makes it clear that the economy is not only seen as an important feature of the concept of power in international relations, it is also assumed to bear a strong relation to the democratic features of a society.

Throughout the estimates, economic power is seen as a strong denominator of power in international relations, but it is also regarded as having a downside. The economic downside of the idea of a liberal market economy (desirable according to the estimates) is undoubtedly founded in the idea of free trade, which is also recognised as having effects on both economic dependence and independence. It is stated in the estimates that economic dependence might be a source of instability, and is a reason for conflict. Conflicts about natural resources (oil) and economic interests are held as examples of that.[50] This view illustrates the duality of general international collaboration prevailing in the estimates. International state collaboration is assumed to be accompanied by a weakened state, due to decreased sovereignty. On the other hand, the state will benefit from collaboration in various ways depending on the character of the cooperation.

Military power
In the estimates, military power is considered as the ability of a state to project power with force outside its own borders to achieve specific interests. However, military power is also a defensive power; it is the power that is considered to be the ultimate protector of the state. Military power is therefore also assessed in the light of threats posed towards the state. In the estimates, the threats directed at the state are not just traditional military threats; a variety of threats are considered.

Military power is articulated as if it is only states that have the ability to project it. At first sight, one might believe that the estimates equate military capability with military power, though that is not the case. Military capability is arranged in combination with military intentions so as to constitute the concept of military power. The concept of military power is rarely discussed explicitly, though these two categories of military capabilities and intentions taken together express the view on what may be understood as military power.

Military capability is discussed in terms of numeraire and level of military education, the technological development of the armed forces, character and effectiveness in military exercises, and the effectiveness of the organisation of the armed forces. These factors are then assembled in an overall assessment: 'Military power, i.e. an overall assessment and comparison of qualitative and quantitative factors, strengths and vulnerabilities of military organisations, is a fundamental factor in determining its strategic usefulness.'[51] However, military power is not represented as just military capability. Military power is represented as a combination of military capability and the possible intention to use that capability.

Military intentions are not so much the intentions of the military, as the intention of the state to use the military. Military intentions are also articulated as decisions based on a rational consideration of calculating pros and cons before using military force. Military intentions are therefore articulated in terms of how willing a particular state is to use military force to achieve its stated interests.

> A threat of armed intervention during the period could only be posed by Russia. Such a threat is very unlikely. This is mainly due to deterrent factors such as lack of interests/goals and Russia's economic dependence to the West. It partly depends on Russian military weakness.[52]

The quotation above illustrates that the decision of whether to use military action is considered a calculated decision. The state's political trade-offs affect its military intentions.

Military threats are a central theme throughout the estimates. The characteristics of military threat are categorised in different contexts. The primary context is the possibility of a military threat to mainland Sweden; that is, territorial defence to maintain sovereignty. A military threat may only materialise from a hostile nation state, and the only such possible nation state is assessed to be Russia.[53] Throughout the estimates, the probability of such a military threat is considered to be a balancing act between Russia's military capability and the political intention of the nation state of Russia.

Other military threats articulated as being of interest to Sweden are the threats that come into play in relation to international missions where Sweden is a partner. In the articulation of these military threats there are a variety of types of aggressors. The aggressor need not be a state in these instances. For example, in the case of Afghanistan, the aggressor is identified as the Taliban movement.

Other threats besides military threats are also articulated in the estimates, and are described as threats to either society or the state. The threats and threatening events that face modern society include environmental threats, military rearmament, development and proliferation of WMD, certain ethnic and/or religious groups, 'new threats', domestic public opinion (the CNN effect), military exercises, IT-related threats, intelligence threats, terrorism threats, threats of sabotage, threats of subversion, threats of criminality, refugees and mass migration of refugees, and so on.[54] However, the vast majority of these threats are not articulated as threats to statehood, which might imply that the response to them will not primarily be by the use of military force. On other hand, it is not explained how these threats relate to military threats, military capabilities, military intention or military power.

Quality of diplomacy and morale
In the estimates there are assumptions about the specific characteristics of different states and their respective populations, and their ability to project power. To be considered as possessing this kind of power, it is assumed that the states need to be characterised by stability and rationality, and must be subject to 'Western logic'. This more intangible element of power is most often implicitly expressed by being portrayed through different concepts or allocated to categorisations implying an assumption of the state's societal features.

Stability[55] is seen as a desirable and necessary trait for a state to be an effective power projector in international relations. Throughout the estimates, the ability for a state to act rationally is denoted as a necessary element of power. This becomes apparent as some states are described and regarded as 'irrational'. When a states is assessed to be irrational or acting irrationally, it is considered ineffective and with little power. The relation between rationality and power is also related to what is interpreted here as whether the state has accepted or is a part of *Western ideas*. It is assumed that being a part of *the West* and *Western ideas* is a sign of being rational. In turn, being rational is one denominator of power.

Balance of Power and State Security

The assumed logic of power as a zero-sum game also has implications for the relation between states concerning the issue of state security. In the estimates there is a prevailing view that the foremost momentum for actors on the international political scene is the effort to increase power. This prevailing idea is visible through the expressed view on the US and Russian relationship. Here is an illustration of the assumption based on the idea of balance of power: 'Russia still wants to see a toning down of America's dominance on the world stage, even if Russian foreign policy under Putin is less stuck in geopolitics and more broad-minded than at the end of the Yeltsin era.'[56] It is not clear whether the estimates consider the balance of power to be a natural process or a construct of political and state leaders. In the estimates, the concept of balance of power is used as logic. The concept is used both for explaining other events as a matter of fact of what has happened, and as a rationalisation of the political leaders' motive for the actions. This is clear in the discussion over a restructuring of the US security sector.

> It is more likely that Rumsfeld's defence review will result in a number of gradual shifts where a few 'projects', such as a heavily reinforced Homeland Defence, the build-up of MD [Missile Defence] and reductions in the strategic nuclear arsenal, will be prioritised – rather than a more rapid and fundamental restructuring of the Armed Forces.[57]

The quotation above illustrates the assumption of logic for balance of power. Hence, if one actor gains power then this automatically means that the other actor decreases in relative power.

SUMMARY

In structuring and approaching the world, interpretation in the estimates is articulated through the ideas and concepts of realism. The idea of statism is clearly a founding assumption. States are the actors that possess power, compete for power and formulate politics; they are the bearers of national interests. These assumptions clearly affect the intelligence service's ability to conceptualise the possibility of other types of societal actors.

The prevailing wisdom in the estimates is that power per se is the vital inner drive for states, and international relations are defined by the competition of promoting national interests in the search for power. Although the references are plentiful, there are few indications of what really constitutes power in the eyes of the intelligence analysis. What is clear is that power is the one societal dimension which draws the attention of the intelligence service. This, again, is a product of familiar realist assumptions. The acceptance of these realist assumptions implies that state action in the international arena tends to be articulated and framed through concepts such as power seeking, balance of power and national interests, while little attention is paid to ideas, ideology or even such a thing as a political programme (for political actors).

The prevailing realist ontological viewpoint of the estimates also leads to gaps in the analysis. The gaps in the estimates hold topics that are for example transnational in character. One such gap is the modest articulation of the phenomena of globalisation. In the mindset of the estimates, globalisation is articulated more as an increase of interaction between states than as a global change of character of interaction, where states tend to mean less as a defining character of identity.

Another gap is the non-articulation of non-state actors. Considering that the estimates do acknowledge that states may be faced with threats of forms other than military, threats very likely posed by actors other than states, it is noteworthy that the articulation of non-state actors is nearly absent. The lack of attention paid to societal actors other than the state is indeed a familiar trait of realist assumptions.

Notes

1. See, for example, Rathmell, 'Towards a postmodern intelligence', Ben-Israel, 'Philosophy and methodology of intelligence' or Kent, *Strategic intelligence for American world policy*.
2. George, *Bridging the gap theory & practice in foreign policy*, pp. 108–14.
3. Morgenthau, *Politics among nations*, p. 13.
4. Waltz, *Man the state and war*, p. 12.
5. Morgenthau, *Politics among nations*, p. 4.
6. Hence, there is little notice taken of other factors that might influence or explain the actions and decisions of the state, and little attention is paid to issues like ethics, moral, ideas and ideology. For a discussion of the inter-

actions between states see for example Bull, *The anarchical society a study of order in world politics*, pp. 62–4.
7 Morgenthau, *Politics among nations*, p. 13ff.
8 Morgenthau, *Politics among nations*, pp. 80–108. Morgenthau's elements of power bear a strong resemblance to Sherman Kent's definition of the intelligence-related term 'substantive content'. The categories of Kent's substantive content are *'Personalities, Geography, Military, Economic, Political, Social, Moral, and Scientific and Technology'*. The categorisation of aspects of power needed in strategic intelligence estimates are similar to Morgenthau's elements of national power. Kent's and Morgenthau's view on the relationship between these attributes and the capacities of national power are strikingly similar, although denoted differently. Kent, *Strategic intelligence for American world policy*, p. 40
9 Morgenthau, *Politics among nations*, p. 87.
10 Morgenthau, *Politics among nations*, p. 88.
11 Morgenthau, *Politics among nations*, p. 96.
12 Morgenthau exemplifies this by the likelihood of the Chinese to strive for stability and the unpredictability of the Russian national character. Morgenthau, *Politics among nations*, p. 96–8.
13 Morgenthau, *Politics among nations*, p. 100.
14 Morgenthau, *Politics among nations*, p. 105.
15 These elements of power were revised by Waltz and thereby came to include 'size of population and territory, resource endowment, economic capability, military strength, political stability and competence'. Waltz, *Man the state and war*, p. 131.
16 Dunne and Schmidt, 'Realism', p. 99.
17 Dunne and Schmidt, 'Realism', p. 99.
18 The different traits of the realist concept of balance of power is both described and critiqued by Bull, *The anarchical society a study of order in world politics*, pp. 97–107.
19 Dunne and Schmidt, 'Realism', p. 102.
20 Waltz, *Man the state and war*, p. 40.
21 George, *Bridging the gap theory & practice in foreign policy*, pp. 109–13.
22 See, for example, Hilsman, *Strategic intelligence and national decision*; Hatlebrekke and Smith, 'Towards a new theory of intelligence failure'; Rathmell, 'Towards a postmodern intelligence'; or Ben-Israel, 'Philosophy and methodology of intelligence'.
23 See for instance Intelligence Estimate 1999, p. 2, or Intelligence Estimate (A) 2000, pp. 2–3, or Intelligence Estimate (A) 2001, p. 3, or Intelligence Estimate 2010.
24 Interview 10.
25 The state is the founding term in the conceptualisation of the world and

international relations used in the intelligence estimates. The references here are not all-encompassing to the passages in the texts, as these would be too plentiful, but suggested references for illustration are: Intelligence Estimate (B), pp. 16, 19, 21 and 36 and Intelligence Estimate (B) 2000, pp. 20, 35, 51.
26 The relation between concepts such as state and nation is only briefly discussed in reference to the situation in the Balkans. In this discussion in the intelligence estimates, this relation is assumed to be a possible problem for the state of Bosnia-Herzegovina, because of the mix of nationalities (also used interchangeably with ethnicity) which is a mismatch to the borders of the state. This is represented as a vital problem to the state and to security, because of the shortness of the time elapsed since the Balkan wars (Intelligence Estimate (B) 2001, p. 111; Intelligence Estimate (B) 2000, pp. 81–82; Intelligence Estimate 1999, p. 74).
27 Intelligence Estimate (A) 2001, p. 19.
28 Intelligence Estimate (B) 2001, p. 86.
29 Intelligence Estimate 1999, p. 54.
30 Although the state is always assessed to be a univocal societal actor in the intelligence estimates in regard to international issues, the domestic political situation is not necessarily assessed in the same manner. In domestic political situations, the state might contain different political viewpoints and competing political groupings. However, as the issues move up to the state level (in the international realm), the political differences are assumed to remain.
31 Intelligence Estimate (B) 2001, p. 18.
32 Intelligence Estimate (B) 2001, p. 39. However, states other than the US (for instance Russia) that are trying to increase their power (like all of the states described are) automatically tend to be portrayed as a bit dubious when opting for multipolarity (the UN) in international decision making.
33 Intelligence Estimate (B) 2001, p. 69.
34 Intelligence Estimate (B) 2001, p. 69.
35 Intelligence Estimate (B) 2001, p. 70.
36 Intelligence Estimate 2001 and later.
37 Intelligence Estimate 2001 and later.
38 Intelligence Estimate (B) 2001, p. 42.
39 Intelligence Estimate (B) 2001, p. 76.
40 Intelligence Estimate (B) 2001, p. 117.
41 Political statements are referred to as *'just politics'* or with the same connotation as *'just rhetoric'*.
42 Intelligence Estimate (A) 2001, p. 36.
43 Intelligence Estimate (B) 2001, p. 124.
44 Intelligence Estimate (A) 2000, p. 26.

45 Intelligence Estimate (B) 2001, p. 60.
46 Intelligence Estimate 1999, p. 13.
47 This is one of the issues regarding Russian economic development, both in terms of crises and in terms of possible economic strength. The economic crises of the mid and late 1990s in Russia raised the concern that the fragile political system might not survive such an extensive economic crisis. At the same time, the succeeding and quite rapid economic growth in the early 2000s created a concern that military expenditure might increase and the possibility of a stronger Russian military might cause security problems in the surrounding countries. This reasoning raises the question of whether there is any way in which Russia's economy could progress for intelligence analysis to assess its effects as being positive for the security situation.
48 Intelligence Estimate 1999, p. 13.
49 Intelligence Estimate (B) 2001, p. 19.
50 In the intelligence estimate the reasons for the wars in Iraq and major parts of the conflicts in Africa are primarily assessed as conflicts about natural resources (Intelligence Estimate 1999, p. 9).
51 Intelligence Estimate (A) 2001, p. 27.
52 Intelligence Estimate 1999, p. 26.
53 This might be said to hold until the 2001 intelligence estimate; after that, the information is classified.
54 Intelligence Estimate 2002, p. 1 and see for example ideas expressed on environmental threats in Intelligence Estimate (B) 2001, p. 14 and Intelligence Estimate (A) 2000, pp. 7–13.
55 It is not clear, however, whether the stability under discussion is internal stability (party politics) or 'rules of the game' stability.
56 Intelligence Estimate (B) 2001, p. 44.
57 Intelligence Estimate (B) 2001, p. 81.

Chapter 9

THE REPRESENTATION OF NATO

This chapter examines MUST's general representation of NATO, covering its view of NATO's role, power and the main actors within international relations. It shows that the description of NATO consistently suggests a representation imbued with positive connotations. Bearing in mind the self-articulated intention of intelligence to present facts with the goal of being value neutral, a representation imbued with positive connotations through language practice and values imply construction of a friend.

CONSTRUCTING NATO

In the eyes of the MUST, NATO is the most influential political actor in terms of war, military action and security issues within international relations.[1] It is suggested in the estimates that NATO has the power and influence to decide which issues are articulated as security issues in the realm of international relations. Furthermore, it is suggested in the estimates that NATO determines how these security issues should be understood and approached for the international community at large. Finally, it is suggested in the estimates that these functions of NATO are desirable and suggest a representation of NATO as an indisputable friend.

THE REPRESENTATION OF NATO

The overall representation of NATO in the estimates is as a provider of stability and security. This representation of NATO involves a concept that this role is needed, wanted and appreciated by the rest of the international community.

In addition, NATO is framed as the most important international political actor for establishing and maintaining security: 'NATO is the most important organisation in terms of security policy cooperation in Europe.'[2] This characteristic of NATO is not just seen in a European context; NATO's dominant role within international security is viewed as valid globally.[3] The assigned role for NATO as formulating norms ranges from overall general security policy to standards for praxis in military cooperation.[4]

The dominant role of NATO is also expressed in statements like *'NATO is the norm for interoperability'*.[5] This outlook is also expressed in regard to the European context: 'ESDP (and to a greater extent NATO) has a particular normative role for the development of [military] capabilities but also to maintain defence spending and defence investments at an acceptable level.'[6]

The estimates indicate that NATO has the role of articulating the correct response to security problems and establishes a norm for which issues are articulated as security problems. NATO is represented as an experienced actor that understands which issues should potentially be understood in a security context and, therefore, should be addressed through security.

> NATO will remain the decisive organisation for military crisis management in Europe for the foreseeable future. Further adaptation to NATO doctrine and to NATO standards is necessary to achieve the required interoperability for international operations, or when a crisis is at risk of escalating.[7]

Here the role of NATO is validated both for making a decision in advance[8] as to how a crisis should be managed and deciding what strategy should be adopted, and to set the standard for interoperability. The representation of its importance and undisputed role is stated in yet another context:

> The Alliance's EU members choose to rely on the North Atlantic Council (NAC) as the primary forum for security policy. (. . .) NATO has a well-developed and well trained crisis management mechanism, exclusive resources and unique expertise. (. . .) The Alliance's [NATO] multinational military planning is the only one of its kind.[9]

The reference to NATO's expertise in planning and operations management in this quotation illustrates that NATO is represented as exhibiting expertise in how to deal with security issues. The quotation also reveals the intelligence view of NATO's abilities and the desirability of NATO articulating what should be understood and treated as a security issue and, thereby, formulating the security agenda, internationally. This is visible in a passage in an estimate that discusses the Balkan issue: 'The extensive involvement in Bosnia-Herzegovina, Kosovo, and Albania, outlined above, could force the creation of a coherent Balkan strategy for the international community, and perhaps primarily NATO.'[10] The quotation illustrates that NATO is considered to have both the mandate and the ability to formulate security strategies for the international community, this time in the context of the Balkans.

NATO IN AN INTERNATIONAL CONTEXT

The construction of NATO in the text of the estimates is a representation and framing of an important political actor in the process of formulating an international agenda for security policy. Considering that Sweden is a partner of NATO (through the Partnership for Peace), the positive framing might not be all that surprising. In terms of the intelligence starting points of objectivity, neutrality and the goal of bringing a greater depth to the analysis, the position on NATO is somewhat disconcerting, analytically. As discussed, the general representation of NATO lacks factual, underpinned arguments. In the investigation of the MUST's view on NATO, the boundaries of NATO's relations and membership are somewhat blurred making the assumptions, analysis and conclusions difficult to distinguish. This could risk analytical conclusions being shaped in the form of factually unfounded representations.

In the estimates, the overall representation gives the impression that NATO is the centre of articulating ideas, strategy and policy for security. For example, NATO is represented in a wide variety of contexts: in relation to its member states, in relation to the United Nations (UN), EU and Russia, standards for interoperability, the expansion process and so forth.

The relationship between NATO and the UN and EU is portrayed as NATO exercising influence over the security agenda and policy in both the UN and the EU.

European security identity will be developed within the NATO framework. Thus, the US can give its support to a greater European role in NATO during the five-year period. However, the dominant role of the US within NATO is expected to continue.[11]

This is apparent in later estimates; in one case a section states that:

NATO remains the dominant organisation for crisis prevention by military means in Europe. NATO is the USA's primary forum for influencing security policy in Europe and the major European powers are the only actors other than the US that have any substantial intervention capability. All NATO members support this role for NATO and want the US to maintain its commitment to Europe. So far, US involvement has been a precondition for any commitment by NATO.[12]

The statement underlines the influence that NATO exercises on the security policy of the EU. The estimates also indicate that NATO is formulating its security policy independent of support from the UN.

NATO is now carrying out military strikes against an independent nation without the support of a UN mandate. This is an expression of America's dominant position within the organisation. (...) This development will strengthen NATO's role and capabilities and, depending on the outcome in Kosovo, could have a deterrent effect in the future.[13]

This statement reveals a view that NATO is an independent actor in international relations and its political power supersedes the UN. The statement also indicates that this role will tend to increase and further strengthen the role of NATO. However, the statements, actions and impact of NATO are not argued or factually demonstrated, nor are the possible consequences of NATO's activities described further elaborated.

The discussion of the relationship between NATO and the member states assessment suggests a difference in types of member states, which gives them varying degree of importance within the NATO structure. The estimates suggest a distinction of importance within NATO between new member states, ordinary member states and the US. However, the analytical distinction and relationship between NATO and the categories of states are neither distinct nor clear. Argued in the estimates is that the first two categories of states are members of NATO, although the assessment suggests that new member states are not equally influential.

> In cases where they do not have security interests, small European nations choose to support and participate because this indirectly promotes their security under the umbrella – 'Security in Europe is inseparable.' The essence of motivating this action is: it helps to preserve U.S. interest in Europe, it strengthens nation's influence in organisations (NATO), this, in itself strengthens organisations' effectiveness (NATO), and crisis management reduces the risk of increasing conflict, all of which collectively strengthen the potential for crisis management and thus stability.[14]

This quotation also illustrates the view of member states within NATO, shows that the states have their own political agendas and have to balance the interest of the state against the interest of the alliance. The quotation also illustrates that states within in NATO are viewed as both trying to promote their own agenda and having to execute the tasks and missions assigned to them by NATO.

Within the context of member states, the relationship between NATO and the US is described in more detail, although it is somewhat analytically blurred. The estimate makes no clear distinction between US and NATO political positions and actions. It is clear that the US is considered the most influential member state within NATO: *'The dominating role by U.S. within NATO is also expected to continue.'*[15] This view is emphasised in later estimates, where it states that the *'US maintains its interest in Europe and its dominant position in NATO'*.[16] The last quotation further suggests that the US articulates the political agenda for NATO and also has a major influence on the European security agenda.

> NATO remains the dominant organisation for crisis prevention by military means in Europe. NATO is the USA's primary forum for influencing security policy in Europe and the major European powers are the only actors, other than the US, that have a substantial intervention capacity. All European NATO members support

this role for NATO and want the US to maintain its commitment to Europe.[17]

Throughout the estimates, a dominant role for NATO in European security policy is assumed. The above quotation also reveals the assumption that the European NATO countries look favourably on the US setting the agenda for the EU.

At the same time, the representation of NATO seems to display an analytical indistinctness that results in an unclear view on political relations between the US and the EU, and in the context of NATO. The facts or factual arguments in support of this representation are vague, if not limited. The relations are stated without corroborating arguments.

NATO is also represented in the estimates as providing security for NATO partners and allies, although this is not the same kind of security as it provides for the member states. The difference is not clearly visible in the text, although some indications may be found. The limited security of partners and allies does not include the security of a definite NATO response if the partner is militarily attacked by another state.[18] The status as a partner or ally makes the state part of a collective, which is represented in the estimates as defined against the outside rather than common or actual security measures.

> That many European NATO countries lack enthusiasm for the continuous expansion of NATO is partly based on a fear of NATO becoming cumbersome and inefficient, and a general unwillingness to incur excessive costs, and not least a reluctance to worsen relations with Russia, thus risking jeopardizing Russia's nascent integration with the West.[19]

This quotation illustrates that the mere presence of NATO or of a NATO member shifts the security situation and increases overall security. The reason, an assumed multiplier for security over a region, is not explicit in the text. However, the strong belief in the geopolitical and geostrategic character of power, which is prevalent in the estimates, accounts for a coherent view on security. In the same way, the security situation might be shifted in negative terms due to NATO presence or NATO membership.

SUMMARY

The prevailing overall representation of NATO in the estimates is of a competent and desirable creator of the international security political agenda. This representation is twofold. It rests on an assumption of fact that NATO has the practical ability and the mandate to fulfil the role of crises manager and articulator of policy. It also rests on a normative assumption of the desirability of fulfilling that role.

Although this representation is based on an assumption that NATO possesses a number of abilities and characteristics, the arguments supporting this way of understanding NATO are unclear or simply not argued. Instead of providing arguments in support of this assumption, the assessment leaves statements to this effect unverified and lacking factual basis. In the representation, a view of NATO as a suitable articulator of an overall international security policy is formulated through an implicit and oft-presented contextualisation of NATO positions and actions.

Notes

1. NATO is the political actor most often referred to in the estimates. It is repeatedly stated in the estimates that NATO articulates both the security strategy as well as various security policies for the 'West' regarding issues of crisis management, conflict resolution and military interventions (Intelligence Estimate 1998, pp. 4, 13; Intelligence Estimate 1999, p. 13; Intelligence Estimate (A) 2000, p. 4; Intelligence Estimate (B) 2001, p. 21).
2. Intelligence Estimate (B) 2001, p. 64.
3. Intelligence Estimate 1999, p. 13, and Intelligence Estimate (A) 2000, pp. 21, 60.
4. Intelligence Estimate (B) 2000, p. 15 and Intelligence Estimate (A) 2001, p. 40.
5. Intelligence Estimate 1999, p. 51.
6. Intelligence Estimate (A) 2001, p. 10.
7. Intelligence Estimate (B) 2001, p. 5.
8. Intelligence Estimate 1999, p. 18 and Intelligence Estimate (A) 2001, p. 21.
9. Intelligence Estimate (B) 2001, p. 66.
10. Intelligence Estimate 1999, p. 75.
11. Intelligence Estimate 1998, p. 4.
12. Intelligence Estimate (A) 2001, p. 21.
13. Intelligence Estimate 1999, p. 52.

14 Intelligence Estimate (A) 2001, p. 20.
15 Intelligence Estimate 1998, p. 4.
16 Intelligence Estimate (A) 2000, p. 17.
17 Intelligence Estimate (A) 2001, p. 21.
18 Intelligence Estimate (A) 2001, p. 28.
19 Intelligence Estimate (B) 2001, p. 73.

Chapter 10

THE REPRESENTATION OF RUSSIA

CONSTRUCTING RUSSIA

This chapter investigates the MUST's representation of Russia in the estimates. During the period being investigated, this representation of Russia entailed elements of both change and continuity, although the overall construction of Russia is that of a hereditary enemy of the West and, thereby, also of Sweden. Consequently, the text regarding Russia is imbued with negative connotations. The language practice is imbued with negative qualifiers and valuations and presuppositions of Russia's motive for action.

THE REPRESENTATION OF RUSSIA

In the representation of Russia specific attributes and characteristics are ascribed to Russian politics and society. Russian politics are viewed as being largely unpredictable and the notion of unpredictability is evident throughout the representation in the estimates and considered valid for Russia, both for domestic and international politics.

A statement that refers to Russia as a political actor within the international political scene suggests that Russian foreign policy lacks a founding idea or consistent political agenda, saying it is, instead, characterised by *'reactive ad-hoc-like actions'*. 'In essence, the pattern of Russian foreign policy was characterised by ad-hoc reactive actions. This pattern is expected to continue.'[1]

Political unpredictability is a general attribute also ascribed to the Russian domestic political arena.

As a result of its new composition, the new Duma is expected to be more willing to cooperate than its predecessors, which increases the President's ability to implement reforms. (. . .) President Putin emphasises the importance of a clear and long-term strategy for Russia. This could mean a more predictable and less capricious policy.[2]

This quotation illustrates how Russian political life is repeatedly represented in the estimates as being unpredictable. This characterisation is mainly argued by referring to the numerous reshufflings of political appointees. The assessed unpredictability in Russian politics is not referred to or argued through unpredictability in the reforms and policies adopted and implemented, instead a close relation between politicians and political outcomes seem to be the assumption underlying the conclusion of unpredictability.

The representation of unpredictability is magnified by the reliance on arguments based on the influence of individuals in Russian politics. The Russian political scene is represented as being defined largely by the personal characteristics of individuals and only in a limited way by political agendas, party politics or ideas/ideology.[3] This is apparent in the limited discussions of the political parties, political ideas and political movements in Russia.[4] Instead the estimates describe political events, actions and incitements in terms of the influence of individuals and the dominant political incentive being the possibility of personal gain through political action.

The representation of Russian politics as being defined by political individuals is also apparent throughout the estimates in discussions of possible political change. The assessments do not report on the possibility of changing policy or political viewpoints, but rather on changes in the political representative in charge of the policies discussed. This, for instance, is detectable in a description of the era of President Yeltsin. 'As long as Yeltsin remains [in power] and no further changes of Prime Minister take place, Russia will most likely keep a low profile.'[5] This quotation illustrates the viewpoint that it is the individual holding the post of prime minister that defines the further course of Russian foreign policy. It is not only that the political viewpoints and course of action that is assumed to be reliant on the individual politician, the political incentive for the individuals holding political positions are assumed to have personal gain as an incentive for their political viewpoints. This view on the incentives for political action is present throughout the estimates and is again visible within domestic politics.

One statement linked a change in appointee to the possibility of political change: 'It is possible that the new Secretary of the Security Council will provide an opportunity to vindicate those power structures that do not belong to the Armed Forces.'[6]

The assumed impact of the individuals holding political positions may be seen more clearly in discussions regarding economics and economic reform. The possibility of economic reform is assessed as being more or less likely in terms of who the politician is rather than in terms of the political position of the politician or on the economic situation or intended reform policy. For instance, this is apparent in the discussion of the economic reform initiated shortly after the financial crises of 1998/1999. The incentives for the politicians within President Putin's cabinet are discussed in terms of possible individual gains and personal ties to the powerful financial elite (oligarchs) in Russian society instead of the ideas and possible results of the economic reforms.

> Intrigues within this circle, where there are also strong financial interests, led to a more unpredictable policy, which included two changes of Prime Minister within the year. Interests of special groups [of self-interest] and the Communist dominated Duma hampered the implementation of reforms, and the reform process slowed down.[7]

The references to 'intrigues' and 'special groups' illustrate traces of the representation of Russian politics as defined by personal viewpoints and motivation rather than by political viewpoints and ideological positions. This is again noticeable in a description of political incentives for President Putin. 'It would also be a loss of prestige for President Putin to return to a relationship of dependency on the IMF [International Monetary Fund], especially in terms of "major political issues".'[8] This quotation shows that it is not the economic downside of a specific economic development that is the basis of President Putin making a decision. Rather, it is the loss of prestige that is decisive.

Another characteristic ascribed to Russian politics is that of politics of rhetoric. Throughout the estimates, the understanding of rhetoric is used to explain Russian political viewpoints and positions that contradict what might seem rational in a *Western political perspective*. The use of the term *rhetoric* could be interpreted as the estimate's descriptions of Russian articulation of foreign policy.

> Russia's strategic interests in the region are considered to be defensive and aim to prevent or slow down NATO's influence. Historically they have always wanted a zone between the Russian heartland and any potential opponents. It is primarily against this background that one should view the repeated rhetoric, and sometimes even various kinds of pressure, from the Russian side on the Baltic States. In Russia, there is a widespread and fundamental reluctance to accept the Baltic States' independence.[9]

In the quotation above, the position of Russian foreign policy in relation to the NATO expansion process is described in terms of *repeated rhetorical proclamations*. In this case, the rhetoric is accepted as the actual political view of Russia, although there is no argument or proof to further substantiate the claim. This claim about rhetoric in is again apparent in the context of the foreign relations with the US. The following statement implies that the rhetoric is coherent with the real political intentions: 'In the aftermath of the Kosovo War Russian foreign policy was characterised by confrontational rhetoric of a "Cold War" nature, which led to overall relations reaching a new low point after 1991.[10]

The term rhetoric is also used as a sort of explanation for an unlikely political position with the connotation that another political position is actually held, although not articulated: 'The loss of a role as a superpower and domestic political considerations led to strong Russian rhetoric opposing U.S. and NATO actions in Iraq and Kosovo.'[11] The quotation uses *rhetoric* to imply that Russia is not actually opposed to the actions of US and NATO in Iraq and Kosovo. Instead the conclusion drawn is that Russia is forced to articulate such a position to please the domestic political scene and because of some sort of identity crisis. Similar aspects of this representation of Russia are apparent in another context.

> Russian reaction to possible NATO expansion into the Baltic is expected to be limited to occasional rhetoric attacking Baltic countries and questioning NATO's motives and logic. (...) Economic sanctions and military action are not expected because they would seem to be counterproductive and contrary to Russia's economic interests.[12]

In this passage, the rhetoric (articulated foreign policy objectives) is the 'real' political position, although this is limited by economic considerations. The expected Russian reactions to the NATO expansion process is still assessed in terms of there being a discrepancy between Russian articulated foreign policy and the political viewpoints held by the Russian political establishment. Yet another passage illustrates this use of rhetoric: 'It is assessed that increased realpolitik and economic considerations will lead to future [Russian] rhetoric does not go [sic] beyond words.'[13] Here the quotation demonstrates a view that the political position held is different from the articulation of the foreign political viewpoint expressed.

RUSSIA IN AN INTERNATIONAL CONTEXT

In the estimates, the state of Russia is constructed around the political situation (domestically and internationally), the economic and industrial situation, the geopolitical situation, and the military (capability and strategy).

The overall representation of Russia is of a former superpower searching for its role, internationally. The loss of superpower status is portrayed as an identity crisis that Russia only reluctantly accepts.[14] Russia is not represented as an important actor within international politics and its role in international politics is represented as declining and more or less reduced to that of obstructing decisions within international forums.

> Nostalgia for the loss of a superpower role and domestic political considerations led to strong Russian rhetoric opposing US and NATO actions in Iraq and Kosovo. Apart from a role in the UN Security Council, however, real opportunities for actions are limited, [and are,] as a rule, more damaging to Russia than the US and NATO.[15]

The diminishing role of Russia within international relations is shown through the viewpoint that Russia's primary means of power in international relations is vetoing or obstructing decisions in the UN Security Council. The decreasing role is also seen in claims that other actors in international politics ascribe to Russia a reduced role.

One estimate suggests that Russia's loss of status in the international arena has led it to actively work for an international world order based on multipolarity: 'However, an overall goal for Russia is still creating a global world order in which international problems are resolved through negotiations or peacekeeping operations within the UN framework.'[16]

Russia is presented as a power-seeking state, which seeks to promote the possibility of power projection and national economic gain. Russia is assumed to seek this power and possibility for power projection through geopolitical and geostrategic reasoning, where the physical attributes, such as borders and access to specific geographical areas, are of vital importance to the state: 'Russian strategic priorities are largely determined from a geo-strategic balance of power perspective.'[17] The quotation refers to a representation of Russia in which the political priorities are defined by seeking power within a geopolitical perspective. This contextualises the representation of Russia, emphasising that Russian political decision making is motivated by power seeking.

In the international setting, Russia is represented as an actor generally opposed to 'the West'[18] and what is referred to as 'Western interests'. Many references show how Russia is trying to limit and oppose the US and NATO, and they constitute the general representation of Russian foreign policy. The view that Russia is trying to limit and oppose the US and NATO is apparent, for example, in a discussion of the NATO expansion process for the Baltic States.

> Russia has long stated that it is opposed to any expansion of NATO in principle, and especially to any expansion including the Baltic States. However, Russia has realised that it cannot prevent expansion and, as a result, President Putin has recently shown increased pragmatism about a future expansion – even to the Baltic States. (. . .) In essence, however, the Russian view persists, meaning that Moscow would prefer not to see Baltic States as NATO members, as this might bring with it a direct US military presence in Russia's immediate vicinity.[19]

This line of argument is displayed in a comment on US/NATO involvement in Central Asia.

> Although Russia and the United States share the anti-Islamist agenda, Moscow sees growing US involvement in Central Asia as

> a threat to its strategic interests in the region. This is especially true if the U.S. military presence in Uzbekistan becomes prolonged and threatens the security structures which Russia has built up over a long period.[20]

In some cases, the representation of the relations between Russia and the US and NATO might be provisional. The estimate, on one occasion, was open to the possibility of Russian membership in NATO.[21] However, the depiction of the animosity of Russia towards the organisation is still evident.

> A possible outcome of potential Baltic NATO membership could be discussions about Russian NATO membership, or more institutionalised forms of cooperation between the parties. Russia's motives for any future NATO membership can be justified both by a genuine interest in participating actively in Western security structures, clearly shown by Russia's actions in connection with the terrorist attacks in the US on 11 September 2011, and probably because such a turn of events would radically change the Alliance's role and undermine its decision-making ability.[22]

This quotation illustrates a duality in the representation of Russia. It depicts Russia as being interested in taking part in Western security structures and at the same time assumes that this interest is based on Russia seeking to undermine NATO's ability to make decisions. This would indicate an official Russian foreign policy seeking further cooperation with *the West*, although with the ambition of decreasing the ability of NATO. Therefore the estimate is in fact again arguing for Russia as opposing instead of cooperating with Western security structures.

The general theme of Russia as an opposing power of *the West* has one exception – economic, trade and commercial interests. The representation of Russia in these issues is characterised by Russia seeking to become an integrated part of Western economic structures and organisations. 'Russia is expected to pursue a pragmatic foreign policy during the period. Above all, because economic dependence on the West place serious limitations on the conduct of foreign policy.'[23] The estimates acknowledge Russia's acceptance of the importance of trade and the economy over security and military issues and relations. Instead of portraying Russia as being opposed to Western economic interests, the assessments represent Russia taking an interactive approach and actively seeking cooperation with Western structures (such as the EU and the World Trade Organization (WTO)). This is displayed in the estimate through statements about Russia seeking cooperation with the EU and the Russian ambition of joining the WTO. Thus, there is a discrepancy in the assessments between the Russian position concerning the expansion of the EU regarding the joining of the Baltic States and the expansion process of NATO for the same reason. Where the economic cooperation of the EU is seen having only positive effects from a Russian point of view, the change in NATO membership is assessed as being essentially negative to Russia: 'With the economic situation prevailing in Russia today, the country is more dependent on good relations with "the West" than vice versa. This bodes for a calmer, more considered Russian reaction [to any Baltic NATO membership].'[24] In this passage in the text the wording suggests that Russia's normal reaction would be to exaggerate, and is only prevented by the economic dependence on the West.

SUMMARY

The overall representation of Russia in the estimates is that of a state deeply affected by the Communist heritage of the Soviet Union. The representation is that of a state unbound by ideological political ties, and its actions are solely explained and interpreted through a realistic power perspective. Russia is still largely defined as something that is the opposite of *the West*, as a rather unpredictable political actor (both domestically and internationally) and as bound by a national and traditional essence.

The Russian political scene is considered to be defined by a set of standards and rationalities that are not *Western politics*. These standards and mechanisms contain, among other things, the notion of being unpredictable, and being governed by individuals driven by personal gain through politics rather than by ideas, ideology or political conviction/agendas. Finally, the public politics are also viewed as a chimera, implying that the real politics are not officially articulated. This representation is influenced by presuppositions about Russian motives.

Notes

1. Intelligence Estimate 1999, p. 34.
2. Intelligence Estimate (A) 2000, p. 35.
3. For example the Russian Constitution is described as *'tailor made for the individual Yeltsin'* (Intelligence Estimate 1998, p. 4).
4. On one occasion in Intelligence Estimates 1998–2001 referral to political parties and ideological viewpoints are mentioned (Intelligence Estimate (B) 2001, p. 39).
5. Intelligence Estimate 1998, p. 6.
6. Intelligence Estimate 1998, p. 8.
7. Intelligence Estimate (A) 2000, p. 37.
8. Intelligence Estimate (B) 2001, p. 51.
9. Intelligence Estimate (A) 2000, pp. 60–1.
10. Intelligence Estimate (A) 2000, p. 39.
11. Intelligence Estimate (A) 2000, p. 21.
12. Intelligence Estimate (B) 2001, p. 36.
13. Intelligence Estimate (B) 2001, p. 90.
14. Intelligence Estimate (A) 2000, pp. 40, 46.
15. Intelligence Estimate 1999, p. 14.
16. Intelligence Estimate (B) 2001, p. 44.
17. Intelligence Estimate 1998, p. 1.
18. In this situation 'the West' not being actually defined, but rather referred to as the idea of the Western hemisphere (in contrast to the former Soviet Union and the former Warsaw Pact). Most commonly, the reference to 'the West' might be understood as the US, NATO and the EU.
19. Intelligence Estimate (B) 2001, p. 74.
20. Intelligence Estimate (B) 2001, p. 60.
21. Intelligence Estimate (B) 2001, p. 91.
22. Intelligence Estimate (B) 2001, p. 43.
23. Intelligence Estimate (A) 2000, p. 35.
24. Intelligence Estimate (B) 2001, p. 74.

Chapter 11

THE REPRESENTATION OF TERRORISM

This chapter examines how the MUST represents terrorism in the estimates. It starts by identifying and discussing how the concept of terrorism is represented over time. The analysis pays special attention to how critical events (such as 9/11) have or have not influenced the understanding and use of the term *terrorism*. Further, the investigation seeks to identify how the representation of terrorism is used throughout the estimates and whether components of the representation are present in other parts of the assessment under a different name. Lastly, the chapter aims to identify and discuss gaps in relation to the representation of terrorism.

THE EARLY YEARS

In the 1998 estimate, the concept of terrorism is only mentioned on one occasion, which is in the context of the conflicts in the Middle East and Northern Africa. In the assessment, there is a growing concern that these conflicts might eventually influence Sweden and Swedish security: *'through immigration and the spread of conflict related terrorism stemming from conflicts in the homeland'*.[1]

The amount of text on terrorism is too limited to indicate what kind of understanding the estimate connotes to the concept of terrorism.

Under the heading *'Crises and Conflicts'*, the 1999 estimate frames terrorism within the concept of *'New Threats'*.[2] The new threats are framed in a world where the Cold War has ended and, in the aftermath, a number of smaller conflicts have surfaced. The estimate represents the resurfacing of the phenomenon of terrorism as being a consequence of this new type of conflict. It is acknowledged in the estimate that non-state actors are a part of these emerging conflicts and also claims that they may be categorised as terrorist or criminal organisations. Later in the 1999 estimate, international political development is discussed in respect to how that might influence the threats that might appear in Sweden or in a Swedish context, and under what circumstances Sweden might be subjected to acts of terrorism. Among other things, the estimate states that Sweden will need both a capacity and a political will to proclaim a *hard line policy* regarding how Sweden should engage with terrorism and to avoid the threat from terrorism increasing:

> The terrorist threat may arise in relation to international activities and is assessed to be dependent on a number of different variables, including . . . perception of the ability, using various means, to deal with threats or actual terrorist acts. A 'soft' approach to these issues, e.g. a lack of will and the lack of capability to meet with might, could mean increased risk [of terrorism].[3]

The lack of further arguments and corroborating evidence regarding the character of or definition of the concept enhances the impression that the MUST's view on how terrorism should be dealt with by states is argued on a value statement without supporting facts.

In the 2000 estimate, terrorism is again discussed as a part of *'New Threats'*.[4] There is no further development or discussion of a definition; rather the only characteristics mentioned are those of a non-state actor and that terrorism most often surfaces in the context of low-intensity conflicts.[5] The estimate also represents terrorism as having an ideological and political meaning and background, but at the same time it narrows the ideological and political viewpoints that could be foundations for terrorist acts:

> Terrorism – there has been a clear decrease in terrorist acts since the end of the Cold War. The peace in Northern Ireland underlines this trend. The decrease can be explained primarily through the disappearance of a number of [terrorist] base areas within the former Soviet bloc and a reduction in ideological support for leftist terrorist organisations. It is not possible to predict any increase in terrorism.[6]

Hence, only leftist ideological viewpoints are considered as possible grounds for terrorism.

AFTER THE RE-EMERGENCE OF TERRORISM

In the 2001 estimate, analytical focus on terrorism seems to have increased. During the time the assessment was written, the terrorist acts of 9/11 occurred in the US which might have affected the way in which and how terrorism was assessed and presented. Although the text offers a bit more than earlier assessments in terms of defining the concept in general and in specific contexts, the issue of terrorism as a phenomenon is still contextualised as a part of the bigger concept of *'New Threats'* and the overall wording is much the same as that in previous estimates (1999 and 2000).

The estimates also contain analysis of the reactions from the US due to the 9/11 incident. One statement acknowledged that the 9/11 events would influence the policies for both the US and the EU and ascribes to terrorism an increasing importance in world politics: 'With the US as the primary driving force it is clear that the War against Terrorism will be high on the agenda, both for the US and EU, for a long time to come.'[7] This is further underlined in another statement in the estimate: 'events such as 9/11 pose a transnational threat to society with potentially enormous consequences, which requires the integrated and effective use of all society's resources'.[8]

As in the earlier assessments, in 2001 the estimate also argues that terrorist acts will likely be carried out in Sweden or affect Swedish interests abroad. Further, it is argued that the risk of this is affected by the will and capacity of Sweden to enforce a *hard line policy* in terrorist issues.[9] The assessment of the possible terrorist threat concludes by stating that: '. . . there is no basis for claiming that the terrorist threat will tend to increase over time. However the current image of threat could change rapidly.'[10] Here again the estimate acknowledges that the threat of terrorism is present, while providing no further substantiation of the meaning of the concept of terrorism. Despite the recognition that terrorism has come to have an increased significance in international world politics, the estimate does not include any further elaboration on what is considered as defining characteristics of the term. It is not defined nor are there any further comments made on what terrorism has come to mean to the organisation and how it might be distinguished from other violent acts.

The chapter dedicated to *'New Threats'* in the 2001 estimate indicates, though vaguely, that the substance of the concept had not changed. The text contextualises terrorism as being a decreasing phenomenon because of the fall of the Soviet bloc and the loss of leftist ideological support for terrorism. The estimate also considers that terrorist acts will primarily be directed towards superpowers like the US. It also indicates that private companies might become potential targets.[11] It also indicates that terrorism might be understood as having roots within unresolved conflicts, suggesting that the reasons for terrorist acts may have a political dimension: 'The breeding ground for international and national terrorism includes long-term unresolved conflicts and the access terrorist groups have to bases.'[12] This statement is not further elaborated.

The estimate contains a historical perspective on the concept of terrorism with a comparison between the historical significance of the attack on Pearl Harbour and the expected importance of 9/11.[13]

> The terrorist acts [of 9/11] will not have the same strategic consequences as the fall of the Soviet Union. They brought about a transition from a bipolar to a unipolar world order. In the US the 9/11 incidents have been compared to the attack on Pearl Harbour during the Second World War. As a psychological phenomenon that might be a reasonable comparison. In terms of strategic consequences the Vietnam War or the Gulf War might be more reasonable parallels.[14]

As the estimate discusses the consequences of 9/11, with a few exceptions, it indicates that the previously expressed notion of terrorism – that there is a decreasing trend (since the end of the Cold War) – and that terrorism, to a lesser extent, is a problem for the 'West':

> The frequency of terrorist attacks has declined during the 1990s. The attacks have also increasingly taken place in the third world. However, several spectacular acts of terrorism with many casualties, most recently 9/11, break this trend. Al-Qaida, a resource-rich transnational network poses a serious international security problem. There is considerable international consensus on the interest in combating international terrorism. As the focus widens to various nationally based groups conflicts of interests come to the surface. The degree of success of the US-led alliance against al-Qaida and the Taliban will be of great significance for the further

development of the international terrorist threat. Terrorism as a phenomenon cannot be eliminated.[15]

The quotation also illustrates the representation of terrorism as an inescapable element of society today. Again, there are no further arguments or explanations for this particular statement. The passage also indicates that terrorism is a major concern for a number of states, creating a consensus for the need to internationally combat terrorism. Later the estimate states that terrorism is a security problem for a number of states: 'Terrorism in various forms is a major security issue for states including US, Great Britain, France, Russia, Turkey and Israel.'[16]

Although a previous statement in the estimate argued that terrorism acts have *'increasingly taken place'* within the third world, the specific states mentioned as being countries where terrorism is a major problem are not from the third world.

Other discussions of terrorism in the estimate comment on the consequences of the 9/11 events, both in terms of the effect on the security threat and on international cooperation.

> Similarly, effective measures against transnational threats/terrorism may have a deterrent effect. Actions taken by organisations such as the UN, EU and NATO, as well as nationally, since the terrorist attacks on 11 September, in the US, are also aimed at reducing the vulnerability of open democratic societies. The incident has resulted in broad international unity against terrorism, but it is still too early to assess the long-term effect.[17]

This quotation indicates that an international consensus exists on the need to combat terrorism through international cooperation. Moreover, it emphasises that the long-term features of terrorism are not predictable. The impact of unpredictability and volatility on international consensus and cooperation is emphasised in another part of the estimate.

> Many Western actors and even Russia have a significant common interest in combating international terrorism. The most important measures in this area are intelligence and security exchanges and measures to deny bases and support to terrorist groups, mainly in bilateral co-operation. Political solidarity in this struggle has proved significant. If the fight [against terrorism] were extended

> to nationally based groups, which are seen by other actors is seen as liberation movements, any common interest could quickly be eroded.[18]

As this statement reveals, the estimate underlines that a consensus on the security problem of terrorism is occurring between states that normally do not agree on international policies (e.g. the US and Russia). It also indicates that this consensus would be rather fleeting if combating terrorism internationally involved nationally based organisations or it affected national interests.

In yet another passage, the assessment states that there are international consequences for Europe as a result of the 9/11 event: 'In the fight against terrorism, apart from the political solidarity, the EU's role is to coordinate legislative action against terrorism and to strengthen security cooperation in Europe.'[19] However, throughout the estimate, the role of the US is emphasised.

In the executive summary of the 2002 estimate,[20] terrorism is not mentioned, although the text contains a description of related issues.

> It is estimated that the consequences of regional conflicts and other threats to Western countries and structures, of which Sweden is a part will increase. Recent threats are by their nature first and foremost asymmetrical, transnational and dependent on the vulnerabilities in society, which makes them difficult to predict. (. . .) [These threats] have in more recent years been accentuated and more concrete, for instance in relation to 9/11 in 2001. These shared threats will be difficult to tackle by individual states.[21]

Terrorism is contextualised as a form of security threat to society. Threats and asymmetrical threats are discussed more extensively and in the 2002 estimate get an entire chapter for the first time. The estimate emphasises that the situation in Sweden is closely connected to the security situation of our neighbouring and affiliated states. The 2002 estimate contains a definition of the organisation's understanding of transnational threats: '[Transnational threats are] non-military and non-state threats that go beyond national borders and either threaten the political or social integrity of a state or its inhabitants.'[22] There seems to be a strategy to incorporate terrorism into the broader concept of transnational threats (also, for instance, incorporating organised crime). At the same time the estimate contextualises the re-emergence of terrorism as a consequence of the end of the Cold War and the globalisation of the world in general and the world economy in particular.

One statement suggests that the international countermeasures taken to decrease the risk of terrorism are assessed to have the desired effect – al-Qaida will have less operational capability: 'reasons that contradict any increasing threat from transnational terrorism are the international counter measures of a military, police or economic nature, directed at, al-Qaida, for example, which have limited the network's operational capability, at least temporarily'.[23] In this quotation, it is also apparent that the estimate equates transnational terrorism with Al Qaida. In combination with the conclusion that *'During the last decade the trend has been for state sponsored terrorism to decrease,'*[24] the quotation illustrates the assessment's conclusion of the decreased importance of terrorism, not only from a Swedish security perspective but also from an international perspective.

The representation of terrorism changed somewhat in the 2003 estimate. Here a paragraph describing terrorism starts: *'Transnational threats are a reality for Sweden today and affect several sectors of society.'*[25] Again, terrorism is included in the broader definition of transnational threats and a distinct definition of terrorism is missing. However, the number of conflicts used as examples (with examples from Iraq and Afghanistan) to contextualise terrorism indicates a new, broader mindset concerning terrorism's components. The estimate states that terrorism occurs most often in regional or domestic conflicts, although Al Qaida is still seen as a reminder of the transnational feature of terrorism.

The 2003 estimate makes a distinction between terrorism and Islamism, without explicitly stating it. This distinction opens up the possibility of such a thing as non-Islamic terrorism. However, the vast majority of examples fall into an Islamist category and the examples used for terrorist organisations are again al-Qaida.[26]

In 2004, the representation of terrorism is similar to that of the previous year, and again provides rather vague indications of the organisation's understanding of the phenomenon of terrorism. Thus, from 2003, a difference in the contextualisation of terrorism occurs, but in the texts there continues to be very little difference made between Islamism and terrorism':[27] 'Poverty and disillusioned youth under authoritarian regimes create a breeding ground for extreme Islamist movements in the Balkans, Africa, South East Asia, the Caucasus, Central Asia and the Middle East.'[28] The quotation illustrates that nearly all efforts to describe and explain terrorism take place within the context of Islamic extremism.

RECENTLY

In the 2005 estimate, the concept of terrorism receives less focus than in previous years. One passage says that the US term *GWOT* (Global War on Terrorism) is an overall concept of understanding and contextualising the phenomenon of terrorism.

> an increased transatlantic consensus in the struggle against terrorism is likely, even if some differences of opinion will affect transatlantic relationships in the future. (. . .) a redirection of strategy, which in practice will mean a broadening of GWOT, to include the increased use of non-military means.[29]

Again, there is no further indication of how the concept of terrorism is defined. The representation recognises tensions exist between different international actors concerning the means needed to conduct this war on terrorism. Other than this passage, the estimate makes few references to terrorism.

The 2006 and 2007 estimates start by concluding that there is no unified definition of terrorism. Although al Qaida is mentioned as an example of a terrorist organisation and terrorism is exclusively contextualised within Islamic movements, Islamism per se is not mentioned. This also illustrate how, without explicitly excluding the possibility of terrorism originating in other movements besides Islamism, the representation underlines the contextualisation of terrorism as an Islamic phenomenon: 'Islamist inspired terrorism . . . which is the primary point of reference for the term terrorism and, in general, also constitutes the biggest threat'.[30] Other than this passage, there are few references to terrorism and none provides indications of the organisation's definition of terrorism.

The 2008 estimate does not discuss or define, per se, the concept of terrorism; rather it is contextualised to the different Swedish military missions abroad and other issues. In one such case, the text relates to a specific type of terrorist threat and the need to adjust the way

Terrorism

of thinking about and acting to counter terror: 'Above all, terminology and operational methods will need to be modified to achieve this [combating terrorism] and avoid future discussions like the ones about Guantanamo and CIA [Central Intelligence Agency] prisons in Europe.'[31] Other than this statement, little text explicitly focuses on the phenomenon of terrorism.

The 2010 estimate does not explicitly discuss terrorism. The contexts and specific situations that previously had been categorised as terrorism/terrorists have been replaced by terms such as *combatants*, *insurgents* and *conflict*. In reference to Afghanistan, for instance, the term terrorism has been replaced with *insurgency*. Previous references to the Taliban identified its members as terrorists. In the 2010 estimate, members of the Taliban are referred to as *insurgents* and contextualised using a vocabulary that indicates that the estimate connotes the Taliban is a permanent and ordered organisation. There is no discussion in the estimate concerning why the change of vocabulary has taken place. Nor are there statements or a discussion of the intended distinction in the two sets of concepts.[32]

SUMMARY

The estimates provide few clues as to how terrorism is defined. Terrorism is assumed to contain an aspect of violence, and to be either ideologically oriented to the left or to Islam.

It is suggested in the estimates that an element of violence needs to be present for actions to be considered as terrorist acts. However, no indications are provided as to what magnitude the violence needs to be for an action to be defined as terrorism. This representation of terrorism makes the definition very broad and leaves a void in defining more violent versions of terrorism. The defining character of terrorism seems to change from it being ideologically left wing to being contextualised as Islamist extremism.

Overall, the intelligence provides little guidance on the assumed reasons and political context for terrorism. The estimates also conclude that there are only a small number of casualties from terrorism compared to other types of transnational threats. In addition, terrorism is most often considered a bigger threat due to the political aspects of its aim. It is also noteworthy that the criteria usually used in defining and categorising terrorism (modus and types of target) is not included as defining criteria in the estimates. The concept of terrorism in the estimate seems to be considered in terms of 'you know it when you see it'.

Notes

1. Intelligence Estimate 1998, p. 5.
2. Intelligence Estimate 1999. The term in Swedish *Kriser och konflikter* and *Nya Hot* respectively.
3. Intelligence Estimate 1999, p. 23.
4. Intelligence Estimate (A) 2000, p. 4. The concept of *'New Threats'* contain four different possible components according to the estimates; weapons of mass destruction, international crime, and computer-based threats and terrorism.
5. Intelligence Estimate (A) 2000, p. 34.
6. Intelligence Estimate (A) 2000, p. 34.
7. Intelligence Estimate (A) 2001, p. 6.
8. Intelligence Estimate (A) 2001, p. 6.
9. Intelligence Estimate (A) 2001, p. 13.
10. Intelligence Estimate (A) 2001, p. 13.
11. Intelligence Estimate (A) 2001, p. 34.
12. Intelligence Estimate (A) 2001, p. 35.
13. Although the text gives little guidance of what strategic consequences serve as a reference and what conclusions to draw from the analogies used. The historical analogies still have several possible interpretations, which in turn leaves it to the reader to interpret and generate the meaning of the concept of terrorism.
14. Intelligence Estimate (A) 2001, p. 35.
15. Intelligence Estimate (B) 2001, p. 31.
16. Intelligence Estimate (B) 2001, p 32.
17. Intelligence Estimate (B) 2001, p. 19.
18. Intelligence Estimate (B) 2001, p. 21.
19. Intelligence Estimate (A) 2001, p. 22.
20. Intelligence Estimate 2002 (the executive summary is unclassified).
21. Intelligence Estimate 2002, p. 1.
22. Intelligence Estimate 2002, p. 31.
23. Intelligence Estimate 2002, p. 32.
24. Intelligence Estimate 2002, p. 32.
25. Intelligence Estimate 2003, p. 71.
26. Intelligence Estimate 2003.
27. The only reference to non-Islamic terrorism is the Japanese cult Aum Shinrikyo that was active in the mid-1990s.

28 Intelligence Estimate 2004, p. 76.
29 Intelligence Estimate 2005, pp. 73–8, 20.
30 Intelligence Estimate 2006/2007, p. 24.
31 Intelligence Estimate 2008, p. 27.
32 Intelligence Estimate 2010.

Chapter 12

THE INTELLIGENCE DISCOURSE

The topics of focus in this chapter are three issues of profound importance in the context of Swedish security policy; thus, they constitute vital issues in the estimates, discussed in Chapters 8–11. Although the goal of the intelligence service is to be value neutral and strive for objectivity, the three issues were constructed on assumptions that were not defined or reflected upon, creating a normative interpretive framework suggesting an intelligence discourse as a consequence of a specific textual discursive practice founded in a 'style of thought'.

This intelligence discourse may be uncovered by searching for traces of assumptions appearing before the analytical conclusions and based on arguments and facts, in the form of value statements and rationalisations. The traces of assumptions can also found in the character of the language practice used in the concepts, terms and adjectives that frame the issues. Informed by the understanding that a discourse is 'a structure of a meaning in use', the empirical study of the language practice in the estimates will be investigated through the analytical method called *predicate analysis* (see Chapter 2 above). To recapitulate, predicate analysis is suitable for analysing the construction of subjects found in representations in texts. Predicate analysis usually focuses on verbs, adjectives and adverbs (hereafter, these are referred to as qualifiers).

LANGUAGE PRACTICE

The overall language practice in the estimates has relatively few qualifiers in relation to the topics in focus (in this case NATO, Russia and terrorism). However, the ones used are value statements, indicating that there is a distinct 'style of thought' in regard to the issues. The frequent use of valuations as qualifiers rather than the use of descriptive or factual qualifiers creates a general character for the text that is based on implicit assumptions and value statements instead of on factual arguments.

The qualifiers used are distinctly different in the assessments of the different issues. There is a distinct coherence of the positive connotation in the descriptive language used for NATO. Throughout the estimates, the qualifiers used in the representation of NATO are positive and/or affirmative. On the other hand, there is a distinct coherence of negatively connoted qualifiers in relation to Russia.

NATO – Constructing a Friend

Throughout the estimates, there are traces and indications of a language practice of using value statements, and valuations are frequently used as qualifiers. All of them indicate a unified positive view on the abilities and actions undertaken by NATO. The language practice and qualifiers defining the representation of NATO are detectable in a variety of contexts:

> As an organisation NATO has inherent, long-established expertise. With a role as a forum for political consultation, for planning and for command and control, the organisation is a force multiplier that cannot be replaced by anything else in the foreseeable future.[1]

The qualifiers 'inherent, long-established expertise' is typical of the framing of the representation of NATO in the estimates. This language practice, in which the organisation cannot be replaced by any other organisation, creates one trace of this overall positive connotation. This is apparent in another context where the capabilities of NATO as a whole are depicted: 'This is partly due to the Alliance's fundamental superiority over any possible opponent. A superiority which increases with time.'[2] Here the phrase 'superiority' is used without being accompanied by factual qualifiers, and is an example of a wording of positive connotation adjacent to a value statement. This use of positive expressions and language practice is detectable again in the estimate that expresses a valuation about the pre-eminence of NATO as an organisation: 'NATO has a well-developed, well-trained crisis management mechanism with exclusive resources and unique expertise. [Military]

Staff functions that ... are difficult to replace in the foreseeable future. The Alliance's multinational defence planning is the only one of its kind.'[3] This quotation illustrates how valuations are realised as qualifiers. The wording and the tone both contain apparent traces of a value statement in favour of NATO and NATO actions. The qualifiers used in reference to NATO are coherently positive and evaluative: *'adequate capacity'*,[4] *'NATO and US superiority in conventional military capacity ... The deterrence is effective'*,[5] *'increased flexibility'*, *'spearhead' 'professionalism'*,[6] *'decisive military organisation'*,[7] *'effective bureaucracy'*[8] and so forth. Throughout the estimates, the representation of NATO implies that NATO represents development, rationality and progress, constantly aiming for improving its crises management ability.[9]

A careful examination of the estimates for views, passages or analytical expressions with traces of a critical perspective on NATO or NATO's actions, reveals a view that borders on naïve. In the representation of NATO, traces of criticism is absent. In situations where a possible critical view might seem to occur, the language practice still creates a representation of NATO imbued with an overall positive impression. With recent history in mind, there are situations in international relations where NATO's actions have been, if not questioned, at least not unanimously approved by the UN and/or established Swedish domestic political actors. For example, in the context of the much debated NATO military action against Serbia in 1999, the estimate states:

> In Kosovo NATO has, once again, shown the capacity to unite in order to make a decision and act. (...) the decision to launch military air strikes, without a UN mandate, indicates a considerable qualitative change in NATO's potential for crisis management.[10]

In the context of the Kosovo conflict, there is yet another example of this particular language practice, which enhances the positive representation of NATO. The use of qualifiers such as 'again, shown the capacity to (...) act' and 'considerable qualitative change', without further substantiating the statement implies an overall positive representation of NATO.

In comments on the NATO military action in Afghanistan in 2001 where the estimates might have created a more nuanced view of the consequences of NATO action, a similar language practice is detectable. The analysis remains one-sided in strong support of both the ability of NATO and the desirability of its actions: 'NATO's use, for the first time ever, of Article 5 of the Washington Treaty in support of the US struggle against terrorism, should primarily be seen as an expression of political solidarity.'[11] By contextualising NATO's actions in the operation Enduring Freedom as an 'expression of political solidarity', the overall representation imbues the qualifiers with positive valuations. In a similar fashion, one of the rare instances where an analytically critical view is possible is undermined with a conclusion that makes sure the paragraph is still favourable to NATO. It is found in the context of a discussion of NATO actions in the Balkans in 1999:

> NATO is now carrying out military strikes against an independent nation without the support of a UN mandate. This is an expression of America's dominant position within the organisation. (...) This development strengthens NATO's role and capabilities and, depending on the outcome in Kosovo, will have a deterrent effect in the future.[12]

The estimate indicates that, despite the lack of a UN mandate, NATO's decision and actions are desirable in the eyes of international society. The use of qualifiers and language practice leaves little or no room for any understanding other than that NATO's actions are commendable. This positive framing is enhanced through the lack of problematisation or critical comments or viewpoints that might have been included regarding the lack of a UN mandate.[13]

Even where possible critical perspectives could be expressed in the estimates, they do not appear. A passage relating to NATO's military operations in the Balkans contains an indication that NATO, as an organisation, might not be flawless.

As they describe and interpret text, the possible criticisms that could be raised (for instance that NATO has acted with a olitical mandate) is "silenced" in the intelligence estimates.

> International crisis management often finds difficulty in achieving sufficient strategic flexibility in rapidly evolving crises. This is mainly due to difficulties in building political consensus in a situation where there are divergent interests. NATO action, including action taken during the various Balkan conflicts, has displayed flaws in this respect. Nevertheless, NATO works reasonably

well because of the acceptance, by other member states, of US leadership.[14]

As the estimate indicates, some aspects of the military operations in the Balkans had been sub-optimised and could (at least in theory) be understood as possible grounds for a critical perspective. It is almost as if the estimate anticipates the criticism of NATO's actions and expresses a normative valuation by stating that the organisation worked 'reasonably well'. The use of valuated qualifiers, such as 'reasonably well' puts an end to potentially critical perspectives, leaving the overall representation on a positive note.

This implicit normative representation is instilled with nothing but admiration for and affirmation of NATO's benign influence on international stability and security. It does not recognise the potential complications of the political influence of NATO on, for instance, the UN or EU security policy. It is this framing of NATO as providing benevolent political influence and power that we will investigate further.

Russia – Constructing a Foe

If the language practice concerning NATO is imbued with positive connotations, the language practice in representing Russia is quite the opposite: a distinct language of negative connotations. There is a distinct presupposition of how to interpret and construct the understanding of Russia. The text and the representation of Russia are imbued with qualifiers of consistently negative connotations. However, the representation of Russia is much richer in arguments and facts.[15]

Given the overall representation of Russia, (as discussed in Chapter 10) as a power-seeking realist nation state, it is not surprising that the language practice is essentially argued within a framework of realism and power. The references to the incentives for Russian political action and the motives for political decisions and viewpoints are described using a terminology of realism and power perspectives, but in a way that implies the representation of Russia to be questionable and distrustful. 'Russian strategic priorities are largely determined from a geostrategic balance of power perspective.'[16] This quotation illustrates that the representation of Russia is firmly established within a framework of realism. This language practice is apparent again in the context of Russian foreign policy.

Russia still wishes to see a reduction in US dominance on the world stage, even if Russian foreign policy under Putin is less stuck in geopolitics and more open than that during the latter period of Yeltsin's term as President. For example, actions in connection with the attacks on the US on 9/11 show that Russia no longer thinks only in zero-sum terms.[17]

A similar language practice is detectable in an estimate on the economy that states:

> The economic situation is undeniably better than ever, since the end of the Soviet era. The scepticism that surrounded the stability of any development, less than a year ago, has now turned to cautious optimism. (. . .) The Russian leadership has decided that all efforts towards reform will be in accordance with the Russian model, which in its turn requires financial independence.[18]

In the language practice used in the two quotations, the qualifiers induce an understanding that the political incentives for Russia are different from those of Western politics, which underlines the MUST's assumed realism perspective given as the basis for Russian political decision making. The language practice of emphasising the difference in political incentives creates a notion that this perspective is negative and the undertone is one of distrust. The estimate does not substantiate in what way Russian politics differ from (or rather oppose) Western politics. Traces of this language practice are displayed in a discussion of the possible Russian reaction to the NATO expansion process in relation to the Baltic States: 'In the economic situation prevailing in Russia today, the country is more dependent on good relations with "the West" than vice versa. This bodes for a calmer and sober Russian reaction [to any Baltic NATO membership].'[19] This quotation illustrates the use of negatively connoted qualifiers. For example, a 'sober Russian reaction' would indicate that the common Russian reactions would be the opposite. The language practice also reveals valuations that assume Russia has an irrational basis for making political decisions. This is expressed by using qualifiers of personal attributes and emotions to frame Russian political decision making. This is, for instance, apparent in a description of the relationship between Russia and the Baltic States: 'In Russia there are historical and psychological reasons for a widespread reluctance to accept the basic idea of the Baltic States' independence. This attitude dictates the Russian position on the Baltic States at least as much as real politic considerations.'[20] A personal attribute is ascribed to Russian political decision making by arguing that the Russian viewpoint is defined by 'psychological reasons'. A similar reasoning is apparent in relation to another discussion of Russian foreign policy objectives.

> Russia's earlier pragmatic and realistic foreign policy is changing to some extent. The change that has taken place has primarily led to a worsening climate in the dialogue between Russia and mainly the US, but also the EU and other Western [states]. Despite the frostier tone, this will probably not mean a break in relations. Therefore, dialogue is expected to continue.[21]

This quotation suggests that Russian foreign policy changes for reasons other than logic or rational, hinting at a whimsicality characterising Russian politics. Further, the representation of Russia refers to the motives for political decision making in terms of emotions. For example, there is a reference to *'For most countries it is the threat of Russian vindictiveness . . .'*[22] This referencing of personal attributes and emotions as the basis for Russian political decision making constitutes a valuation of Russian politics, portraying it as becoming less rational and uncertain.

The language practice framing Russia underlines the focus on recession, deterioration, poverty and so on, and, as a result there is a continuous use of a negative connotation through the use of certain qualifiers.

The estimates concerned with Russian politics use terms and concepts of recession, decline and poverty. . . maybe 'degrading' would almost be the right word?

Since the period being examined was a troublesome time for Russia (the financial crisis of 1998, and the transition from Soviet communism towards a democracy and a society going through rather harsh reforms), the situation could quite naturally explain the use of terms and words with negative connotations. Still, it is noteworthy that the qualifiers used are often valuating words with consistently negatively connotations. The consistent use of negatively connoted qualifiers without further determining factual or evidential underpinnings creates the impression of the existence of a predetermined 'style of thought'.

Discourse 175

For example, by using the reference 'developing country', one estimate creates a rather vivid description of the status of Russia, while providing little information about the actual social, economic or political situation: 'Russia is increasingly perceived by the West as a developing country with huge economic, political and social problems, which may contribute to less account being taken of Moscow's concerns in the security policy field.'[23] This quote illustrates the language practice of qualifiers referring and determining the image of Russia throughout the estimate. By using the reference of 'developing country' it creates a rather vivid description of the status of Russia, although providing little information about the actual social, economic or political situation. Without denying that Russia has economic, social and political problems, facts have not been used to further substantiate the Russian situation. This language practice is again apparent in the context of the demographic situation in Russia.

> The investigations presented ominous scenarios where Russia's population will fall to about 130 million in 2020. In addition, they revealed the embarrassing fact that the life expectancy for men is at the same level as developing countries, [and is expected] to persist for at least a decade.[24]

While this quotation has factual underpinnings, the use of words such as 'embarrassing' allows the qualifiers to have the character of a value statement, rather than use qualifiers that would provide a basis for discussing factual consequences. This use of negatively connoted qualifiers is also apparent in a description of various aspects of the Russian armed forces.

> A threat of armed attack during the period could only emanate from Russia. However, such a threat is very unlikely. This [lack of threat] is primarily [due to] deterrent factors such as a lack of interest/goals and Russia's economic dependence on the West. It is also linked to Russian military weakness.[25]

Without elaborating or further specifying what this 'military weakness' is or how it should be understood, it is the only sign of a characteristic of the Russian armed forces. The referral to the 'military weakness' of Russia is consistent throughout the language practice of the estimate, and is apparent in yet another context: 'The weakness of Russian conventional capabilities brings about increased significance for nuclear and other methods.'[26] Here again this is a statement made without further elaboration using factual or empirically based qualifiers. The language practice is enhanced when the estimate describes the military budget: 'The financial framework for the Russian Armed Forces will continue to be tight. Some respite from the persistent and draconian cuts the armed forces have suffered might be possible under the new political regime.'[27] Here, the qualifier 'draconian cuts' amplifies the understanding of the armed forces in Russia as being constantly weakened, while providing little depth for understanding the actual impact of the economic cutbacks made. Instead, this language practice creates a negative connotation for the representation of Russia.

A thorough examination of the language practice of the representation of Russia in the estimates revealed only a few positively connoted qualifiers. When economic progress in Russia is discussed, there are qualifiers used such as *'cautious optimism'*.[28] Positively connoted qualifiers are also used in describing the new political possibilities for Russia when Putin became the Russian president.

> Not only through the reforms mentioned previously, has Putin proven to be a man of action. As early as his first year in office, he began a campaign to regain influence over Russian central policy, which – during Yeltsin's rule – was dominated by financial magnates and regional leaders.[29]

Here the ability of President Putin is framed using positively charged qualifiers. This is found again in the context of discussing Russia's involvement in Balkan conflict: 'The Kosovo war placed a heavy burden on relations between NATO and Russia. It became clear to Moscow that Russia was seen as a third-rate power without influence. Nevertheless, Russia played an important role in terminating the war.'[30] The latter part of the quotation reveals an acknowledgment of Russia's role in the war's termination in Kosovo, although the overall impression is that Russia is an unimportant actor in international relations, with qualifiers such as 'third-rate power' being used. Although the language practice concerning Russia contains a few positive qualifiers, the general impression is that of doubt and a negatively charged 'style of thought'.

In the estimates, the analysis of NATO and Russia contain similarities

Discourse

and differences. In the case of both NATO and Russia, the text contains a distinct, coherent language practice imbued with valuating qualifiers that create an impression of a pre-established 'style of thought'. The difference between the two cases is that the valuations used as qualifiers are virtually opposite. The language practice for NATO is instilled with positively charged qualifiers, while the Russian practice is charged with primarily negatively charged qualifiers.

TERMS AND CONCEPTS

The exploring of language practice includes not only exposing what and how qualifiers are used, but also implies investigating what concepts and terms are used to describe societal phenomena, if and how these concepts are defined and if they are used consistently (as discussed in Chapter 3).

Conceptual Coherence and Change

Between 1998 and 2010 the concept of terrorism seems to have changed in essence. In the estimates of 1998 to 2001, fragments of characteristics can be found on which a definition of terrorism can be based. In these documents, terrorism is portrayed as organised violence used for political and/or ideological purposes from a non-state actor. The texts clearly state that it is necessary to be left-wing oriented (communism) to be labelled a terrorist.[31] The violence may, according to this working definition, be directed against state as well as against civilian, military and private organisations. To be a bit more explicit, the idea seems to be that this non-state actor (the terrorist) is organised, uses asymmetrical methods and is focused on critical vulnerabilities in society *and* has a specific ideological foundation (communism).

It is also of interest to identify what is not mentioned in the context of terrorism. For instance, there is no mention of Islam or the Taliban in Afghanistan in the estimate of 2001. Al Qaida is briefly mentioned as an organisation affiliated with Saddam Hussein in Iraq; however, no reference is made to the concept of terrorism. Islam or Islamic fundamentalism is not mentioned once in the estimates of 2001 and 2002 in connection with terrorism. The first time Islamic fundamentalism/extremism is mentioned is in the 2003 estimate.[32]

From 2003 on, the phenomenon of terrorism seems to be essentially equated to Islamic extremism, and simultaneously the possibility of other ideological foundations existing for terrorism seem to vanish. Terrorism is not mentioned in another context or with a different fundamental idea. Strangely enough, the vague yet embryonic definition of terrorism from the early years, where the methods and targets of terrorism were briefly discussed, is no longer present in the discussion of terrorism. Hence, from being a definition containing an idea of the characteristics of terrorism as well as an essence (ideology/founding idea), the definition has transformed into a one-dimensional view of terrorism as merely being organised violence stemming from Islamic extremism. As the characteristics of terrorism change, they are again never argued, elaborated or explained, which makes understanding the use of the term quite wide, blurred and essentialist (and with necessity based on Islam).

The investigation of consistency in the use of the term terrorism in the estimates looked at situations in which the text discussed geographical areas other than what the MUST view as 'the West'. The goal was to find out if the concept of terrorism was used coherently, that is, if situations describing a non-governmental actor with a political foundation that conducts violent actions towards civilian, governmental and military targets were described and labelled terrorism.

The investigation revealed that when the estimates described and analysed 'non-Western' parts of the world, there was a change in vocabulary in depicting similar situations that was seemingly dependent on what part of the world was being analysed. Contrary to the earlier statement that the vast majority of terrorist acts are conducted in the third world, these situations, when described individually in the estimates, were not labelled as 'terrorism'.

In the estimates, the language practice seems to limit the use of the term terrorism to specific geographical parts of the world (Europe, the US and Japan). From the years 1998 to 2004, quite early in the text, for example, the estimates refer to the situation in Northern Ireland as an example of terrorism, but do not describe similar conflicts in the Caucasus (Dagestan, Chechnya) as terrorism.[33] Although the situation in the Caucasus is described as one where non-governmental actors are using organised violence against governmental and military institutions, the term terrorism is not used; instead the actions are described as *'political violence'*.[34]

Similarly, in other situations that fit the definition of terrorism but occur in different geographical contexts (Russia, Africa and Middle East), different terms are used to describe the use of violence (and the violent actor). Instead of using the language practice of terrorism, expressions such as *'political struggle'*, *'struggle for power'*, and *'civilian violence'* are used. This change is apparent in a portrayal of Algeria:

> In Algeria, political violence, which has claimed 100 000 casualties since 1992, continues. (. . .) However, there are signs that the radical Islamists, who wish to continue the armed struggle . . . which will mean continued violence against the civilian population.[35]

The quotation refers to actions undertaken by radical Islamists (i.e. a non-governmental actor conducting organised violence aimed at civilians). Terms such as *'power struggle between different Islamic groups'* and *'violent attacks by Islamic organisations'* are used to describe the conflict between the Islamic groups (among others GIA – The Armed Islamic Group and FIS – The Islamic Salvation Front) and the government troops in Algeria.[36] In the context of Algeria, for instance, several non-state actors used organised (on some level) violence to obtain political goals, targeting both civil and governmental targets, a situation that fits the definition of terrorism implicitly suggested by the estimates. Yet these organisations are not labelled terrorist organisations, while the IRA and Hamas are. A situation that in a European context would most likely have been referred to by the term terrorism is described as an *'armed struggle'*. It should also be noted that the text in the estimates makes no distinction, provides no contextual understanding and makes no further determinations between these concepts to provide an explanation of the difference in meaning.

This incoherent use of the concept of terrorism raises the question of whether the ideological viewpoint of the terrorist organisation or the geographical (and cultural) context makes the difference. There is a possibility that the idea prevailing in earlier estimates, namely that the leftist ideology (communism) needs to be the founding idea for any situation to be understood as terrorism, is so firmly rooted that the ideological base for Islamic fundamentalism is not recognised as political. After the terrorist act of 9/11, the understanding of the concept of terrorism has gradually shifted from being a leftist ideological-oriented activity to a modus of violent political action, no matter what the ideology, to a phenomena completely framed by Islamist extremism.

	West (Europe and the US)	Other (Russia, Africa and Middle East)
Leftist ideology	Terrorism (for instance, IRA)	Armed resistance, political violence, political struggle etc. (Angola)
(Islamic) Fundamentalism	Terrorism (for instance, al-Qaida)	Violence, political violence and political struggle (GIA in Algeria, PLO, Hamas, Hezbollah)

Figure 12.1 Language practice for the term terrorism

The language practice in the estimates for the term terrorism in respect to geographical aspects may be summarised. The geographical and cultural distance between these conflicts could also somehow explain the change in language practice (see Figure 12.1).

Figure 12.1 illustrates that *terrorism* seems to be exclusively used in relation to the Western parts of the world. Similar acts and actions undertaken in other geographical areas are described using a different language practice. It need not be the actual geographical position that creates this distinction. An ethnocentrism that favours the 'Western hemisphere' may also have created this difference, thereby making it difficult for consumers of the estimates to recognise the possibility of terrorism being conducted in other parts of the world.

In addition, the breadth and indistinct characterisation used in defining terrorism makes it possible to use the term for a wide variety of actions and organisations, for example both Greenpeace and Reclaim the Streets, even though they are not terrorist organisations. The choice to use the term terrorism in certain situations but not in other, similar, situations seems highly arbitrary and might be understood as an unreflected choice of language practice with political consequences. Since 9/11 and the acceptance of the GWOT, the language practice of labelling situations and specific organisations with the term terrorism has had political consequences. This makes the use of clearly defined terms and factual underpinnings urgent in order to avoid the language practice being perceived as arbitrary and as containing normative subjectively unfounded truth claims.

Hence, a term such as terrorism is given a political connotation, which indicates that the determining factors for using it do not correspond to logic, reason or a consistent use of a defined term. Rather, the choice is based on uncontested, implicit and unreflective assumptions, which suggests terrorism should only be used in relation to Western liberal democracies while political violence in other parts of the world should be contextualised and depicted with greater understanding and acceptance.

FACTS, ARGUMENTS AND ASSUMPTIONS

In the estimates, the representation of NATO, Russia and terrorism consists of statements concerning their essence, characteristics and context, presented in the text as analytical conclusions. These analytical conclusions create meaning as to how the issues are perceived and understood. This raises the question of whether the discussions and conclusions about these issues are underpinned by facts and arguments and, if so, by what kind of facts and arguments. If the statements and conclusions are not underpinned by facts and arguments, there is a risk that the analytical conclusions are drawn partly with assumptions and normative viewpoints as the founding arguments.

The statements and analytical conclusions in the estimates are rarely substantiated by facts or factual arguments. Rather, the text contains important statements and conclusions that are made without an empirical basis or reasoning and are either assumptions or conjectures. Here the assumptions are the starting points, because the empirical data should be contextualised and interpreted, but instead has become the truth claim of the text itself. The conjectures about situations could (and should) be backed by empirical facts.

Analytical Qualifiers and NATO

This is, for example, visible when the estimates conclude that NATO membership is desirable, and contain numerous statements and conclusions on the positive effects that membership of NATO entails for member states. Here, the conclusion of the estimates of the desirability of NATO membership is shown in several parallel lines of arguments, none of which is empirically founded or argued.

The positive effects connoted with a NATO membership are apparent in the estimates in regard to the NATO expansion process involving the Baltic States. The estimate states that a NATO membership would imply *'a higher sense of security'*, without indicating what that *'sense of security'* holds. The estimate continues by stating that the general status of security would increase and that NATO membership for the Baltic States, therefore, is desirable.[37] Again, the statement is not substantiated with facts or empirical evidence nor is this general status of security further defined. Hence, the analytical conclusion seems to be based on realism assumptions on what membership in a security alliance would imply – the statements have become the truth claim itself.

The estimates argue that NATO membership is desirable because it provides security against an aggressor (primarily founded in a military threat). This is apparent in a text in which the estimate accounts for the benefits for the Baltic States of full membership in NATO.

> All of the Baltic States are very interested in the security guarantees under Article 5 of the NATO Charter, while NATO's motives for Baltic membership have more of a political and moral dimension and may be seen as a step in building a European security structure.[38]

This passage from the intelligence analysis allows us to see that the primary reason for states becoming members of NATO is to ensure that NATO will automatically respond to military intervention. Here too no further details are provided. There is nothing on what membership in NATO would mean to the national security of the Baltic States or how relevant the threat of military intervention is for the Baltic States. The estimate does acknowledge the possibility of Russian aggression in relation to the NATO expansion process, assessing the risk as being minor and unlikely.

A statement parallel to the one above, which states that military intervention in another state is highly unlikely in, for instance, Europe, is prevalent throughout the document: 'In 2000 NATO has, for the first time, dismissed the threat – in the foreseeable future – of a large scale armed attack against the territory of member states.'[39] Although the estimate states that military intervention (in specific regions) is not likely in the foreseeable future, and does not specify what state or what kind of state might constitute such an aggressor, creating security for such a threat is represented as the primary reason for a NATO membership. Despite the lack of a threat of military intervention, the representation in the estimates to provide security against a threat is repeatedly given as the reason for joining NATO. Again, the improbability of military aggression is also apparent in assessments of the Russian context: '*At a time when the military threat from the East seems to be insignificant*'.[40]

In addition, the estimate counters the already argued conclusion that NATO membership would be advantageous to new member states based on increased security. While arguing that NATO would provide security against military intervention, the estimates are simultaneously arguing that the current security threat is terrorism.[41] NATO could, for instance, provide another kind of security (against terrorism, for instance), although this is neither specified nor argued in the estimates.

The estimate gives other reasons for NATO membership (or, as in the case of Sweden, close cooperation) being desirable. The estimates include statements on the desirability of Sweden's continuing close cooperation with NATO and preferably as an integrated part of NATO: 'Also, maintenance of the Euro-Atlantic Security Community, of which Sweden is an active part, requires active participation. A robust Euro-Atlantic security system also means stability in the Baltic Sea region, as evidenced by NATO's expansion into the Baltic States.'[42] The inherent meaning of this quotation is that it is of great importance for Swedish security to continue and deepen its cooperation with NATO, which and again underlines of the favourable effects of the NATO expansion process. This is also apparent in a statement that it is of great importance for Sweden to continue and increase adaptation to NATO standards for interoperability to be feasible.

> For the foreseeable future, NATO will remain the decisive organisation for military crisis management in Europe. Further adaptation [by Sweden] to NATO doctrine and NATO standards is necessary for the interoperability needed in an intervention or when a crisis is at risk of escalating.[43]

These statements on the perceived desirability of continued Swedish cooperation with NATO are made without being argued from factual evidence or arguments and can hardly be understood in any way other than as value statements.

The analytical conclusion of the advantages of NATO membership and the positive view of NATO per se are made without factual arguments or evidence and could, therefore, be interpreted as a rationalisation, a valuation expressed as a fact. This valuation is prevalent in that the analytical process either does not recognise there are factors that counteract that presupposition or does not recognise that the argument in support of NATO membership being desirable does not support the analysis. In such a case, the lack of analytical precision makes the estimates appear unfounded.

Similarly, the lack of explicit factual underpinnings and reliance on implicit assumptions as the basis for conclusions is apparent in the context of Russia. In one instance, the analysis diametrically contradicts facts concerning the same issue, yet still ends up with the same conclusion. In the estimates, the description and analysis of the poor economic situation during the period being studied provide a troubling picture. In the representation of Russia, there is a clear analytical connection between economic developments and the possibility of Russia being a possible (military) threat or Russia being framed as a possible military adversary. It is as if the writers of the assessments constantly assume that Russia has the political will to be a military adversary or enemy, even though it has limited military capabilities to pose such a threat. Here the military capability is being depicted as dependent on economic (and technical) development, although the nature of that relationship is analytically blurred.

Analytical Qualifiers and Russia

In texts where the economic situation in Russia is represented in the estimates as weak, without any chance of improving and technical development as lagging behind, the conclusions assume that Russia poses a threat[44] or that military types of threats are created: 'Unclear chains of command, [issues concerning] loyalty and major maintenance problems are expected to be predominant issues during the assessment period. The social problems and demoralisation of the Armed Forces with the consequent political risks are expected to persist.'[45] This quotation illustrates the overall conclusion of the estimate that poor performance of the Russian economy implies negative effects on the Russian armed forces, saying that *'political risks'* affecting the security situation in the Russian 'near abroad' are created and existent. Thus, the estimate suggests an unpredictability in Russia's military actions due to the difficult economic situation within the armed forces. Although the overall actual military threat posed by Russia is assessed as unlikely due to a lack of military operational ability, the representation still encompasses the idea of Russia as an enemy.

As Russian economic development looked more positive, these improvements, along with the military reforms, were assessed as having a positive effect on the Russian military operational status, suggesting Russia is still assessed as posing a threat. However, the assessments also say that Russia's ability to act on its assumed antagonism towards its opponents is still restricted by the inferiority of its operational capacity.[46]

When the Russian economic situation was poor, the political risks stemming from Russia were assessed as being unpredictable. When the new more stable economic situation changed the character of how the threat was argued, there was still an assumption that Russia held an essentially antagonistic position. The estimates seem to imply an assumption that Russia is, in its essence, an antagonist of 'the West'. The assessments seem to rely on facts that point in different directions to draw the same conclusion – that the situation in Russia poses threats and creates security risks.

One possible explanation for this continued assessment could be that the frame for interpretation is so vividly active in the process of analysis that the a priori knowledge of how the available information should be understood means that facts and evidence become secondary. Thus, either the economic situation does not define the possibility of threats or security risk, in which case the facts provided for the conclusion are an analytical fallacy, or the economic situation does define the risk of threats and security risks and the analysis presented is not specified sufficiently for the chain of reasoning to prevail. The analysis here is not suggesting that the conclusion that Russia poses threats is wrong, merely that the facts and evidence to underpin this conclusion are not presented nor argued.

This analytical situation is a case of rationalisation, in which there seems to be a clear lack of evidence and argument underpinning the conclusion. This poses further problems, for instance in relation to the intelligence consumer.[47] Hence, the intelligence consumer may not recognise the reliance on the a priori knowledge and draw a conclusion based on assumptions rather than on facts and factual arguments.

SUMMARY

As we have seen, the representation of NATO appears to be analytical processed without a critical perspective. This absence of a critical perspective is apparent both in the reoccurring indistinctness in the analytical qualifiers and the under-problematisation of the consequences of the analytical assertions made. Instead the intelligence analysis seems to be written with an uncritical analytical eye and factually unsubstantiated. Correspondingly the representation of Russia also holds a reoccurring indistinctness in the analytical qualifiers and inexplicit factual substantiation, although from a distinctly critical perspective.

The indistinctness in the analysis is also visible in the text in the estimates in relation to the definitions and use of terms and concepts. In the estimates, the concepts and terms used are rarely reflected on, elaborated or defined. For example, the estimate uses the term 'terrorism' without elaborating its defining character. Rather, the estimate seems to adopt a position of 'you know it when you see it'. Furthermore, the text displays inconsistency in the use of the concept of terrorism. As a result of the lack of definition and the inconsistent use of the concept the analysis and the conclusions drawn are open to interpretation by the intelligence consumer. Additionally, the prevailing view on language as 'only a mediator' of information fails to recognise the possible political implications of the use of specific concepts for description. The arguments, concepts and language and, thereby, the articulated meaning of the intelligence analysis are problematic. The problems are plentiful.

The text contains valuations and normative viewpoints, despite the expressed goal of the intelligence service to the contrary. These values and valuations may in some cases be the result of unarticulated theoretical assumptions. The valuations are also seen in other forms throughout the intelligence analysis, indicating another analytical problem. The rationalisations are valuations disguised as facts. We have seen that the texts include rationalisations in arguing for a specific analytical conclusion. To do this, the intelligence analysis is using normative viewpoints as grounds for knowledge and predictions. In addition, the language used in the intelligence analysis is problematic in respect to the terms used both to articulate and to discuss the issues. It is also problematic in respect of the use of adjectives and adverbs. Again, the valuations and pre-existing normative viewpoints and assumptions permeate the

Discourse 187

intelligence analysis in a manner that seems to be unreflected, creating an uncritical analytical perspective.

The unreflected approaches in the analytical conclusions are further underlined through frequent occurrence of unargued representations or what sometimes appear as truisms. The text might consist of claims charged by the values that are conventions or jargon within the intelligence service (i.e. important claims and conclusions made even though they lack an empirically argued basis). Furthermore, some postulations are assumptions or attempted predictions, which are assertions without empirical underpinnings. Here, unclear and unreflected assumptions are used as both the starting point as well as the corroboration for the analytical conclusions, rather than predictions being argued using data, factual arguments or other kinds of evidential arguments.

The representation of NATO and Russia could also become instilled with valuations because of a lack of an overall critical perspective in one case and a predetermined critical perspective in the other. This unreflected approach can emerge through the use of imprecise analytical distinctions and definitions, leaving little possibility of the analysts recognising contradictions and complex conditions. This could leave the representation with an imprecise analytical perspective, allowing the 'style of thought' to emerge and overpower a critical and nuanced representation. As seen, the articulations made in the intelligence analysis, taken together with the problems outlined, create an aura of indistinctiveness in the text. An uncritical analysis allows the representation of NATO to become the creating of a friend, while the representation of Russia allows for the creation of a foe.

Notes

1. Intelligence Estimate (A) 2001, p. 23.
2. Intelligence Estimate (B) 2001, p. 67.
3. Intelligence Estimate (B) 2001, p. 66.
4. Intelligence Estimate (B) 2001, p. 28.
5. Intelligence Estimate 1999, p. 19.
6. Intelligence Estimate 1999, p. 57.
7. Intelligence Estimate (B) 2001, p. 9.
8. Intelligence Estimate (B) 2001, p. 21.
9. See, for example, Intelligence Estimate (A) 2001, p. 23.
10. Intelligence Estimate 1998, p. 8.

11 Intelligence Estimate (A) 2001, pp. 21–2.
12 Intelligence Estimate 1999, p. 52.
13 The lack of reflection on the NATO action without a UN mandate is especially noteworthy since the Swedish government repeatedly underlines the importance of international security policy being formulated within the UN in the Foreign Policy Declarations during 1998 to 2009. Even if one of the founding ideas of the intelligence service in general is to be independent of government policy (politisation) arguments should be put forward and reflections of the consequences should be brought to light, even if only to persuade the intelligence consumer (the government) of the probability of the assessment.
14 Intelligence Estimate (B) 2001, p. 66.
15 The more frequent use of facts and factual arguments are especially visible in the estimates where economic issues are discussed.
16 Intelligence Estimate 1998, p. 1.
17 Intelligence Estimate (B) 2001, p. 44.
18 Intelligence Estimate (B) 2001, p. 47.
19 Intelligence Estimate (B) 2001, p. 74.
20 Intelligence Estimate 1999, pp. 64–5.
21 Intelligence Estimate 1999, p. 34.
22 Intelligence Estimate 1999, p. 54.
23 Intelligence Estimate 1999, p. 53.
24 Intelligence Estimate (B) 2001, p. 49.
25 Intelligence Estimate 1999, p. 26.
26 Intelligence Estimate (B) 2000, p. 27.
27 Intelligence Estimate 1999, p. 30.
28 Intelligence Estimate (B) 2001, p. 47.
29 Intelligence Estimate (B) 2001, p. 39.
30 Intelligence Estimate (A) 2000, p. 61.
31 Intelligence Estimates 1998–2000.
32 Intelligence Estimate 2003, p. 75.
33 The chapters on the Caucasus region in the Intelligence Estimates 1999, 2000 and 2001.
34 Intelligence Estimate 1999, p. 80.
35 Intelligence Estimate 1999, p. 80. See also the description of Sudan and the Sudan People's Liberation Army (SPLA) as a violent non-governmental actor in Intelligence Estimate 1999, p. 91.
36 Intelligence Estimate (A) 2001, p. 44.
37 The intelligence estimate does acknowledge that there are possible downsides with the NATO enlargement process in regard to possible Russian negative reactions.
38 Intelligence Estimate (B) 2001, p. 92.

39 Intelligence Estimate (B) 2001, p. 67.
40 Intelligence Estimate (B) 2001, p. 66.
41 Intelligence Estimate (A) 2001, p. 31.
42 Intelligence Estimate 2002, p. 1.
43 Intelligence Estimate (A) 2000, p. 4.
44 Although it is made clear that there is not the threat of military intervention from a Swedish perspective under these conditions.
45 Intelligence Estimate 1999, p. 41 and Intelligence Estimate (B) 2001, pp. 55–6.
46 Intelligence Estimate (B) 2001, pp. 55–6.
47 In this particular case the Swedish Government (the intelligence consumer) did not agree with the conclusions made by the estimate of 2006/2007 in regard to the threat from Russia. The wording by the defence minister indicates that they presumed that the intelligence service had a presupposed idea of Russia as the government didn't agree with the conclusion of the estimate and therefore demanded an independent assessment. Interview 11.

Chapter 13

THE INTELLIGENCE 'STYLE OF THOUGHT' AND 'COLLECTIVE OF THOUGHT'

The institutional setting and the formal social practice within which intelligence is produced is characterised by two sets of features. The production process is formally ordered and hierarchically structured in a way that identifies and directs various actions and interactions within the MUST and in the MUST's external relations with intelligence consumers. The roles, routines and procedures for the analytical process within the MUST (structuring the actions of analysts and managers) are characterised by a set of informal social and textual discursive practices. These informal practices imply a disregard for discussing, reflecting on and critically reviewing vital aspects of the analytical process. The intelligence social discursive practices at the least discourage a reflective and critical perspective on the analytical foundations and conduct of the intelligence analysis. The intelligence knowledge is created, upheld and affirmed within a specific intelligence 'collective of thought' and an intelligence 'style of thought'.

The intelligence 'style of thought' is founded within a worldview corresponding to political realism, which defines what the intelligence holds as being important objects of knowledge. Hence, the worldview becomes primarily state-centric, arguing and interpreting world events through a (undefined) concept of power, and becomes inattentive to factors such as non-state actors, ideology and ideas. However, the analysts do not consciously recognise that realism is the frame of interpretation. Hence, the assumptions underlying the intelligence analysis are not argued, discussed or defined; rather they might be conceived as complying with an established way of thought – a tradition of conceptualising.

Rather than an explicit reliance on a defined worldview, it is the emphasis on seeking consistency and continuity within the established 'style of thought' (and the traits of the 'collective of thought' to cohere with the social and textual practices) that directs the approaches used for problematising, articulating issues and drawing conclusions. The search for continuity and consistency with accepted approaches to issues and to how conclusions have been argued and substantiated constitute an intelligence knowledge discourse. The drive for continuity and consistency in the intelligence knowledge discourse dominates the analytical distinction between assumptions, arguments and conclusions. The arguments and facts used for substantiating the analysis are not distinctly separated from assumptions and valuations. Hence, the intelligence knowledge discourse suggests a reproducing of knowledge rather than a creation of new insights.

INTELLIGENCE SOCIAL PRACTICE

The intelligence knowledge is produced within an institutional social context encompassing the formal and informal rules, tasks, roles and procedures that constitute a social practice. This social practice embodies certain formal conditions and instructions that define the social practice of the MUST. These conditions and instructions structure the activities of the MUST and affect and direct the actions and behaviours of the intelligence analysts. Both the MUST and the individuals have to relate and adjust to this set of rules, roles and procedures as they carry out their activities and assignments.

The social practice is guided by a formal institutional set of rules and procedures. This study suggests that the formal institutional setting structures the work process on an overall level by defining the processes governing instructing the MUST, the means of dissemination and how transparency and review are organised. This structure defines the purpose of the intelligence service, the high-level tasking of what issues and regions are in focus and the organisational structure within the MUST.

In relation to the external political and institutional setting, the process of directing the focus of the intelligence service is based on a formal and annual dialogue with the government (via SUND) and the other intelligence consumers defined in the legal framework. The dialogue results in a document of prioritised issues and regions. These issues are then internally processed within the MUST by management, resulting in a reprioritised list. Thereafter, the social discursive practice directs the process through an informal set of routines, procedures and roles.

The basic conceptual idea of the internal working process is the MUST intelligence cycle, which specifies the main components of the work process in terms of directing, collecting, systemising, analysing and disseminating. The formal social practice expressed within the organisation also outlines the process of management approving and releasing estimates before they are disseminated to intelligence consumers. However, the formal social practice does not cover aspects of the analytic process (such as systematising information, making analytical choices and developing methodologies). These aspects of the process are primarily structured within informal norms of how the analysts should act, thus creating a highly influential, informal social discursive practice that structures the action of the analysts.

The view of the analysts is that they individually define the analytical process (thinking and writing) within the formal structure laid down. The individual analyst decides what and how to more precisely articulate the issues of intelligence requests. The individual analyst chooses what information to include in the analysis. The individual analyst chooses which terms and concepts to use and what conclusions to draw. Nevertheless, this study suggests that the analysts are highly affected by their social context and adjust their behaviour and analytical process to this social discursive practice.

INTELLIGENCE SOCIAL DISCURSIVE PRACTICE

The discursive social practice of intelligence seeks continuity, letting implicit assumptions and tradition guide the analysis, and neglects the role of interpretation as a vital part of drawing and articulating conclusions. This allows the desire for conformity of thought to override the need for discussion and critical examination of the analysis, thus discouraging reflection, evaluation and criticism.

Continuity

The search for continuity is visible throughout the analytical process. In the articulation of the issues and topics under investigation, the analysts tend to rely either on their preconceived idea of the needs of the intelligence consumer or on the articulation in previously written assessments. Occasionally (and depending on the individual interrelationship between analyst and consumer), the articulation is further shaped according to the intelligence consumer's need and intended use. The social discursive practice suggests that the appropriate behaviour for the analyst is to follow is the established conception of how an issue is usually described within estimates.

Continuity is also a vital element in the thinking and writing process for intelligence analysts. This mindset is well known to the analysts, who adjust their analytical processing accordingly. In general, the analysts say they intend to base their current analytical task on the previously written assessments and only add new information. Even if they do not use this process, the analysts intend to do so. This mindset is enhanced by reminders from management that a continuum of assessments is preferable so as to not to make the organisation look ambivalent.

Individuality and Reflection

The lack of formal routines and procedures for the analytical work creates logic of appropriateness within the social discursive practice. There is no procedure or routine for discussing or reflecting on the assumptions on which the analyses are based. In addition, the methodological approaches are unarticulated, leaving the analysts with the impression they can make individual choices. Even during the formal procedure before the assessments are approved when management representatives have an opportunity to raise objections, methodological and analytical considerations are not discussed. Rather, the discussions focus on seeking continuity and making sure there is consensus on the conclusions.

In the intelligence discursive practice, there is no routine or procedure that enables reflection and evaluation of previous assessments, the analytical process or the basis for the analysis. As a result, the analysts do not necessarily reflect upon the assumptions, the information used or the analytical process or why certain conclusions were drawn. Thus, the individual analyst is responsible for making (what they perceive as) relevant and reasonable articulations, choices and demarcations. This unreflective approach is a recurrent trait in several aspects of the textual discursive practice and is further underlined by an unarticulated view of interpretation.

Analysis without Interpretation

Within the intelligence analysis, the interpretation and interpretative process are unarticulated and tacit, thus making it difficult to uncover, conceptualise and reflect upon from internal and external perspectives. Although the analysts consider the interpretation an individual action, social context plays a crucial role in the process of systemising and interpreting the information and analytically approaching specific topics and throughout the process of writing.

The social discursive practice suggests that striving for continuity discourages change and controversial interpretations or reconceptualisations. The striving for continuity is apparent in all sequences of the analytical process. This study indicates that in the initial phase of articulating issues the analysts are prone to accept the articulation of previously accepted knowledge. This reliance is evident in what the analysts choose to use when they research a subject, as they choose information to use in their analysis, in how they conceptualise and contextualise issues and in the language they use in the written estimates.

Because of the reliance on previous assumptions and conclusions, the intelligence analyses, in most cases, tend to reproduce not only a similar kind of knowledge, but also lack a critical and evaluative reflection of the previous conclusions and assumptions and thereby reproduce similar assessments and conclusions.

The intelligence social discursive practice suggests that there is a consensus on conclusions made within the organisation. This consensus is sought through informal discussion between analysts and consent must be obtained from management for the assessment to be disseminated. The discussions cover the conclusions, which are presented as statements, and how they are argued with reference to previously written assessments and to incoming information at hand. The emphasis on relying on previously established knowledge and the prevailing idea of knowledge creation reduces the importance of the interpretation within intelligence analysis.

Critiquing

The MUST rarely carries out an extensive discussion on the assumptions, interpretation and conclusions, making critique problematic too. Discussions on issues of analytical or methodological concern are rarely initiated, critiqued or commented on. Issues of what assumptions are made, how the interpretation is done or why specific conclusions have been made are, in the same manner, almost never debated or critiqued. In general, the possibility of raising questions is structured according to area of expertise. For an analyst working within one area of expertise, it is nearly impossible to question or comment on the assessment on another issue area. Even in the unlikely case of analysts raising questions in their own area of expertise, it is a sensitive issue. Any questions are almost exclusively about language or editorial concerns.

There are several reasons for the difficulty in raising questions about assumptions, interpretations and conclusions within the intelligence social discursive practice. The first reason for this socially induced habituation to not criticise is related to the prevailing view in the organisation on how the intelligence knowledge is produced. The organisation considers that the intelligence knowledge is being constructed with little emphasis on the role of interpretation and of how analytical conclusions are derived. Rather, the prevailing image is one of creating knowledge by 'just telling how things are' and making the assumptions and the frames for interpretation implicit and, thereby, less visible in the (text of the) assessment.

The second reason is that there seem to be a prevailing idea that knowledge is compartmentalised in the organisation and, as a consequence, critique is equally compartmentalised. Thus, critique is only possible if the critic has access to the same information or area of expertise.

Third, the analysts are reluctant to question a fellow analyst because of the social and organisational interrelationship among them. The analysts, being well aware of the importance of being right and obtaining consensus for the assessments, hesitate to raise questions because they do not want to make fellow analysts 'look bad'. In other instances, analysts avoid questioning the work of another analyst due to difference in status. The overall social discursive practice of the intelligence service is characterised by a socially imbedded reluctance to initiate discussion or critique or to comment on analytical issues. Thus, this social discursive practice of the 'collective of thought' making and identifying, and above all, critiquing conclusions and the analytical process is a socially difficult task.

Searching for Status

Within the social discursive practice of the intelligence service, it is important to have status. The interrelationships between analysts and between analysts and management are defined by formal as well as informal status. Having status is important because it helps analysts to have assessments approved and released. Status helps analysts avoid criticism and to have the opportunity to articulate issues and affect the frames of interpretation.

Analysts gain status in various ways, such as being perceived as making stable and solid analyses. That means that the analysts seek consistency with the previously written assessments. It also implies that the analyst seeks to write analyses and assessments so as to avoid change. Analysts that regularly change their analyses and assessments would be considered ambivalent and would most likely not gain status within the organisation. Moreover, analysts need to be considered as uncontroversial to gain status. Thus, the analysts seek consistency with what is considered the norm of assessing and writing about issues. Analysts have a few ways to increase their status. They need to be engaged with an issue or a topic that is considered important and vital. An analyst making excellent assessments on a marginalised topic will not draw the attention of management and not increase their status.

The status of the analyst also increases if the analysis is considered to be correct. On several occasions, the analysts expressed a reluctance to be as precise as possible for fear that the conclusions might be considered partly incorrect. It is better to write analyses that are imprecise and conservative in order to increase one's status. The analysts are worried about being considered bold or controversial, and so it is more rewarding to produce assessments consistent with the established 'style of thought'. While there is no expectation that the analysts should constantly make accurate assessments and predictions, it is important not to be wrong. It is not unheard of, as we have seen, for analysts to adjust their analytical distinctiveness to reduce the chances of being wrong. This is one reason for the analysts' keenness 'to stay close to the information' and reluctance to define concepts. The analysts' keenness to stay close to the information is visible in their recurrent argument that 'we can't make an assessment of what they will do, until they have actually started doing it'. The emerging view on knowledge production of an unarticulated interpretative process (by systemising and stacking new information upon old) also encourages the analysts to 'stay close to the information' – re-infusing the unarticulated analytical approach.

Among the intelligence analysts is a core of members who have a greater impact on how certain issues are articulated, conceptualised and interpreted. The intelligence 'collective of thought' consists of an *esoteric group* of analysts and the less influential analysts form an *exoteric group*. The esoteric analysts possess higher status, which does not necessarily correspond to a formal role of increased responsibility.

The status of the informal group of esoteric analysts leaves them analytically unchallenged to a higher degree than other analysts. The esoteric group is trusted more by management and is less likely to receive criticism from other analysts or management. If criticism is ever articulated about assessments written by analysts belonging to the esoteric group, it is unlikely to be incorporated or dealt with. Rather, critics risk lowering their status by raising questions. The disinclination to criticise and the greater trust given by management also suggests that management more frequently considers assessments done by the esoteric analysts to be valid. Hence, the esoteric analysts need to argue less and use fewer facts and information in making their assessments and deriving conclusions. Their 'gut feeling' is trusted to a higher extent.

The esoteric analysts also influence which concepts and terms are used and how assessments are written, thus influencing the assumptions underlying the analysis and creating a preferred frame of interpretation. The preferred frame of interpretation is transferred to other and to new analysts through consensus seeking and explicit statements about seeking an analytic continuum of written assessments. It is evident within the social discursive practice that analysts are taught how to write, and when they try to portray issues differently from what was done in the past, they are corrected, which instils the preferred frame of interpretation and literary style.

INTELLIGENCE TEXTUAL DISCURSIVE PRACTICE

Knowledge in a Continuum

Not only is previously established knowledge vital in the analytical process of the analysts, it also functions as a norm for a continuum to which new information is added. Within the analytical work it is not uncommon for the analysts to rely heavily on the previous assessments.

The routines and procedures reveal that analysts reuse previous assessments and conclusions for background reading and as components of new assessments. Although the relation to and reliance on previously established knowledge is vital in several ways, its greatest importance is the formative role it plays in the knowledge produced. The intention of the assessments (and thereby the knowledge) to 'be in line with' previously written assessments defines the discursive space within which new knowledge is produced. The effort to create the new assessments within the continuum does not suggest only searching for consistency but also avoiding change. This is noticeable in several ways.

First, the influence of the need to stay within a continuum is noticeable in the actual assessments and conclusions. The interpretation of how possible future events will evolve is considered as a prolongation of previous assessments. This is seen in the text of the estimates where state actors are argued to act in a specific way because they have done so before. The practice has become an institutionalised routine. This leads to the organisation not recognising (or at the least, not discussing the possibility of) how a different set of conditions might change a state's behaviour.

Second, this reliance on previously established knowledge creates a troubling situation, because there is no institutionalised routine for evaluating the accuracy of previous assessments. In the organisation's view, the piecing together of new and old information and the contextualisation creates the knowledge added value of intelligence analysis. Hence, the contextualisation is not interpretation, and interpretation per se is not needed or desirable for intelligence knowledge. This suggests a view within the intelligence service that knowledge is cumulative.

Third, within this continuum established knowledge serves as building blocks for cumulative intelligence knowledge. Again, this is troubling because of the lack of critical reflection and evaluation of whether previous assessments were correct.

Finally, the explicit search for producing knowledge within a continuum extends to the language used in the estimates. Thus, established knowledge defines the concepts and terms used for conceptualising the issues under current analysis. This further underlines that the disinclination towards change extends to a resistance to change in understanding concepts and introducing new terms and concepts, as seen in

Chapter 11 in the resistance to change the defining characteristics of terrorism after the events of 9/11.

Facts and Arguments

In the estimates, the assessments and conclusions are substantiated through statements. These statements are partly argued using facts and factual underpinnings, and partly argued using assumptions and valuations articulated as facts. The former are argued according to an expected line of reasoning based on the intelligence worldview. This became apparent in the kind of facts used to substantiate the assessments and conclusions about what constitutes a state's power. The estimates recurrently referred to different states gaining or losing power in the international political arena. Since the estimates discuss power in this context, the arguments share the features of power using ideas of realism as the foundation.

As we have seen in Chapters 9 to 12, the discussion in the estimates does not make clear distinctions between facts and factual underpinnings, and assumptions and interpretation, nor do they seem to recognise the role of the valuations used as foundation for analysis and conclusions. This raises a concern about assumptions and valuations being used as a factual foundation, something that happened frequently. For example, in the estimates that articulated the character of NATO, the assessments were based on positively connoted valuations, even though little factual evidence was presented to support the effectiveness and expertise ascribed to NATO. Although the articulation of the representation of Russia was, to a larger extent, supported by facts, a not insignificant number of assumptions and valuations were argued as facts. The use of qualifiers reveals the ambiguity of the arguments used to substantiate conclusions. In the text, the way in which events, phenomena and actors are named and represented help reveal the assumptions that may underlie the frame of interpretation and the impact of the language. Therefore, the use of qualifiers will tell us something about how well knowledge is argued and substantiated.

The textual discursive practice also suggests that assessments based on information collected by the organisation are preferred. The analysts, to a large extent, tend to rely on information collected by or available within the organisation. The analysts ascribe to this information from accepted sources higher credibility per se. Thus, the choices of what information to use are primarily made in terms of its origin rather than its relevance. The focus of collecting new information is, to great degree, guided by the previously accepted knowledge and the underlying assumptions. This makes a certain kind of information more available to the analyst.

Contradictory Facts

If recognised, information that contradicts established knowledge is considered less credible than information affirming previously written assessments. This could be the effect of the worldview and the 'style of thought' on the information sought and infused into the intelligence analytical process, which limits the range of diversity. Alternatively, this could be a result of the textual discursive practice permeating the routines and procedures of the analytical process to such an extent that contradictory information is not recognised. As we have seen, the directing effect of the worldview and 'style of thought' do affect the possibility of having diversity in the incoming information. The search for logical consistency to the established 'style of thought' is so profound that the analysts recognise and engage with contradictory facts only with difficulty. This is, for example, noticeable when analysts with more ten years' experience state that they have never really seen contradictory incoming information or reports that contradict established knowledge. Analysts say facts that contradict the previous assessments might be an indication that something is about to change or something 'is happening' in regard to the questions. If the difference between the established 'style of thought' and the new contradictory fact is too great, the new information (fact) is not considered credible.

The Intelligence Literary Style

The estimates have a particular literary style. Overall, the character of the intelligence literary style seems to suggest an intention to introduce and underline new information. The style has no expectation of making distinctions between assumptions, valuations and facts, making the interpretative process implicit, tacit and indistinct. The organisation expects new analysts to comply with this literary style.

The intelligence literary style is partly articulated in formal instructions from management, which imply that the assessments should be written so the conclusions are expressed as the only possible interpretation. The estimates should be expressed in such a literary style so the consumer does not need to form interpretations of their own. Although many of the issues and topics analysed in the assessments are complex societal and political issues, the intelligence literary style expresses the conclusions so they do not depend on a process of interpretation. Rather, the assessments are to be expressed as definite conclusions with only one viable answer – not demanding a process of interpretation. If the interpretation is accepted, the distinction between information and facts, and interpretation, is not explicitly expressed to the intelligence consumer. The use of definite answers is seen, for example, in the way assessments should express the probability of a predicted issue or event. The acceptance of one possible interpretation may create a risk of not communicating alternative interpretations or the limitations of the assessment to the intelligence consumer.

It is important to note that there is no explicit intention in the formal instructions about withholding information or possible interpretations from the consumer. However, the analysts' expectation that they will express their assessments as the only possible interpretation and, thereby, adhere to the norm of the literary style, results in them withholding information and possible interpretations.

Choosing Concepts

In the view of the analysts, the choices of the concepts used in the contextualisation and explanation of different topics and regions are, in general, left to them as individuals. Yet, as we have seen, the choices they make are affected by their social context and the practices in place. The analysts know the organisation expects them to use the existing concepts. The analysts are also affected by the concepts being used by fellow analysts and other experts engaged in the same issues or regions. They argue they are a part of a specific group of experts and, therefore, adjust to the established use of language within this group.

In general, the concepts used within the assessments are not explicitly defined. Instead, there seems to be an expectation of implicit and informal consensus on the intended meaning of different concepts. For example, the estimates refer to concepts such as *power* and *terrorism*. Both are highly contested concepts in almost all the other contexts in which they are used, but are undefined in the estimates. There are clues in the estimates of the intended meaning of these concepts. Power, for example, is referred to in different contexts and with different attributes. The estimates refer to different kinds of power (i.e. political, real, informal and economic), and with frequent references to increase or decrease in power, although nowhere is there an extended discussion on the character of that power or on how it might have increased. The same approach is taken for other concepts, such as the concept of terrorism, as seen in Chapter 11.

The difficulty of defining concepts is recognised by the analysts. The analysts consider definition as difficult both because of the lack of consensus (within and outside the organisation) and because it makes the analysis more difficult. The analysts view defining a concept as limiting the possibility of expressing their arguments, assessments and conclusions. The striving within the organisation to seek a continuum of the use of concepts suggests that a loosely defined concept makes the need for changing definitions less acute and the desired continuum is more easily achieved. If the clues presented in Chapters 11 and 12 about the intended meaning of terrorism are summarised, an implicit definition of terrorism can be found: 'organised violence by a societal actor directed at other different kinds of (societal) actors with political purpose'. This or any other definition is never written or expressed explicitly in the estimates; rather, it is the product of a sympathetic reading and a rationalisation of what might be the intended meaning. Thus, it appears that the vague definition enables a tradition of concept use to be kept intact.

Loosely defined concepts also make it possible for them to be used inconsistently throughout the estimates. The inconsistent use of concepts in estimates between different regions and issues is visible in regard, for example, to the concept of terrorism. Highly flexible and debated concepts such as 'power' are not defined or reflected upon, as we saw in Chapter 8 when examining the intelligence worldview. The apparent reluctance to define concepts or of consistent use of specific terms and concepts are present throughout the text in the estimates.

Changing Concepts

In spite of the intention to use the established concepts within the estimates, change in their use does occur. The types of change are replacement of one concept by another, the way in which concepts are used, and a shift in the intended meaning of a concept. The reasons and the intended meaning of a concept are not explicitly argued in the estimates nor do they seem to be discussed within the organisation. The change or shift is only detectable through a careful reading of the implicitly intended meaning revealed by the context, hints and shifts of nuance in the adjoining qualifiers. If the name or labelling of an event or phenomenon is changed, from one estimate to the other, it occurs without explanation of why the event demands another label, what circumstances have changed or why the new label is better suited to describing the issue. Moreover, this kind of change in concept is not stressed in the text so the intelligence consumer is less likely to notice that a changed has occurred.

The reasons for changing concepts is not a topic of discussion among analysts or something that the analysts seem to reflect on in their daily work, as seen in Chapter 12. The closest the analysts seem to come to reflecting on if and why they change the use of a concept happens when they detect such a significant change within the issue that the previous concept no longer seems appropriate. Hence, the change does not seem to be the product of a deliberate and explicit analytical position. The lack of discussion or intentionality means when a change occurs it does not result in a new and explicitly defined concept; the result is a different partial, implicit intended meaning. Since the change is not discussed, argued or susbstantiated it results from the intuitive character of the intelligence analysis. However, I argue that the decision to change the concepts in specific topics is not unaffected and solely based on the individual analyst's intuition. Rather, the choices of concepts and change of concepts are shaped by the social and textual discursive practise within the MUST.

Nevertheless, it is clear that the overall intention is to try to avoid changing the use of concepts for specific issues. Again, to illustrate: after the events of 9/11, the importance of terrorism was assessed to be decreasing, substantiated by the fall of the Soviet Union and the decline of leftist terrorist organisations. The tentative conclusion was that the 9/11 events were perhaps not to be considered as terrorist acts. The intention of maintaining continuity in the use of concepts in relation to the unarticulated definitions makes the process of changing concepts opaque within the MUST.

Reflecting on Impartiality and Objectivity

The intelligence analysts hold impartiality and objectivity to be fundamental features of their work. The analysts often returned to the importance of these features as they described their analytical process, as seen in Chapters 6 and 7. The analysts underlined that assessments needed to be objective and impartial so that policymakers could rely upon them. Simultaneously, they recognised two possible difficulties in maintaining impartiality and objectivity. One was the danger of being influenced by the intelligence consumer (ending up writing what they want to hear – politisation). The second was not just describing and explaining, but ending up writing policy. Both of these are considered as endangering the role of the intelligence analysis as impartial and objective.

The analysts also recognised that there is a risk of not being objective in their daily analytical work, although the possible problems of impartiality were more unarticulated and intangible to the analysts. The analysts argued that objectivity and impartiality is threatened by making personal and subjective valuations on the issues and that this is revealed by the use of a 'personal and subjective language', using words as 'good or bad'. This is commendable, although doesn't acknowledge that subjective assumptions and valuations might play a significant role in the analyses through the language practice in use. That is, they did not recognise that the use of concepts, terms and valuations as qualifiers might create problems for the impartiality and objectivity that they strive for.

Although the intelligence service's prime purpose is to provide policymakers with objective, impartial intelligence to help them make informed decisions, this study suggests this is sub-optimised. This study suggests that the biggest threat to objectivity and impartiality is the indistinctiveness in the analytical and interpretative processes for the assessments. As discussed, the text in the estimates does not make a clear distinction between facts, arguments and valuations/viewpoints, making it difficult for an intelligence consumer to recognise the conditions for the analysis. The textual discursive practice holds a lack of transparency of the assessments and interpretations, indistinct division between facts, assumptions and viewpoints, and limited transferral of the conditions of the analysis to the intelligence consumer.

INTELLIGENCE KNOWLEDGE DISCOURSE

As noted in Chapter 8, a pre-established worldview influenced and permeated all the estimates through the study. This worldview is not consciously acknowledged, but silently permeates and underlies the thoughts and wording in the estimates. This underlying and immanent worldview guides the choice of relevant actors and problems, and functions as a frame of interpretation. The intelligence worldview defines how the intelligence service conceptualises its representation and defines the problem horizon and interpretative horizon. In short, this worldview affects which information is sought, selected and used, and influences all interpretations, thereby structuring and defining the meaning of the objects of knowledge in the intelligence discourse.

This study shows that this worldview is an internalised version of political realism, which is displayed in the choice of social and political actors. As seen in Chapter 8, political realism has a long history and has played an important and vital role in international relations (and within intelligence studies). Political realism is also highly debated and contested over its normative and to descriptive claims. The foremost critique of political realism as a foundation for explaining international relations is state centrism. State centrism makes political realism inattentive to other kinds of political actors and, therefore, makes it difficult to conceptualise actors and phenomena that are not state related. The argument in this study is not to judge the suitability of the intelligence service using political realism as its frame of interpretation. Nevertheless, political realism defines what are considered as objects of knowledge and thus may be said to have a structuring effect on the objects of knowledge of intelligence. Hence, the focus of the estimates assumes that states are the sole constitutive political actors that strive for power and are the sole driving force for state action, and that ideology or ideas are unimportant as a driving force for political action. Furthermore, the estimates' perception of power is the same as that of political realism, in other words focusing primarily on military, economic and geopolitical power. The estimates further reveal a disinterest in other types of political actors holding power in international relations. The analysts also hold on to the importance of the geopolitical perspective as a defining frame of interpretation for state action and for contextualising and explaining world events. The intelligence worldview may, therefore, be argued to be based in a general theory of political realism.

At the same time, the worldview is not explicitly articulated in the estimates, nor is it discussed among the analysts or within the organisation. There is limited or no discussion or reflection on how to formulate analytical hypothesis or discussion of the assumptions underlying the analysis. Instead, the analysts are eased into what is considered a correct frame of interpretation through socialisation. What are deemed as important questions are largely determined by previously written assessments and an informal tacit knowledge of what an assessment 'should focus on'. The worldview seems to be a tradition rather than the result of conscious reflection. The intelligence analysts direct their analytical focus to issues and problems that are consistent with the worldview. This is displayed, inter alia, in the analysts' choices of which political actors should primarily constitute the object of investigation.

The intelligence worldview affects not only the intelligence analysis in the construct of states and power. The worldview also implies the use of a certain set of terms' and concepts' description and conceptualisation in the estimates. This is, for example, evident in the intelligence analyses' difficulty in conceptualising non-state actors and in the estimates' tendency to explain state action that is not power seeking as irrational, dubious or framed by valuating (occasionally in reference to emotions as the cause for state action) qualifiers. The choice of a framework of terms and concepts and a worldview founded in the general theory of political realism is not articulated or reflected upon. Rather, the analytical choices of which terms and concepts to use seem to be largely determined by an established tradition of how it is usually done. The use of terms and concepts are highly affected by which language and its accompanying worldview has been used in previously written assessments.

The worldview of the intelligence discourse does not explicitly define what sources are acceptable to use for information gathering, although it influences what kind of information is sought and used for intelligence analysis. The constitutive role worldview in the almost exclusive focus on coherent state actors and power and the emphasis on the search for power as the primary momentum of state action significantly influences the sorting of information. For instance, information about non-state actors holding power within international relations or making an impact on security situations is left unexplored or neglected. This risks making the intelligence analysis neglect events and phenomena that may be important to future events that are not easily conceptualised within the existing frame of interpretation.

The worldview of intelligence affects both the conceptualisation and the assumed logic in understanding and explaining different societal phenomena. The textual discursive practice of how this worldview affects, influences and constrains approaches, problematisation, articulation and conclusions in the knowledge production creates an intelligence 'style of thought'. Within the intelligence 'style of thought' are underlying assumptions, presuppositions, viewpoints and arguments that affect the character of intelligence knowledge. These are not explicitly stated, articulated or discussed. Nor are they systematically reflected upon by the analysts or within the organisation. I argue that it is important to note that political realism seems to be unconsciously used as a frame of interpretation. It is a crucial defiance of the knowledge production that the normative and descriptive assumptions underlying the intelligence knowledge production are neither explicit nor clarified. Nor are the assumptions and logic related to such a worldview openly declared or argued; rather, they constitute a tacit frame of interpretation present throughout the estimates. The lack of explicit awareness and of discussion and reflection about this connection to realism within the textual discursive practice suggests that the worldview is more of a tradition of thought, rather than the conscious choice of viewpoint.

CONCLUDING REFLECTIONS AND SUGGESTIONS

Reflections

This study has shown that there is a strong interpretive framework within intelligence, one that is not articulated or explicitly stated within the discursive practices. The frame of interpretation continuously influences and guides the knowledge production and makes the knowledge dependent on one perspective, contrary to the intention of the intelligence service.

It is also argued within this study that the social and discursive practices for intelligence knowledge production denote a logic of appropriateness induced by the existence of a 'collective of thought' and a 'style of thought'. The routines, procedures and roles are taught through both formal training and socialisation into the intelligence 'collective of thought'. The practice of how assessments (and, thereby, the intelligence knowledge) are produced is dense with formal and informal routines and procedures. The formal and explicit social practice is for the most part concerned with the administrative procedures of how an assessment is processed from an intelligence request to the dissemination of an approved assessment. The informal routines, procedures and roles are partly transferred and reproduced through social and practical 'trial and error' to accustom analysts to the logic of appropriateness in the discursive practices. Thus, the actions and choices of the individual are transformed to create conformity to the norms present within the social discursive practices, thus constituting a 'collective of thought'.

In addition, there is awareness among the analysts of the organisation's search for continuity and stability regarding assessments and conclusions. The organisation's strive for continuity is explicitly expressed by management and the analysts adjust accordingly. Thus, the inherited frame of interpretation as well as the norm of staying within the previously accepted interpreted meaning and understanding of issues implies that analysts adapt to the intelligence 'style of thought'. Overall, the character of the 'collective of thought' and 'style of thought' suggests that the intelligence knowledge discourse remains unchallenged, to a great extent, and tends to encourage reproduction of knowledge and reaffirmation of the established intelligence knowledge discourse. In addition, it tends to discourage reflection and critical scrutiny. This study shows the structuring effect that the discursive practices have on the actions of the individual, thereby re-enforcing the organisation's logic of appropriateness, which constitutes a 'collective of thought' and a specific 'style of thought'. The character of the existing 'style of thought' is problematic, given the intelligence service's purpose of providing new insights on and explanations for world events in an objective and value neutral manner.

Our world is very complex and rich in relations, mechanisms and people, and even richer in information and facts (in whatever shape and form they might come). When trying to understand this complex situation, we humans have to make choices of what to understand, how to understand it and how to investigate it. We make these choices from a predetermined and simplified view of how the world is constituted. Intelligence is no exception. Thus, the intelligence knowledge per se and the assumptions and presuppositions it rests on, and how the knowledge is created are of importance for the analytical outcome and, in turn, for the policy decisions based on that knowledge. Because it is important to understand and critically investigate what these assumptions are and how they come to affect knowledge produced within policy-related institutions, this study inquired into the knowledge production of intelligence. In addition, while the critical policy analysis research is rich in theoretical debate, there are few empirical case studies. From the perspective of critical policy research, this study might be said to contribute with an empirical case – that of investigating the knowledge produced within intelligence analysis.

At the core of political science in general and within the research tradition of critical policy analysis in particular, resides the question of what and how policy is shaped. Even though this study has focused on one organisation in a specific policy field, it provides insights to the knowledge and policy nexus. Hence, this study argues that the MUST (as an example of an intelligence service) produces and reproduces one kind of knowledge that is somehow infused into the policymakers' frame of reference. The view both within the MUST and in the wider institutional setting (including the intelligence consumers) is that the primary purpose of the intelligence knowledge is to inform policy decisions. However, it is unclear how intelligence knowledge is infused or incorporated into policy. Therefore, one possible research focus could be an inquiry into how the intelligence knowledge is or is not used by the intelligence consumers in developing policy. For example, it raises the question of whether the intelligence knowledge is negotiated or co-constructed in relation to the knowledge and beliefs held by the intelligence consumer or other intelligence agencies or knowledge producers.

It is further suggested in this study that there is an intriguing dualistic relation in the view held by the agents (analysts and managers) and the structure of the institution, the MUST, as outlined in the social and discursive practices. Throughout the process, the characterisation of individuality in producing knowledge and the individual responsibility of making analytical choices is emphasised in the social discursive practice. However, this study has also shown that the actions of agents are highly affected by the logic of appropriateness constituted within the intelligence 'collective of thought' and 'style of thought'. The failure to recognise the impact of the social context for knowledge production makes the processes inattentive to the constraining analytical implications that the social and discursive practices have on the knowledge produced. Instead, within the MUST, the view prevails that expert knowledge is vested in individual analysts and the process of creating knowledge is for the most part an individual action. This is related to the notion present in the organisation that knowledge is nearly equivalent to information. The individual analysts have access to different amounts of information, and systemising and interpreting it is considered an individual process. This is further underlined by the lack of articulation of the analytical techniques and methods used, thus implying an understanding of the analytical process as intuitive and relying on the individual analysts' 'gut feeling'. It also implies a lack of recognition of the effect of the social context.

Second, the empirical findings suggest there is a relation between the roles of analysts and managers that needs further research. As we have seen, the formal social practice embodies a hierarchical and ordered process revolving around the production of intelligence. The informal discursive practices shape the analytical process and choices. The hierarchical and ordered production process suggests that managers play an important role and might be conceptualised as 'gatekeepers'. The prevailing view in the empirical material points to power being vested in the gatekeeping function of sanctioning some intelligence analysis and conclusions and not others. This function is allocated by the power of judging what analysis and conclusions are sufficiently probable and can be allowed to be disseminated. Thus, the role of managers could be conceptualised as that of gatekeepers of the 'style of thought', of keeping the established analysis and conclusions intact and opposing views away from the knowledge process. Further, the awareness of and need to comply with the 'style of thought' within the discursive practices affects how the analysts approach the issues. Hence, it could be that complying with the 'style of thought' becomes as important to the analysts as making a well-argued and accurate analysis. This could happen because it is important for the analysts to gain the support of managers and gain status within the organisation, which they can do by safeguarding the established 'style of thought'. Hence, in the logic of appropriateness for the intelligence, analysts could conceivably be understood as 'custodians' of the 'style of thought'. The roles of managers as gatekeepers and analysts as custodians would benefit from further study to acquire insights on the relation between the individuality and structure within intelligence analysis.

Suggested Points of Reform

The theoretical approaches and concepts that have framed and structured this study share an understanding of the practices of the intelligence service as non-static. The constraining effect of the social and discursive practice on the actions of agents and on the knowledge produced is widely and readily accepted. These discursive practices have come to have features that discourage transparency, critical perspectives and reflection. At the same time, it is important to recap that the structuring impact of social contexts and social discursive practices also make coordinated collective action possible. Therefore, I suggest intelligence organisations in general and the MUST in particular need to accept and acknowledge that knowledge is socially embedded and contingent. That is, the nature and the character of the discursive practices to be found in intelligence (and MUST's) contexts are possible to alter – if desired. The critical perspective of the intelligence knowledge process and its context may be altered (if desired) because the relationship between the individual and the structure holds an element of contingency.

The following suggestions are made with awareness of the limitations of making concrete proposals for reform and with the proviso that the study allows only for a few cautious (and interrelated) suggestions. First, there is a need to have a more *reflective* approach to knowledge production. As discussed, the study suggests that the intelligence social and discursive practices seem to be enshrouded in non-reflective approaches, which pave the way for troubling consequences. Therefore, I would argue that overall the social and discursive practices in intelligence knowledge production (and within the MUST) need to encompass a more reflective approach to the knowledge production per se and for the specifics of the analytical process.

Second, a *recurrent dialogue* is required within the discursive practices, by acknowledging that knowledge production is not a process done by atomistic isolated individuals, but rather is dependent on and affected by its social context. Nevertheless, the persistent view that the individual agent is able to produce new knowledge free from the social environment may be a way of expressing the normative ideal picture of how 'good knowledge' ought to be created, though neglecting the effect of how things 'are really done' in everyday practice. Allowing the image of the normative ideal to function as a description of the real makes the difficult intelligence analytical work performed by the agents unarticulated and unrecognised. If the discursive practices instead held a recurrent and ordered interaction between the individuals within that social context, the analytical distinction of what is considered to be assumption and fact and the added value of the analysts' interpretive work would come to the surface. Therefore, I would argue that a systematic dialogue about analytical and interpretative aspects and the characterisation of the social discursive practices would be useful.

Finally, relying on increased reflection and frequent dialogue would allow for further *explicitness* in various aspects of knowledge production. It would allow for further definition of the analytical and interpretative added value. A greater explicitness in regard to analytical distinctions would also be possible. The analytical distinction and transparency of worldview, assumptions, valuations, and facts and arguments would be further enhanced. As discussed above, the interpretative work done by the analysts is to a large extent unarticulated and merely referred to as intuition.

I believe intelligence analysts do much more refined work than merely listening to their gut feeling. They carry out advanced analytical processes, which are difficult to discuss, criticise and recognise because they are unarticulated. Therefore, the contribution of the analysts within the intelligence knowledge production need to be truly recognised, the focus of attention, and viewed through a lens of critical and constructive evaluation and improvement. Because, ultimately, it is the analytical process that turns information into intelligence.

BIBLIOGRAPHY

LITERATURE

Adler, P., Adler, P. (1994), 'Observational techniques' in Denzin, N. K., Lincoln, Y. S. (eds) *Handbook of qualitative research*, Thousand Oaks: Sage Publications.
Agrell, W. (1998), *Konsten att gissa rätt*, Lund: Studentlitteratur.
Anton, A. (1980), *Administered politics: Elite political culture in Sweden*, Boston: Martinius Nijhoff Publishing.
Aronoff, M. J., Kubik, J. (2013), *Anthropology and political science a convergent approach*, Oxford: Berghahn Books.
Atkinson, R. (2002), 'The life story interview' in Gubrium, J. F., Holstein, J. A. (eds) *Handbook of interview research: Context and method*, Thousand Oaks: Sage Publications.
Bacchi, C (2009), *Analysing policy: What's the problem represented to be?*, Frenchs Forest, Sydney: Pearson.
Berger, P., Luckmann, T. (1966), *The social construction of reality*, London: Penguin Books.
Bjerled, U., Demker, M. (2006), *Främlingskap: Svensk säkerhetstjänst och konflikterna i Nordafrika och Mellanöstern*, Lund: Nordic Academic Press.
Boreus, K., Bergström, G. (2000), *Textens mening och makt*, Lund: Studentlitteratur.
Bruce, J. B. (2008), 'Making analysis more reliable: Why epistemology matters to intelligence' in George, R. Z., Bruce, J. B. (eds) *Analyzing intelligence: Origins, obstacles, and innovations*, Washington, DC: Georgetown University Press.
Bull, H. (2002), *The anarchical society a study of order in world politics*, 3rd edn, New York: Palgrave.
Bunge, M. (2009), *Philosophy of science from problem to theory*, New Brunswick: Transactions Publishers.
Burr, V. (2006), *An introduction to social constructionism*, London: Routledge.

Butler, F. E. R. (2004), *Review of intelligence on weapons of mass destruction*, London: The Stationery Office.
Carlgren, W. M. (1985), *Svensk underrättelsetjänst 1939-1945*, Helsingborg: Liber Allmänna Förlag/Försvarsdepartementet.
Christians, C. G. (2005), 'Ethics in qualitative research' in Denzin, N. K., Lincoln, Y. S. (eds) *The SAGE handbook of qualitative research*, London: Sage Publications.
Clark, R. M. (2004), *Intelligence analysis: A target centric approach*, Washington, DC: CQ Press.
Collier, D., Elman, C. (2008), 'Qualitative and multi-method research: Organisations, publications, and reflections on integration' in Box-Steffensmeier, J. M., Brady, H. E., Collier, D. (eds) *Oxford handbook of political methodology*, Oxford: Oxford University Press.
Davies, P. H. J., Gustafson K. C. (eds), (2013), *Intelligence elsewhere: Spies and espionage outside the Anglosphere*, Washington, DC: Georgetown University Press.
de Graaf, B., Nyce, J. M. (eds), (in press), *Handbook of European intelligence cultures*, Lanham, MD: Rowman & Littlefield.
Denzin, N. K., Lincoln, Y. S. (2005), *The SAGE handbook of qualitative research*, London: Sage Publications.
Dunne, T., Schmidt, B. C. (2008), 'Realism' in Baylis, J., Smith, S., Owens, P. (eds) *The globalization of world politics*, Oxford: Oxford University Press.
Einarsson, C., Hammar Chiriac, E. (2002), *Gruppobservationer teori och pratik*, Lund: Studentlitteratur.
Ekengren, A. M., Oscarsson, H. (2006), *Det röda hotet: De militära och polisiära säkerhetstjänsternas hotbilder i samband med övervakningen av svenska medborgare 1945-1960*, Lund: Nordic Academic Press.
Eliasson, U. (2006), *I försvarets intresse: Säkerhetspolisens övervakning och registrering av ytterlighetspartier 1917-1945*, Lund: Nordic Academic Press.
Eriksson, G. (2013), *The intelligence discourse: The Swedish military intelligence (MUST) as a producer of knowledge*, Örebro: Örebro Universitet (Doctoral Thesis).
Esaiasson, P., Gilljam, M., Oscarsson, H., Wägnerud, L. (2007), *Metodpraktikan*, Stockholm: Norstedts Juridik.
Fägersten, B. (2010), *Sharing secrets – Explaining international intelligence cooperation*, Lund: Lund University (Doctoral Thesis).
Fairclough, N. (1992), *Discourse and social change*, Cambridge: Polity Press.
Fisch, S. E. (1995), *Is there a text in this class? The authority of interpretive communities*, Cambridge: Harvard University Press.
Fischer, F. (2003), *Reframing public policy*, Oxford: Oxford University Press.
Fischer, F., Forester, J. (1993), *The argumentative turn in policy analysis and planning*, London: Duke University Press.

Fleck, L. (1979), *Genesis and development of a scientific fact*, Chicago: Chicago University Press.
Fleck, L. (1979), *Genesis and development of a scientific fact*, Chicago: Chicago University Press.
Fleck, L. (1997), *Uppkomsten och utvecklingen av ett vetenskapligt faktum*, Stockholm: Brutus Östlings Bokförlag Symposion. (In original: Fleck, L. (1935), *Enstehung und entwicklung einer wissenschaftlichen tatscache*, Basel: Schwabe.)
Flick, U. (2002), *An introduction to qualitative research*, London: Sage Publications.
Fontana, A., Frey, J. H. (1994), 'Interviewing the art of science' in Denzin, N. K., Lincoln, Y. S. (eds) *Handbook of qualitative research*, Thousand Oaks: Sage Publications.
Fontana, A., Frey, J. H. (2008), 'The interview – from neutral stance to political involvement' in Denzin, N. K., Lincoln, Y. S. (eds) *Collecting and interpreting qualitative materials*, Thousand Oaks: Sage Publications.
Frick, L. W., Rosander, L. (2004), *Bakom hemligstämpeln*, Lund: Historisk Media.
Fry, M. G., Hochstein, M. (1994), 'Epistemic communities: Intelligence studies and international relations' in Wark, W. (ed.) *Espionage: Past, present, future?* New York: Frank Cass.
George, A. L. (1993), *Bridging the gap theory & practice in foreign policy*, Washington, DC: United States Institute of Peace Press.
Gerring, J. (2007), *Case study research*, Cambridge: Cambridge University Press.
Giddens, A. (1979), *Central problems in social theory action structure and contradiction in social analysis*, Berkeley: University of California Press.
Gustafsson, A. (2009), *Pamfletter! En diskursiv praktik och dess strategi i tidig svensk politisk offentlighet*, Lund: Lund University (Doctoral Thesis).
Gustavsson, J. (2002), 'Hemliga tjänster och det öppna samhället' in Statens Offentliga Utredningar, *Forskarrapporter till Säkerhetskommissionen*, Stockholm: Regeringskansliet, SOU 2002:95.
Heclo, H., Madsen, H. (1987), *Policy and politics in Sweden*, Philadelphia: Temple University Press.
Heuer, R. (1999), *Psychology of intelligence analysis*, Washington, DC: Center for the Study of Intelligence.
Hilsman, R. (1956), *Strategic intelligence and national decisions*, Glencoe: The Free Press.
Howarth, D. (2000), *Discourse*, Buckingham: Open University Press.
Janis, I. L. (1982), *Groupthink*, 2nd edn, Boston: Houghton Mifflin Company.
Johnson, J. M. (2001), 'In-depth interviewing' in Gubrium, J. F., Holstein, J. A. (eds) *Handbook of interview research*, Thousand Oaks: Sage Publications.

Johnson, L. K. (2007), 'Introduction to intelligence studies literature' in Johnson, L. K. (ed.) *Strategic intelligence understanding the hidden side of government*, London: Preager Security International.

Johnston, R. (2005), *Analytical culture in the U.S. intelligence community: An ethnographic study*, Washington, DC: Central Intelligence Agency.

Jorgensen, D. L. (1989), *Participant observation a methodology for human studies*, Thousand Oaks: Sage Publications.

Kent, S. (1949), *Strategic intelligence for American world policy*, Princeton: Princeton University Press.

Kuhn, T. (1996), *The structure of scientific revolutions*, 3rd edn, Chicago: Chicago University Press.

Kuhns, W. J. (2003), 'Intelligence failures: Forecasting and the lessons from epistemology' in Betts, R., Mahnken T. (eds) *Paradoxes in strategic intelligence: Essays in honour of Michael Handel*, London: Frank Cass.

Kvale, S. (1996), *InterViews: An introduction to qualitative research interviewing*, Thousand Oaks: Sage Publications.

Kvale, S. (1997), *Den kvalitativa forskningsintervjun*, Lund: Studentlitteratur.

Kvale, S. (2008), *Doing interviews*, London: Sage Publications.

Lakoff, S. A. (1966), *Knowledge and power: Essays on science and government*, New York: Free Press.

Legard, R., Ward, K. (2003), 'In-depth interviews' in Ritchie, J., Lewis, J. (eds) *Qualitative research practice: A guide for social science students and researchers*, London: Sage Publications.

Lidskog, R., Soneryd, L., Uggla, Y. (2010), *Transboundary risk governance*, London: Earthscan.

Lundberg, S. (2004), *Ryssligan: Flyktingarna från öst och morden i Bollstanäs 1919*, Lund: Nordic Academic Press.

Lundqvist, L. J. (1980), *The hare and the tortoise: Clean air policies in the United States and Sweden*, Ann Arbor: University of Michigan Press.

March, J. G., Olsen, J. P. (1989), *Rediscovering institutions*, New York: Free Press.

March, J. G., Olsen J. P. (2004), *The logic of appropriateness*, Arena working paper WP 04/09, Centre for European Studies, University of Oslo.

Morgenthau, H. (1949), *Politics among nations*, New York: Alfred A. Knopf.

Moses, J. W., Knutsen, T. (2012), *Ways of knowing*, New York: Palgrave Macmillan.

Myrdal, G. (1969), *Objectivity in social research*, New York: Pantheon Books.

Odendahl, T., Shaw, A. M. (2002), 'Interviewing elites' in Gubrium, J. F., Holstein, J. A. (eds) *Handbook of interview research: Context and method*, Thousand Oaks: Sage Publications.

Oredsson, S. (2003), *Svensk oro: Offentlig fruktan i Sverige under 1900-talets senare hälft*, Lund: Nordic Academic Press.

Ottosson, J., Magnusson, L. (1991), *Hemliga makter: svensk hemlig militär underrättelsetjänst från unionstid till det kalla kriget*, Stockholm: Tiden.
Palm, T. (1999), *T-kontoret några studier i T-kontorets historia*, Stockholm: Kungl. Samfundet för utgivandet av handskrifter.
Patel, R., Tebelius, U. (1987), *Grundbok i forskningsmetodik*, Lund: Studentlitteratur.
Peräkylä, A. (2005), 'Analyzing text and talk' in Denzin, N. K., Lincoln, Y. S. (eds) *The SAGE handbook of qualitative research*, London: Sage Publications.
Peräkylä, A. (2008), 'Analyzing text and talk' in Denzin, N. K., Lincoln, Y. S. (eds) *Collecting and interpreting qualitative materials*, Thousand Oaks: Sage Publication.
Persson, P.-A., et al. (2008), *Från koncept till öppet system – utveckling av operativ och taktisk underrättelsetjänst i den militära insatsorganisationen, för att verka, synas och respekteras*, Stockholm: Försvarshögskolan.
Peters, G. (2005), *Institutional theory in political science: The 'New Institutionalism'*, London: Pinter.
Petersson, O. (1994), *The government and politics of the Nordic countries*, Stockholm: Fritzes.
Popper, K. (1963), *Conjectures and refutations the growth of scientific knowledge*, London: Routledge.
Ragin, C., Amaroso, L. M. (2001), *Constructing social research*, Thousand Oaks: Pine Forge Press.
Ruin, O. (1981), *Att komma överens och tänka efter före: politisk stil och 1970-talets svenska samhällsutveckling*, Stockholm: Statsvetenskapliga Institutionen, Univeristet.
Sartori, G. (1984), *Social science concepts*, London: Sage Publications.
Schmidt, W. (2002), *Antikommunism och kommunism under det korta 1900-talet*, Lund: Nordic Academic Press.
Schön, D. A., Rein, M. (1994), *Frame reflection: Toward a resolution of intractable policy controversies*, New York: Basic Books.
Scott, L. V, Jackson, P. (eds), (2004), *Understanding intelligence in the twenty-first century*, New York: Routledge.
Stake, R. (2005), 'Qualitative case study' in Denzin, N. K., Lincoln, Y. S. (eds) *The SAGE handbook of qualitative research*, London: Sage Publications.
Törnebohm, H. (1975), *Inquiring systems and paradigms*, Report No. 72, Department of Theory of Science, University of Göteborg.
Törnebohm, H. (1983), *Studier av kunskapsutveckling*, Bodafors: Doxa.
Treverton, G. (2003), *Reshaping national intelligence for an age of information*, Cambridge: Cambridge University Press.
Vetenskapsrådets (2002), *Forskningsetiska principer inom humanistisk-samhällsvetenskaplig forskning*, Stockholm: Vetenskapsrådet.

Waltz, K. N. (2001), *Man the state and war*, 3rd edn, New York: Columbia University Press.

Wirtz, J. (2007), 'The intelligence-policy nexus' in Johnson, L. K. (ed.) *Strategic intelligence understanding the hidden side of government*, London: Preager Security International.

Wohlstetter, R. (1962), *Pearl Harbor warning and decision*, Stanford: Stanford University Press.

ARTICLES

Agrell, W. (2012), 'The next 100 years? Reflections on the future of intelligence', *Intelligence and National Security*, 27: 1, 118–32.

Anton, T. J. (1969), 'Policy-making and political culture in Sweden', *Scandinavian Political Studies*, 4: A4, 88–102.

Armed Forces Communications and Electronics Association (AFCEA) Intelligence Committee (2005), 'Making analysis relevant: More than connecting the dots', *Defense Intelligence Journal*, 14: 1, 23–46.

Bar-Joseph, U. (2010), 'The professional ethics of intelligence analysis', *International Journal of Intelligence and Counterintelligence*, 24: 1, 22–43.

Bar-Joseph, U. (2013), 'The politicization of intelligence: A comparative study', *International Journal of Intelligence and Counterintelligence*, 26: 2, 347–69.

Ben-Israel, I. (1989), 'Philosophy and methodology of intelligence: The logic of estimate process', *Intelligence and National Security*, 4: 4, 660–718.

Betts, R. (2007), 'Two faces of intelligence failure: September 11 and Iraq's missing WMD', *Political Science Quarterly*, 122: 4, 585–606.

Bloor, D., Edge, D. (2000), 'For the record', *Social Studies of Science*, 30: 1, 158–160.

Dargie, C. (1998), 'Observation in political research: A qualitative approach', *Politics*, 18: 1, 65-71.

Davies, P. H. J. (2001), 'Spies as informants: Triangulation and the interpretation of elite interview data in the study of the intelligence and security services', *Politics*, 21: 1, 73–80.

Grey, C., Sturdy, A. (2009), 'Historicising knowledge-intensive organizations: The case of Bletchley Park', *Management & Organizational History*, 4: 2, 131–50.

Hansen, F. S. (2012), 'An argument for reflexivity in intelligence work', *Intelligence and National Security*, 27: 3, 349–70.

Hart, T. (1976), 'The cognitive dynamics of Swedish security elites: Beliefs about Swedish national security and how they change', *Cooperation and Conflict*, 11: 2, 201–19.

Hastedt, G. (2013), 'The politics of intelligence and the politicization of intel-

ligence: The American experience', *Intelligence and National* Security, 28: 1, 5–31.
Hatlebrekke, K. A., Smith, M. L. R. (2010), 'Towards a new theory of intelligence failure? The impact of cognitive closure and discourse failure', *Intelligence and National Security*, 25: 2, 147–82.
Hulnick, A. (1986), 'The intelligence producer-policy consumer linkage: A theoretical approach', *Intelligence and National Security*, 1: 2, 212–33.
Kahn, D. (2001), 'An historical theory of intelligence', *Intelligence and National Security*, 16: 3, 79–92.
Kent, S. (1964), 'A crucial estimate relived', *Studies in Intelligence*, 8: 2, 1–18.
Maier, S. L., Monahan, B. A. (2009), 'How close is too close? Balancing closeness and detachment in qualitative research', *Deviant Behavior*, 31: 1, 1–32.
Mazey, S. (2000), 'Introduction: Integrating gender – intellectual and "real world" mainstreaming', *Journal of European Public Policy*, 7: 3, 333–45.
Meyer, R. E. (2006), 'Review essay visiting relatives: Current developments in the new sociology of knowledge', *Organization*, 13: 5, 725–38.
Mikezc, R. (2012), 'Interviewing elites: Addressing methodological issues', *Qualitative Inquiry*, 18: 6, 482–93.
Milliken, J. (1999), 'The study of discourses in international relations: A critique of research and method', *European Journal of International Relations*, 5: 2, 225–54.
Millstone, E. (1978), 'A framework for the sociology of knowledge', *Social Studies of Science*, 8: 1, 111–25.
Mole, C. (2012), 'Three philosophical lessons for the analysis of criminal and military intelligence', *Intelligence and National Security*, 27: 4, 441–58.
Nyce, J. M. (2011), 'Hindsight bias, scientism and certitude: Some problems in the intelligence literature', *Kunglig Krigsvetenskaplig Tidskrift*, 2, 115–125.
Räsänen, M., Nyce, J. M. (2013), 'The raw is cooked: Data in intelligence practice', *Science, Technology & Human Values*, 38: 5, 655–77.
Rathmell, A. (2002), 'Towards a postmodern intelligence', *Intelligence and National Security*, 17: 3, 87–104.
Russel, K. (2004), 'The subjectivity of intelligence analysis and implications for the U.S. national security strategy', *SAIS Review*, 24: 1, 147–63.
Schmidt, V. (2008), 'Discursive institutionalism: The explanatory power of ideas and discourses', *Annual Review of Political Science*, 11, 303–26.
Schmidt, V. (2010), 'Taking ideas and discourse seriously: Explaining change through discursive institutionalism as the fourth institutionalism', *European Political Science Review*, 2: 1, 1–25.
Scott, L., Jackson, P. (2004), 'The study of intelligence in theory and practice', *Intelligence and National Security*, 19: 2, 139–69.
Selznick, P. (1996), 'Institutionalism "old" and "new"', *Administrative Science Quarterly*, 41: 2, 270–77.

Shelton, C. (2011), 'The roots of analytical failure in the U.S. intelligence community', *International Journal of Intelligence and Counterintelligence*, 24: 4, 637–55.
Wesely, A. (1997), 'Philosophy of science and sociology of knowledge', *Innovation: The European Journal of Social Science Research*, 10: 1, 7–15.
Whittington, R. (1992), 'Putting Giddens into action: Social systems and managerial agency', *Journal of Management Studies*, 29: 6, 693–712.

PUBLIC INQUIRIES

Regeringens Proposition 2006/07:63, *En anpassad försvarsunderrättelsetjänst*.
Review of Intelligence on Weapons of Mass Destruction, 14 July 2004, Report of a Committee of Privy Counsellors, London: The Stationery Office.
Statens Offentliga Utredningar, *Den militära underrättelsetjänsten*, SOU 1976:19, Stockholm: Regeringskansliet.
Statens Offentliga Utredningar, *Underrättelsetjänsten – en översyn*, SOU 1999:37, Stockholm: Regeringskansliet.
Statens Offentliga Utredningar, *Forskarrapporter till Säkerhetskommissionen*, SOU 2002:95, Stockholm: Regeringskansliet.
Statens Offentliga Utredningar, *Försvarets underrättelseverksamhet och säkerhetstjänst integritet – effektivtet*, SOU 2003:34, Stockholm: Regeringskansliet.
The Commission on the Intelligence Capabilities of the United States Regarding Weapons of Mass Destruction Report, 31 March 2005, <http://www.fas.org/irp/offdocs/wmd_report.pdf> (last accessed 8 April 2013).

INTELLIGENCE ESTIMATES AND POLICY DOCUMENTS

Intelligence Estimates

Intelligence Estimate 1998, Försvarsmaktens Strategiska Omvärldsbedömande 1998; 1998-11-05, 01 600:73940
Intelligence Estimate 1999, Försvarsmaktens Strategiska Omvärldsbedömande 1999; 1999-03-29, 01 600:63422
Intelligence Estimate (A) 2000, Försvarsmaktens Strategiska Omvärldsbedömande 2000; 2000-04-28, 01 600:64733
Intelligence Estimate (B) 2000, Försvarsmaktens Strategiska Omvärldsbedömande 2000; 2000-04-28, 01 600:64734
Intelligence Estimate (A) 2001, Försvarsmaktens Strategiska Omvärldsbedömande 2001; 2001-11.08, 01 600:72004
Intelligence Estimate (B) 2001, Försvarsmaktens Strategiska Omvärldsbedömande 2001; 2001-11.08, 01 600:72003

Intelligence Estimate 2002, Försvarsmaktens Strategiska Omvärldsbedömande 2002; 2002-11-06, H10 600:81190
Intelligence Estimate 2003, Försvarsmaktens Strategiska Omvärldsbedömande 2003; 2003-12-04; H10 600:81775
Intelligence Estimate 2004, Försvarsmaktens Strategiska Omvärldsbedömande 2004; 2004-11-23; H 10 600: 81972
Intelligence Estimate 2005, Försvarsmaktens Strategiska Omvärldsbedömande 2005; 2005-12-02; H/S 10 420:82091
Intelligence Estimate 2006/2007, Försvarsmaktens Strategiska Omvärldsbedömande 2006/2007; 2007-02-28; H/S 10 420:80384
Intelligence Estimate 2008, Försvarsmaktens Strategiska Omvärldsbedömande 2008; 2008-03-11; H/S 10 420:80776
Intelligence Estimate 2010, Försvarsmaktens Strategiska Omvärldsbedömande 2010; 2010:03:19; H/S 10 420:80656

Policy Documents

Förordning (2009:969) Instruktion för statens inspektion för försvarsunderrättelseverksamhet (Government decree).
Försvarsmakten (2008), *Försvarsmaktens grundsyn underrättelsetjänst 08*, Stockholm: Försvarsmakten.
Försvarsmakten (2010), *Försvarsmaktens underrättelsereglemente 2010*, Stockholm: Försvarsmakten.
Lag (2000:130) om Försvarsunderrättelseverksamhet (Defence Intelligence Act).
MUST Årsöversikt för verksamhetsåret 2000, Bilaga 1, 23 386:617 44 (MUST Annual report for the year 2000).
Policy Documents on the Military Intelligence and Security Directorate – MUST (unclassified), Defence Headquarters (2009).
Regeringens styrning av Försvarsunderrättelseverksamheten – Försvarsdepartementet Sekretariatet för underrättelsefrågor (2009) (Government policy documents).

INTERVIEWS

Interview 1 (14 November 2009), the respondent is male, officer, academic background, aged between 30 and 45 years.
Interview 2 (12 February 2010), the respondent is female, academic background, aged between 30 and 45 years.
Interview 3 (19 December 2009), the respondent is male, academic background, aged between 30 and 45 years.
Interview 4 (21 January 2010), the respondent is male, academic background, aged between 30 and 45 years.

Interview 5 (11 June 2010), the respondent is male, officer, aged between 30 and 45 years.
Interview 6 (10 November 2009), the respondent is male, reserve officer, academic background, aged between 30 and 45 years.
Interview 7 (23 April 2010), the respondent is male, academic background, aged between 30 and 45 years.
Interview 8 (3 January 2010), the respondent is male, academic background, aged between 40 and 60 years.
Interview 9 (19 May 2010), the respondent is male, reserve officer, aged between 40 and 60 years.
Interview 10 (21 May 2010), the respondent is female, academic background, aged between 30 and 45 years.
Interview 11 (3 June 2010), the respondent is male, officer, aged between 45 and 60 years.

OBSERVATIONS

Observation 1, MUST 13 October 2009
Observation 2, MUST 14 October 2009
Observation 3, MUST 26 January 2010
Observation 4, MUST 27 January 2010
Observation 5, MUST 8 February 2010
Observation 6, MUST 9 February 2010

INDEX

Page numbers in italics refer to figures

Administrative Division (Stödkontoret – StödK), 57
Afghanistan, 165, 170–1
Algeria, 179
al-Qaida, 127–8, 160–1, 163, 164
analysis without interpretation, 69–72, 194
Analytical Department, 57
analytical qualifiers, 186
  and NATO, 181–4
  and Russia, 184–5
appropriateness
  code of appropriate behaviour, 23–4
  logic of, 21, 24, 33, 207–8, 209
arguments and facts, 75, 98–101, 172–7, 181, 191, 199–200
Aronoff, Myron J., 15n
articulatory aspect of discursive practice, 9, 26, 29–32
assumptions, 9–10, 34, 194–5, 199, 212
  implicit and explicit, 2–3
  theoretical and methodological, 11

Bacchi, Carol Lee, 8, 9
balance of power and state security, 121–2, 135
Balkans, 142, 171–2, 176
Baltic States, 151, 153–4, 173–4, 182–3

Caucasus, 178
Central Asia, 153–4
classical realism, 118–19
code of appropriate behaviour, 23–4
Cold War, 157–8, 160, 163

Collection Coordination Intelligence Requirements Management (CCRIM), 57
'collective of thought' (Denkkollektiv), 28–34, 38n, 62, 90, 190–212
company policy, the, 78
concepts
  changing, 106–7, 177–81, 202–3
  choosing, 101–3, 201–2
  coherence, 177–81
  consensus, 6, 41–4, 75–87, 102–6, 160–4, 193–7, 201–2
consistency, 30, 108–10, 115, 190–1, 196–200
constraints, 4, 18n, 21–3, 27–33, 94, 108–9, 209–12
contingency, 21–3, 30, 33, 211
continuity, 23, 95, 98–105, 190–4, 208
  of language, 31, 72, 203
corporatism, 43
credibility, 73–4, 79–87, 114, 199–200
'Crises and Conflicts', 157
critical discourse analysis, 10–11, 24–7, 33
critical policy analysis, 8–11, 20, 24, 32, 33–4, 209
criticism, 23, 29–30, 78–87, 171–2, 194–7
customer needs, 64–6

Defence Intelligence Act (Försvarsunderrättelselagen), 46–7
Defence Intelligence Board (Försvarets Underrättelsenämnd – FUN), 56

223

Defence Staff, 55
defensive power, 132
democracy, 131–2
Department for Information Security, 57
Department for Support of International Missions, 57
Der Derian, James, 20
Development and Long-Term Policy Department (Utvecklingsavdelning – UTV), 57
diplomacy, 120–1, 134
discourse, 9–10, 22–7, 32, 38–9n, 67, 72
  Fairclough's model, 25, 33
  intelligence, 33, 168–89, 191, 205–8
  language, 3, 107
discourse analysis, 10–11, 24–7, 33
discursive event, 25–6
discursive practice, 9–10, 25–34, 193, 207–12; *see also* social discursive practice; textual discursive practice

economic power, 131–2
Enduring Freedom operation, 171
environmental regulation, 9
ESDP, 141
esoteric circle, 32, 197
ethnocentrism, 7, 180
Europe, 128, 182
  and NATO, 141
European Union (EU), 125–7
  and NATO, 142–5
  and Russia, 155
  and terrorism, 159, 161, 162
exoteric circle, 32, 197
explicitness, 212

facts, 6, 113–14
facts and arguments, 75, 98–101, 172–7, 181, 191, 199–200
Fairclough, Norman, 24–7, 36n
  model for discourse, 25, 33
Fischer, Frank, 8, 9, 10
Fleck, Ludwik, 28, 30, 31, 38n
formal set of rules and routines, 21–4, 190, 191–2, 207–8
Foucault, Michel, 36n
framework for researching intelligence knowledge, 20–40
framing, 19n, 101–7

General Staff, 56
geography and power, 130–1, 172–3
geopolitics, 130–1, 172–3
  Russia, 153
Giddens, Anthony, 21
'gut feeling', 63, 75, 90, 98–100, 197, 210, 212
GWOT (Global War on Terrorism), 164, 180

hard line policy, 158, 159
Hilsman, Roger, 6–7, 7–8, 18n

impartiality, 111–16, 204
individuality, 70, 90, 102, 193, 209–10
industrial capacity, 120
informal procedures, routines and roles, 21–4, 62–90, 190, 192, 208
Information Bureau (Informations Byran – IB), 56
institutional setting, 3, 10, 11, 209
  MUST, 33, 46–54, 49, 190, 191–2
institutionalism, 21–4, 59
insurgency, 165
intelligence
  definition, 1–8
  politicisation of, 91n
intelligence analysis, 1–2, 209
  aligning and creating support, 75–87
  getting the question right, 64–6
  making, 62–90
  and policymaking, 5–6, 8–10, 209
  reading up, 66–8
  releasing the assessment, 87–90
  thinking and writing it down, 68–75
  value of, 111–12
  wrong conclusions, 1–2
Intelligence and Security Management (Underrättelse – och Säkerhetsledningen – USL), 56
intelligence cycle, 50–2, 53–4n, 59, 192
Intelligence Department, 57
intelligence discourse, 33, 168–89, 191, 205–8; *see also* discourse
intelligence discursive practice, 9–10, 25–34, 193, 207–12; *see also* social discursive practice; textual discursive practice

Index

Intelligence Division
    (Underrättelsekontoret – UNDK),
    57–8
intelligence in Swedish political
    culture, 41–5
intelligence knowledge
    creation, 91–117
    definition, 1–8
    direction and prioritisation, 94–101
    framework for researching, 20–40
    production, 3, 10–11, 62–90, 207,
        209
intelligence realist position, 118–39
intelligence research, 4–5
intelligence work process, 48–52, 52
intelligence worldview, 118–39, 190–1,
    199, 205–7, 212
international dependence, 126
interviews, 3–4, 14–15n
'intuitive feeling', 63, 75, 90, 98–100,
    197, 210, 212
IRA, 179
Iraq, 151, 152
Islam and terrorism, 163–4, 164, 165,
    177–81

Jackson, Peter, 16n
Johnson, Loch K., 6
Johnston, Rob, 18n
Joint Intelligence Bureau
    (Gemendamma byrån för
    Underrättelser – GBU), 56

Kent, Sherman, 5, 7–8, 17n
knowledge
    in a continuum, 197–9
    creation, 91–117
    production, 3, 10–11, 62–90, 207, 209
    view on, 2–3, 24–8
Kosovo, 151, 152, 170, 171, 176
KSI, 56
Kubik, Jan, 15n
Kuhn, Thomas, 27–8, 29–30, 37n

language, 81–2, 115, 201–2
    articulatory aspect of discursive
        practice, 9, 26, 29–32
    literary style, 31–2, 101–7, 200–1
    practice, 168–81, *180*
    of representation, 186, 199

language discourse, 3, 107; *see also*
    discourse
Ledningsavdelningen Department
    (LED), 51–2, 57
liberal market economy, 131–2
Lidskog, Rolf, 9
logic of appropriateness, 21, 24, 33,
    207–8, 209
Lundqvist, Lennart J., 45n

March, James G., 22–3
market economy, 131–2
Mazey, Sonia, 8
Middle East, 157
military
    capability, 133
    intentions, 133
    preparedness, 120
    threats, 133–4
    weakness, 175–6, 184
military power, 132–4
Milliken, Jennifer, 38–9n
Milosevic, Slobodan, 109
Ministry of Defence, 48
Mole, Christopher, 17n
Morgenthau, Hans J., 120–1
MUST (Swedish Military and Security
    Directorate), 1, 3–4, 8, 13n
    history, 55–8
    legal framework, 46–54
    overview of the organisation, *58*
    work process for the, 50–2, *52*

national
    character, 120
    interests, 119, 124, 128
    morale, 120–1
NATO, 127, 128, 151–5, 173, 176–7, 186,
    199
    constructing a friend, 169–72
    and EU, 142–5
    and Europe, 141
    in an international context, 142–5
    interoperability, 141, 183
    membership, 181–4
    positive expression, 169–72, 181–2
    representation of, 140–7, 187
    Russia, 145
    security, 140–7
    and stability, 140–7, 172–3, 183

NATO (*cont.*)
  and UN, 142–5, 188n
  and US, 142–5
natural resources, 120, 132
New Institutionalism, 11, 24, 33; *see also* institutionalism
'New Threats', 157–8, 159–60
9/11, 159–62, 179–80, 203
non-state actors, 127–8
North Africa, 157
Northern Ireland, 158, 178
Nyce, James M., 13n

objective truth claims, 2, 7, 11
objectivity, 5–6, 94, 111–16, 142, 168, 204
observations, 3–4, 15n
Olsen, Johan P., 22–3
openness, 18n, 43–4

participant observation, 3–4, 15n
Pearl Harbour, 160
Persson, P. A., 13n
PLAN (planeringssektion), 57
policymaking and intelligence, 5–6, 8–10, 209
political realism, 118–39, 190, 205–7, 206
politicisation of intelligence, 91n
Politics among Nations, 120
politics and power, 129–30
population, 120
power, 129–34, 201–2
  defensive, 132
  division of, 42
  economic, 131–2
  geography and, 120, 130–1, 172–3
  military, 132–4
  politics and, 129–30
  state, 199
  of states in international arena, 119, 120–1
predicate analysis, 38–9n, 168–81
prioritisation, 94–8
proofreading, 87–90, 107, 114
Putin, Vladimir, President, 149, 150, 153, 173, 176

qualifiers
  analytical, 181–6
  valuations as, 168–81

Räsänen, Minna, 13n
realism, 172–7
  classical, 118–19
  in the estimates, 123–39
  intelligence position, 118–39
  political, 118–39, 190, 205–7
  structural, 122
recurrent dialogue, 211–12
reflections, 207–10
reflective approach, 211
Rein, Martin, 9–10, 19n
representation
  of NATO, 140–7, 187
  of Russia, 148–56, 187
  of terrorism, 157–67
Russia, 128, 130, 133, 182, 186, 199
  constructing a foe, 172–7
  as developing country, 175
  economy, 139n, 173, 184–5
  and EU, 155
  geopolitics, 153
  in an international context, 152–5
  loss of superpower status, 152–3
  military weakness of, 175–6, 184
  and NATO, 145
  negative expression, 172–7
  political personnel, 148–50
  politics of rhetoric, 150–2
  representation of, 148–56, 187
  as unpredictable, 148–9, 161, 184–5
  and US, 131, 135, 151, 152–5, 172–3
  and WTO, 155

SÄPO (Swedish Security Police), 80
Sartori, Giovanni, 39–40n
Schmidt, W., 22–3
Schön, Donald A., 9–10, 19n
Scott, L. V., 16n
Second World War, 55
Section for Operations 5 (Operativ Sektion 5 – Op 5), 56
security, 46–8, 168–89
Security Department, 57
Security Division (Säkerhetskontoret – SÄKK), 57
Serbia, 109, 170
Situation Centre, 57
SIUN, 49–50

social context, 7–11, 27–8, 201–2
  institutionalism, 21, 24, 33
  social discursive practice, 31, 209, 211–12
social discursive practice, 12, 26–33, 62–90, 190–7, 207–12
socialisation, 7, 23, 100, 206–7
socialised knowledge, 27–8
Soviet bloc, 55, 158, 160
Soviet Union, 155, 203; *see also* Russia
speaking truth to power, 5–7
Special Collections Division (Kontoret för Särskild Inhämtning – KSI), 57
Special Collections Unit (Kontoret för Särskild Inhämtning – KSI), 56
stability, 23, 31, 112, 122, 126, 131–4, 208
  and NATO, 140, 144, 172–3, 183
state
  centrism, 190, 205
  collaborations, 125–7, 132
  irrationality, 134
  power, 199
  as rational actor, 124–5
  security and balance of power, 121–2, 135
State Inspection for Military Intelligence (Statens Inspektion för försvarsunderrättelseverksamhet), 49–50
statism, 119, 123–5, 127, 135
status, 81–7, 196–7
Strategic Intelligence and National Decision, 6–7
Strong Programme, 27
structural realism, 122
Structure of Scientific Revolutions, The, 27–8
'style of thought' (Denkstil), 28, 28–31, 32, 168–89, 190–212
suggested reforms, 210–12
SUND (Enheten för samordning av försvarsunderrättelsefrågor), 48–50, 50, 51, 57
Supreme Commander's headquarters, 56
Swedish Military and Security Directorate (MUST), 1, 3–4, 8, 13n
  history, 55–8

legal framework, 46–54
overview of the organisation, *58*
work process for the, 50–2, *52*
Swedish Military Intelligence Directorate, 55–61
Swedish model, the, 42
Swedish National Defence University (NDU), 13n
Swedish political culture, 41–5
systemising information, 68–75, 111, 113, 192, 194, 210

Taliban, 160–1, 165
T-Bureau (Tekniska Kontoret – T-kontoret), 55–6
terrorism, 183, 186, 201–2, 203
  after the re-emergence of, 159–64
  and EU, 159, 161, 162
  and Islam, 163–4, 165, 177–81
  recently, 164–5
  representation of, 157–67
  and UN, 161
  and US, 159–64, 171–2
textual discursive practice, 12, 26–31, 33, 168–89, 190, 193, 197–204, 207
Tornebohm, Håöökan, 37n, 38n
tradecraft, 7, 18n, 63, 82
transnational threats, 162–3
Treverton, Gregory, 17n
Turkey, 130

UN, 153, 170–1
  and NATO, 142–5, 188n
  and terrorism, 161
UN Security Council, 152
United States, 128
  and NATO, 142–5
  and Russia, 131, 135, 151, 152–5, 172–3
  security, 135
  and terrorism, 159–64, 171–2
USL, 56
Uzbekistan, 154

valuations, 11, 186–7, 199, 212
  and facts, 113–14
  implicit and explicit, 2–3
  as qualifiers, 168–81

Waltz, Kenneth N., 122
War against Terrorism, 159
Warsaw Pact, 55
Washington Treaty Article 5, 171
WMD Commission Report, 16n

worldview, 118–39, 190–1, 199, 205–7, 212
WTO, and Russia, 155

Yeltsin, Boris, President, 149, 173, 176

EU representative:
Easy Access System Europe
Mustamäe tee 50, 10621 Tallinn, Estonia
Gpsr.requests@easproject.com

www.ingramcontent.com/pod-product-compliance
Lightning Source LLC
Chambersburg PA
CBHW051056230426
43667CB00013B/2322